**ADDITIONAL PRAISE FOR** *NEW MARKET TIMING TECHNIQUES*

"Tom DeMark is one of the most innovative and insightful technicians of the last twenty years. His contribution to technical analysis is irrefutable. *New Market Timing Techniques* narrows the focus of many points from Tom's first book, *The New Science of Technical Analysis*, and extends its applicability. Essential reading."

> —William Abrams
> Senior Partner, Stern Brothers
> Specialist on the floor, NYSE

"Tom DeMark's technical systems lead you to examine all markets with an orientation to buy low and sell high rather than chase market consensus. The hardest thing for any investor to do is to buy something that everyone hates or sell something that everyone likes. *New Market Timing Techniques* details the mechanics of Tom's techniques to indicate the points at which you should do just that. Fortunately, many of his best indicators are long-term in nature so big investors need not be concerned with slippage, and small investors can make longer-term investments without having to worry about day-to-day volatility."

> —Chris Evans,
> Principal, Spectrum Global Management LLC

# WILEY TRADING ADVANTAGE

# New Market Timing Techniques

## Innovative Studies in Market Rhythm & Price Exhaustion

Thomas R. DeMark

**John Wiley & Sons, Inc.**

New York • Chichester • Weinheim • Brisbane • Singapore • Toronto

Copyright © 1997 by Thomas R. DeMark
Published by John Wiley & Sons, Inc.

This publication is designed to provide accurate and authoritative information in
regard to the subject matter covered. It is sold with the understanding that the
publisher and author are not engaged in rendering legal, accounting, or other
professional services. If legal advice or other expert assistance is required, the
services of a competent professional person should be sought.

## DISCLAIMER

**Although both the author and the publisher believe the information, data,
and contents presented are accurate, they neither guarantee their accuracy
and completeness nor assume any liability. It should not be assumed that
the methods, techniques, or indicators presented in this book will be profitable or that they will not result in losses. Trading involves the risk of loss,
as well as the potential for profit. Past performance is not a guarantee of
future results.**

*Library of Congress Cataloging-in-Publication Data:*
DeMark, Thomas R., 1947–
    New market timing techniques : innovative studies in market rhythm
& price exhaustion / Thomas R. DeMark.
        p.   cm.—(Wiley trading advantage)
    Includes index.
    ISBN 0-471-14978-0 (cloth : alk. paper)
    1. Investment analysis.   2. Stock price forecasting.   3. Financial
instruments—Prices—Forecasting.   I. Title.   II. Series.
HG4529.D458     1997
332.63'222—dc21                                                    97-19962

To my wife Nancy, who for many years has lived the life of a trader's widow, for her tolerance, insight, common sense, and encouragement

To my children, T.J., Carrie, Meghan, Rocke, Evan, and Dominic, of whom I am deeply proud, for their love and respect

To my parents, for their direction, support, and values

To Frank Mersch and Tony Popowich, for their interest in new ideas and market applications

To Tim Mather, Rick Knox, Ernie Popke, and Matt Storz, for their help, time, and most of all for their friendship

To Leon Cooperman, for his support of me and my work, as well as his enduring friendship throughout the years

To Duane Davis, for his unselfish willingness to contribute his programming and technical expertise and time

To the management and software pioneers at ADP, Aspen Graphics, Bloomberg, Bridge, CQG, Dow Jones Markets, GFIC (formerly Knight Ridder), Future-Source, Omega Research, Telerate, and TeleTrac, for their confidence in and commitment to my indicators and for the recognition of their value and contribution to the investment community

To Jason Perl, Anthony Orphanos, Joe Bernardo, Ginger Szala, Ron Michaelsen, Mark Etzkorn, Bill Abrams, Jeff Henderson, Dick Pfister, Rex Wilmore, Chris Evans, John Praetorius, Gibbons Burke, Rick Redmont, John May, Stuart Okorofsky, Sam Tennis, Pat Raffalovich, Courtney Smith, Mark Ellington, Peter Fiedelholtz, Karen Thomas, George Farley, Milton Barnes, Rob and Scott Madden, Ron Williams, Pat Kowalski, Rick Bensignor, Wayne Babler, Robert Stehlik, Lucille Kirkpatrick, Bill Griffith, Ron Insana, Sue Herrera, Richard Saxton, and John Murphy, as well as many others, for their interest in my work throughout my career.

# Contents

# Trademarks

All of the following indicators are registered trademarks and protected by U.S. Trademark Law. Any unauthorized use without the express written permission of Market Studies Inc. or Tom DeMark is a violation of the law.

TD Absolute Retracement
TD Alternative Oscillator
TD Arc
TD Breakout Qualifiers
TD Carrie (TDC)
TD Channel I, II, III
TD CLOP
TD CLOPWIN
TD Combo
TD Combo Reinforcement
TD Countdown
TD Critical Price
TD Critical Qualifier
TD Daily Range Projection
TD Dead Zone
TD Demand Line
TD DeMarker I, II
TD Diff
TD Dollar-Weighted Put/Call Ratio
TD Double Price Range
TD Double Retracement
TD Double TD Point

TD Duration Analysis
TD D-Wave
TD Exit 1
TD Fibonacci Intraday Indicator
TD Final Filter
TD Gap
TD LV
TD Lines
TD Line Gap
TD Magnet Price
TD Meghan (TDM)
TD Moving Average I, II
TD One Tick One Time Rule
TD Open
TD Pivot
TD Plurality
TD Point
TD Point Reversal
TD "Power of Nine"
TD Pressure
TD Price Flip Trend
TD Price Oscillator Qualifier (TDPOQ)

TD Propulsion
TD Range Expansion Index (TD REI)
TD Range Expansion BreakOut (TD REBO)
TD Range Projection
TD Relative Retracement
TD Rocke (TDR)
TD ROC I, II (TD Rate of Change)
TD Sequential
TD Sequential Reinforcement
TD Setup Trend (TDST)
TD Spring
TD Stop Reverse
TD Supply Line
TD Termination Count
TD TJ (TDTJ)
TD Trap
TD Trend (TDT)
TD Trend Factor
TD Triangulation
TD Two Day Stop

# Foreword

The year was 1986 and I was the director of research at Tudor Investment Corporation. With Paul Tudor Jones, we were in a new field of investing now known as managed futures and hedge fund management. Paul's job was to increase client capital by buying and selling the global futures, foreign exchange, and fixed income markets. My job was to help him make better-informed trading decisions. I thought, "No problem!" because at the age of 26, I knew I was perfectly equipped for the challenge. My background from the Federal Reserve Bank of New York provided the foundation for the task at hand: collect, massage, and interpret data from many markets around the world. And, I had the latest technology—an IBM PC with two floppy drives and Lotus 123.

Unfortunately, futures markets were emerging in more countries and on more markets than my two floppy drives could handle. Developing models similar to the regression models I had created at the Fed was either impossible or irrelevant. Given the slow speed of the computer and the vast amount of data, these models would have taken until 1990 to explain 1986—not very useful to a money manager whose average holding period was two weeks. There had to be a better approach to the problem.

Paul based most of his trading on technical analysis. At Tudor, technical analysis was broadly defined to include all relevant factors that could be gathered from within a market and which could affect its price, including volume, open interest, seasonality, spread relationships, and relative performance to related markets. One of Paul's favorite indicators was the "market analog"—that is, the behavior of a market after the reoccurrence of a previously observed price pattern—an "outside day," for example. It became very clear that the only way to gain an edge in these markets was to combine technology, a disciplined approach, and technical analysis rigorously. The growing number of markets in multiple time zones required a methodology that did not depend on human insight alone.

In 1986, as well equipped as I thought I was, I had to learn the whole new science of technical analysis. My passion for markets led me to read everything I could get my hands on. The name "DeMark" kept appearing in my research. Tom published a newsletter and a chart book. His newsletter was rated number one for profitability. His chart book had the most indicators and cleanest data.

At the time, I was developing a hierarchical approach to market analysis. This approach relies on the multi-stage filtering of data beginning with indicator development and ending with specific buy-sell rules. The indicator development would help Paul make better risk-reward trades. Additionally, we hoped the buy-sell rules could stand alone as a trading system. To aid this effort, I sought consultation from a guru of technical analysis. I decided to give Tom a call.

I found Tom DeMark on a visit to his home in Racine, Wisconsin. Coming from New York, my sense of Racine was that there were only two things to do—work and sleep. It was the perfect environment for a man with my passion for markets and the available time to do something about it. I remember that Tom was incredibly creative and a fountain of ideas. For days on end we would discuss markets, new trading indicators, and system ideas. *The DeMark Chart Books* required Tom to collect and scrub data from every market around the world. I was computer literate and very quantitative and Tom had programmers to run the indicators for his newsletter. Our creative energy overwhelmed the programmers. I was in market heaven. I flew back to New York full of new ideas and ready for a good meal and a night out. It was a perfect business match. It was also the beginning of a beautiful friendship.

Of course, Paul had more ideas than anyone. But before his theories could be traded, they first needed to be tested. We would rigorously test his ideas and apply money management and portfolio rules. Ultimately, we found we could implement a systematic trading approach. From this effort, Tudor Systems Corporation was born and its success would be greatly enhanced by the hiring of Tom DeMark. He joined TSC in 1988 as executive vice president and worked virtually around the clock with me until 1990.

As technology advanced, our work together progressed. I wish I could have taken a computer cable and downloaded all the market information contained in Tom's head. Instead, I settled for many stimulating conversations and rigorous testing. We examined every conceivable idea, and some not so conceivable. We began with sequential and ended with the four systems described in the book. I can categorically state that the systems I trade today could not have been developed if Tom had not laid the foundation of systems knowledge for me.

Eleven years after having met Tom, I still have his phone number committed to memory. There is many a time I have a question about a market or am using one of his indicators on a real-time quote machine and a thought pops into my head. We chat a bit about the way we think the market works and discuss different trading strategies and refinements. After all these years, Tom's work is still original and stimulating. It is a pleasure to speak with him and learn from him his latest market strategies.

The most wonderful of Tom's insights are often the most frustrating. There is no right answer; there are only probabilities. As a result, one can use Tom's work simply as a discretionary indicator, as the basis for a trading system, or in a multidimensional trading model. The choice is up to the user. I think its extremely important not just to read, but to study Tom's ideas and his charts. While each approach may appear to be independent, they build upon themselves into a harmonious orchestra of technical market instruments. It is worthwhile to take out a pencil and work through what is being presented. Don't skip over the difficult material. Trading markets is about discipline and making money—there are no shortcuts.

It is so easy to gossip about the markets—"I think the energy market is going up because it is cold outside." This approach is a sure way to part with your capital. Remember that the objective of trading is to make money—not to be right. The analyst never gets stopped out of a position on the low tick. The reality is that traders do. It is essential, therefore, to develop a game plan and stick with the approach. The trader is quite similar to the coach of a football team who must constantly remind the players of the little things it takes to win the game. Prepare for the worst and do not commit mental errors such as moving a stop lower or taking too large a position.

Technical analysis lets the trader follow the game plan. It provides a price level from which to initiate a trade; it also provides profit levels and stop loss levels. The discretionary trader uses technical analysis as an art. The systematic trader uses it as a science. Both can be successful. It is up to the practitioner to choose the method.

The technical analysis of Tom DeMark provides a good framework for both the systematic and discretionary trader. Tom does not mince words and he certainly does not gossip. He provides insight found nowhere else in the technical analysis literature. But, as brilliant and insightful as Tom can be about markets, he does not make the trading decision. Every trader must develop his or her own personal strategy. Such a system must include a risk profile, time frame, and market selection. Tom's book will help in each of these areas.

One thing is certain: Tom's work, if studied, will help every trader. No one can ask for more than this. Even so, it is only a start. Trading encompasses a lot more than entry and exit levels. Without them, however, one would have only a vague idea on how to approach the problem of making money in the markets.

I consider myself most fortunate to have a friend who cares as passionately about markets as I do. It is indeed very rare to find someone who is still innovating after so many years. Tom is a good friend and has been a powerful mentor. This book belongs in every trader's toolkit. Use it wisely and profitably.

Peter F. Borish
President, Computer Trading Corporation
Chairman, Futures Industry Institute
New York, New York
May 1997

# Acknowledgments

It's not often that an author involved in a complex project such as this book is able to receive special assistance, guidance, and attention from so many people and, at the same time, thoroughly enjoy these individuals' company and friendship.

Although I alone have written this book in its entirety, the development of the indicators and their accompanying graphics, displays, and tables would not have been possible were it not for the support I received from Tim Mather, Rick Knox, Ernie Popke, and their exceptional team.

Pamela van Giessen, my editor at John Wiley & Sons, provided encouragement and direction along the way. She was an effective cheerleader and director. Ms. Christine Furry at North Market Street Graphics played an integral part in the editing process.

The fine staff at *Futures* magazine and Futures Learning Center, including Joe Bernardo, Ginger Szala, Mark Etzkorn, Ron Michaelsen, and Wendy Grassley Speckerman, have helped enormously with the dissemination of my ideas and trading models throughout the years.

I would like to thank those readers of my first book, *The New Science of Technical Analysis*, who took the time and made the effort to supply me with the feedback I needed before I attempted to write this book.

I would also like to thank CQG (800-525-7082 or 970-945-8686), Duane Davis, DeMark Indicators c/o Futures Learning Center (800-601-

8907 ext. 2590 or 319-277-7892 and fax 319-277-7982), and Bloomberg (800-448-5678 or 212-318-2000) for their assistance in the production of the graphics included in this book. Their efforts and contributions have simplified and enhanced both the discussion and the overall presentation of the DeMark indicators.

# Introduction

Prior to writing my first book, *The New Science of Technical Analysis*, the sum total of my entire life's writing experience was limited to occasional, frantic, last-minute term papers dealing with topics with which I had a limited understanding and only a casual interest. Once I had undertaken the assignment to write the book, the rigid schedule and massive demands imposed by my publisher weighed heavily upon me. Daily, I cursed the project for its intrusion upon my time, life, and profession. Upon its completion, I was disappointed with and critical of the book's content and presentation. I vowed never again to undertake such a major commitment. Despite the fact that I was pleased with the reviews I received from even some of the industry's most staunch and vocal critics, I was determined not to waiver from my decision to retire from book writing—that is, until now.

What changed my mind? First of all, I was disturbed by the feedback I received from a handful of readers that some questions they had were left unanswered in the original book. Although I was satisfied the studies I presented were fresh, creative and, to some degree, revolutionary, I was frustrated that a few individuals misconstrued the correct interpretation and proper application of some indicators presented in the book due to the indicators' apparent incompleteness and perceived ambiguity. In addition, I was concerned that I had limited the book's scope by failing to address in sufficient detail all the variations and combinations the indicators presented. Most important, however, is the fact that subsequent to the release of the book, many authorized electronic quote vendors and research software providers added a number of these indicators to their databases. As a result of jointly working with them, I have had the opportunity to review and evaluate from a panoramic perspective all these studies in real time, as well as numerous adaptations and derivations of them. I am now comfortably equipped to introduce many qualifiers and enhancements to my original set of indicators. Furthermore, I am also able to provide more explanations and interpretations, which should improve their efficacy and, at the same time, your understanding by dispelling any confusion that may have previously existed due to either partial explanations of the indicators or unintentional disparities between the text and the accompanying charts. In addition, I am prepared to disclose for the first time ever many exciting trading indicators and studies that should challenge your analytical creativity and, hopefully, inspire you to experiment and develop new methods and indicators of your own. I assure you that it is not my intention to overwhelm or intimidate you by showering you with a deluge of new studies. Rather, my goal is to make this a true learning experience by presenting a number of key indicators, discussing their composition, and suggesting various alternative settings, applications, and interpretations. This process should enable you to introduce improvements and variations of your own, which will serve to improve your market timing abilities and analytical success.

I realize I have set an ambitious goal by attempting to write a book sequel and expecting it to have the same impact as my first book. While my original book may have inadequately dealt with some topics and concerns regarding indicator interpretation and implementation, I will address these shortcomings, as well as focus in more detail upon indicator construction and application. I do not plan to embrace in this book every aspect of the research I have conducted throughout the years. Limitations of time and space do not permit such a comprehensive agenda. I am confident, however, that I am now better prepared to write a book than I was before. The major technological alliances I forged with many data vendors and research networks have allowed me to introduce a more varied and complete presentation of my trading ideas and concepts. Not only am I able to devote entire sections of the book to improvements of the techniques discussed in my original book, but I am also able to allocate a considerable amount of time and attention to discussions regarding many other trading strategies I have developed throughout the years.

Subsequent to reading my first book, many readers expressed a strong interest in the TD Sequential market timing method. For years this indicator has served as the cornerstone of my trading strategy. Specifically, TD Sequential has operated as my market timing compass by consistently anticipating shifts in market sentiment and direction. Singularly, TD Sequential accomplishes the goal of most traders. It objectively and mechanically identifies low-risk and high-risk price zones. In this book, I introduce a number of enhancements to this special indicator, as well as present a market timing relative of TD Sequential, which I call TD Combo. I regard this new indicator as the "mother of all price anticipatory methods" I have developed. For over 16 years, I have been applying this indicator successfully to various markets, and it has proven to be an indispensable companion to the TD Sequential confirmation process. In fact, on many occasions, it has proven to be more definitive than TD Sequential in the detection of potential price-reversal levels. More important, however, by combining these two unique techniques, the potency of the identification process of low-risk and high-risk price zones is enhanced considerably. Further, I assure you that my attention to these two indicators will neither diminish nor detract from my presentation of numerous other trading techniques that I'll also share with you. I am confident that, once learned and properly applied, any number of these indicators will produce a profound impact upon your market timing research and trading success.

Also, I will present many heretofore proprietary trading techniques I have created over the years for use by a number of well-known traders. By sharing these methods with you, I hope to broaden your market timing awareness to a level enjoyed by them when they profitably and aggressively applied these techniques. Given the degree of computer horsepower and software sophistication currently available, I believe the time could never be better spent for you to experiment with these ideas and to make improvements and adaptations of your own that are compatible with your trading style. Unfortunately, I was not afforded a similar luxury and opportunity at the time I began my research career over 25 years ago. Notwithstanding the significant advances made in computer technology over the past few years, however, I am disappointed with the dearth of market timing research currently available to the trading community. I hope this book will help fill this void, as well as serve as a catalyst inciting you to conduct additional studies of your own.

In order to trade successfully, most traders rely upon trend-following techniques. This practice is emotionally satisfying and pragmatically straightforward since it serves to reinforce one's predisposed trading instincts to buy strength and to sell weakness. So widespread among traders is the practice of using trend-following techniques that it is not uncommon to hear a trader remark that "the trend is a trader's friend." I believe, however, that this expression must be qualified to include the phrase "unless the trend is about to end," and at that time it becomes a trader's worst enemy. By their very construction, trend-following techniques ensure entry only after price tops and bottoms have been completed. To counteract this shortcoming, two basic themes permeate most trading indicators I have developed—namely, market rhythm and price exhaustion. By design, most of my trading concepts contradict the conventional trading wisdom and style employed by the trend-following community, since both approaches evaluate price patterns and relationships that unfold as a market moves up or down, attempting to identify those price periods commonly associated with the culmination of a trend and the inception of a price reversal. Specifically, my extensive market research indicates that price bottoms develop not because smart buyers or groups of buyers operate in concert, but rather, figuratively speaking, the last seller sells, supply diminishes, and, by default, price advances. Furthermore, my studies suggest that market tops are not made because omniscient top pickers or informed trading syndicates with massive financial resources coordinate their selling campaigns; rather a diminution in buying occurs at that particular point in time and price declines of its own weight. The following example should illustrate this phenomenon more clearly. In early 1980 I served as a consultant to a large metals' trader. I instructed him in the basics of my TD Sequential indicator, and I explained to him that I had designed this market timing tool to anticipate high-risk price zones and that a trader should be prepared to sell into market strength at that time since demand is plentiful. Throughout the month of January, I prepared him for the ultimate high in the precious metals' markets. Each day I reported the indicator's status until the completion of Countdown day 13 occurred and the anticipated zone of high risk approached. As the market rallied, the release of fundamental news became decidedly more positive, and most analysts enthusiastically forecast the continuation of the upside move indefinitely. Just prior to recording the thirteenth Countdown day, I had an extended discussion with the trader, and the outcome of this conversation influenced my analytical career forever. By means of numerous historical examples, I demonstrated to him the vulnerability of the market to decline once a 13 high-risk TD Sequential Countdown was recorded. He understood, but when pressed by me to liquidate, he chose to postpone selling until he was confident price had in fact peaked. Repeatedly, I urged him to sell. Once the market price accelerated downside, he countered my exhortation to sell by responding, "Sell? Sell to whom?" These words ring true to my ears to this day. His description of the market environment was unknowingly insightful, and at the same time, its implications held dire consequences for his portfolio. The market had rallied for an extended period of time. All those individuals who were positively disposed toward the market were fully invested and their subsequent lip service and hopes alone were insufficient to move price higher, let alone support it. The trend followers were positioned in the market. My warning to exit the market had been insistent and repetitive and, at the same time, totally ignored by my client. He was confronted with a dilemma—the trend-following sellers were now in control, and it was too late for him to attract sufficient bids for his sizable position in the market. My theory of price exhaustion had been applied to a real-time market experience, and my expectations were fulfilled.

Subsequently, I researched and improved my trend-reversal detection process by developing additional market timing models and techniques that also anticipate and confirm exhaustion tops and bottoms. My goal has been to avoid the competition and pitfalls generally associated with traditional trend-following approaches by developing contratrend trading indicators. Early on, I realized that by researching and creating trend-following techniques, like so many other analysts, I merely invited unwanted trading risks such as slippage, price vacuums, gaps, and unfilled orders. I noted that few, if any, stock specialists or futures or options market makers ever file for bankruptcy. What distinguishes their trading styles from those of the typical trader? I concluded that they operate against the prevailing trend—in other words, they provide supply as price moves up and they furnish demand as price moves down. To illustrate this phenomenon further, I cite an observation made while commuting daily to work from the suburbs into the city in dense, early-morning traffic, competing with other drivers and frustrated by delays and gridlock. I became envious of those drivers who were leaving the city to work in the suburbs, unimpeded and traveling at their own pace. I find this situation analogous to trading against the flow or the consensus of market trend followers. By doing so, the trading benefits derived are obvious. They include positive price slippage on market orders (price fills, regardless of size, at levels often better than the price limit entered), minimal market impact, and enhanced trading performance results. Consequently, the thrust of my research tends to avoid techniques that can be described as trend following and that are designed to buy strength and sell weakness.

Despite the fact that many of the indicators presented in this book were created many years ago, I am confident that these ideas are still applicable to current markets. Unfortunately, at the time I conducted my research and development, I did not possess the technology, data, information, and resources available to market analysts today. My work evolved over time as a result of rigorous manual calculations, inspection, and trial and error. In recent years, sophisticated software and technology have been developed to simply and effectively apply these research methodologies to intraday, daily, weekly, and monthly time intervals. Consequently, research regarding optimal price and time interrelationships can be conducted more easily and productively, and conclusions can be reached much quicker than ever before.

Hopefully, gone are the days when market timers have to hide their chart books in a bottom desk drawer, lest others perceive them as practicing voodoo analysis or using occult powers to formulate their market forecasts. Market timing has become acceptable, even fashionable, and is a major component in the decision-making process of many highly regarded financial institutions. I recall my own experience many years ago when my fundamental research boss assigned me to write a report evaluating General Motors. He gave me four weeks to prepare and present the fundamental outlook for this company. Once I had completed my research report on the company, he stood at my desk, looking over my shoulder, awaiting my interpretation of the market timing outlook for the company's stock. Obviously, he had no appreciation for the time and information required to complete a technical appraisal of the stock. Whereas fundamental forecasts are typically couched in vague "buy," "sell," or "hold" recommendations and most lack specific entry price and exit levels, the role expected of market timers or technicians by the uninformed is to operate and produce forecasts on short notice with little preparation or forethought. Depending upon both the level and degree of analytical sophistication of the market technician and the availability and application of computer software and resources, a technical forecast generally requires more than a quick perusal of price charts. Certainly, this process is not a casual, matter-of-fact exercise; rather it requires concentration, proper tools, and market timing expertise to execute effectively. I can't emphasize enough the fact that success in any endeavor, and especially one as challenging as trading, which attracts some of the brightest individuals and minds in the world, requires many years of training and experience.

The success and recognition I've enjoyed in developing and applying market timing techniques have instilled in me a high degree of confidence and comfort. All of the indicators discussed throughout this book are presented in the context of a market timing tool kit, as a package, rather than as a series of complete and separate systems. This is intentional, since I prefer to have you integrate these methods into a research amalgam specifically adapted to your trading style. In my first book, I described three distinct levels of market timing analysis that can be employed to predict price behavior:

1. *Casual chart inspection.* Since this method requires nothing more than the subjective interpretation of price patterns (in other words, "gut feel"), by definition, it is vague and general, lacks consistency, and is deficient to the extent that "beauty is definitely in the eyes of the beholder" and that which is perceived as positive or negative by one analyst may, in fact, be totally contradicted by another analyst or even the same individual at a different time. In other words, I often refer to the fact that I have broken down the word *chartist* into what I believe to be the proper description of this type of market timer—namely, a "chart artist."

2. *Indicator construction and interpretation.* This technique is a significant improvement over item 1, since the approach is defined and prescriptive; however, the necessary structure required to generate buy and sell signals is lacking. More important, however, the link between this level and actual systemization is but a minor one.

3. *System creation and implementation.*    This level is totally objective and mechanical, and the benefit derived from this type of analytical approach is the development of real-time systematic buy and sell generators. The description of this type of market timer can be aptly described as a "chart scientist."

Intentionally, I have restricted this book's content to a discussion of a series of market timing indicators. Although I have worked on these techniques for many years, the technology and software required to test and determine their ideal composition is ongoing. Hopefully, your inquisitiveness will enable you to craft improvements to these methods, thereby affording you the opportunity to build them into workable market timing models that will serve to enhance your potential of trading success.

I have often described my role in the educational training process as the supplier of the fuel and the road map necessary for a student trader's analytical journey. At the same time, I have repeatedly emphasized my unwillingness to chauffeur his or her car. I am a firm believer that independent thinking is critical to trading success. I'm certain that after devoting time and effort to the mastery of the basic indicator concepts I present, you will appreciate this fact. In any case, at the conclusion of each indicator discussion, I will present the generic default settings I currently use in my own trading and consulting operations. Please note that I have expanded the variability of the indicator parameter settings to introduce you to both the numerous possible selections, as well as the comprehensive composition and nature of each indicator. Had I not discussed these various options, I believe my assignment as an instructor would be incomplete. Merely presenting a fixed series of settings would suggest that the systemization process was rigid, when in reality it is dynamic and fluid, since a myriad of combinations and permutations exist that can produce respectable trading performance results. Unfortunately, my quest for the selection of both the optimal composition of the indicators, as well as the ideal matrix for the interrelationships between the various indicators, has not been completed at this time.

I learned at an early age that anything worthwhile is attainable with effort and determination and then only with a lot of luck. I caution you that the application of the research material I am sharing is somewhat complex, unorthodox, and its vernacular may initially appear foreign and confusing. Don't be intimidated or discouraged. As with learning any new methodology, it requires a period of time to both understand and then apply the concepts successfully. It took me over 25 years to develop these indicators. It should take you considerably less time to become proficient at the use of these techniques once you review the text and examples presented. I will share the observations I have made as a result of the extensive market timing research I have conducted throughout this long development process.

Ultimately, nothing would be more gratifying to me than for you to acquire a similar appetite to research, develop, customize, and successfully apply variations of these indicators to your own trading activities. While I know that these indicators are effective, they alone are not the answer. In short, successful trading requires much more than just a set of solid indicators. Fortitude, conviction, discipline, and money management are each important components of trading success and are often overlooked by the apprentice trader. Without consideration of these additional factors, trading tends to become an exercise in gambling and futility.

A common denominator existing among most all of the indicators and the ideas presented throughout this book is the readers' ability to apply them mechanically and to interpret them objectively. Technical analysis has evolved from its simple and humble beginnings to complex market timing models incorporating neural networks, optimization techniques, chaos theory, artificial intelligence, and, ultimately, full circle back to basic, meat-and-potatoes methodologies from whence my research began over 25 years ago. Despite the fact that the approaches may superficially appear homogeneous, however, there exists an obvious distinction between this reincarnated version of technical analysis and its former composition. In a significant regard they are different—I have replaced the subjectivity and the vagueness that characterized the usage and application of these basic techniques historically with mechanical, systematic, and objective rules and methodologies, which when applied properly serve to eliminate guesswork. Unfortunately, from my perspective, I have witnessed no meaningful, value-added improvements as a result of the increased technology, software, formulas, and theories developed to decode market price activity by those complex, sophisticated, computer-driven techniques employed by some market timing rocket scientists. There is, however, a definite coordinated effort to revert back to the technical basics. In any case, I have concluded that in order to be successful, a trader must study market price behavior and then develop simple, basic, and mechanical models designed to anticipate price movements, and no better starting place exists, I believe, than applying variations of the objective techniques and market timing approaches presented in this book.

Profitable trading is a combination of three distinct and unrelated factors, the least important of which is a good market timing indicator or system. Two more critical elements are money management skills and self-discipline. With the exception of one chapter in this book devoted to general money management principles, the discussion of these two topics will be incidental to this book's primary focus, which is market timing techniques. My goal in writing this book is to provide an introduction to a series of new and exciting market timing approaches, as well as fresh and original perspectives for a trader to view and operate within the markets. In the process, I hope to dispel any misconceptions or misperceptions regarding many widely used market timing methods. In conclusion, I strongly suggest that before you implement any of the indicators presented in this book, you conduct an inventory of your money management methodology, as well as develop a thorough psychological trading profile of yourself. To ignore either would be akin to a carpenter building a house with tools but no plans. Certainly, an accomplished journeyman will be able to construct a respectable structure by using only equipment; however, by following a set of architectural plans and drawings, the task is simplified immensely and the potential for success is enhanced considerably as well. Once again, I emphasize the fact that successful trading requires a similar combination of activities and abilities: a strict adherence to a trading philosophy and methodology, an appreciation of sound money management principles, an awareness of your trading emotions, and a recognition of your trading limitations.

Note that throughout this book, unless stated otherwise, for purposes of discussion and illustration, I will generally refer to daily charts and data, when in fact any other time period can be easily substituted as well. My reasons for selecting daily information are threefold:

1. It is the most readily available data and has been the most widely followed time period for decades.
2. It not only relieves the trader of the necessity of constantly following the market on an intraday basis, but it also reduces the risk of price revisions from the various exchanges, such as those that historically have plagued intraday databases.
3. It increases the chance that when market indications are generated based on this information, the trader can be confident the trades will in actuality be executed.

# Chapter

# 1

# Oscillators

*Observation:* In late summer 1982 the stock market registered one of its steepest advances in history. At that time, many market commentators and analysts were quick to report the extreme overbought levels recorded by most conventional market timing oscillators. Incorrectly, they associated severely overbought, extremely stretched indicator readings with the expectation of an imminent market collapse or at least a sharp downside correction. A similar but reverse situation occurred in October 1987 during the stock market crash. Few market timers were aware in either instance that such exaggerated and unrelenting oscillator movements over an extended period of time are generally associated with a continuation of a price trend rather than its termination. Extensive research suggests that a clear distinction exists between what can be described as either a *severe* or a *modest* overbought or oversold indicator reading. For example, extreme market oscillator readings are like patients who are suffering from potentially fatal illnesses or who are involved in life-threatening accidents. Although in rare instances recovery can be miraculous and immediate, in most cases it is gradual and beset with numerous setbacks. Only after the condition has been upgraded from critical or guarded to stable is the patient able to commence recovery in earnest. So, too, only when an oscillator level is mildly, as opposed to severely, overbought or oversold is a price reversal likely to occur. However, to distinguish correctly one market condition from the other can be a difficult diagnostic process. It requires the successful development and application of an effective market timing oscillator. Furthermore, subsequent to a determination of the overall market environment, there must be a trigger mechanism or device installed, sufficiently sensitive to identify when potential trend reversals are imminent. In other words, the steps required to evaluate and implement a trade as a result of an overbought/oversold oscillator reading are as follows: (1) The overall condition or environment of the market must be defined as either overbought or oversold. (2) The extent, level, or degree of overbought or oversold must be measured temporally (in terms of time) in order to classify the oscillator as either mildly or severely overbought or oversold. (3) A set of prescribed conditions and rules must be defined and then fulfilled in order to establish whether the existing price trend is about to reverse or the current market movement is more likely to continue or even intensify.

You should be skeptical of many conventional market timing oscillators. For a number of reasons, the widespread acceptance and use of a few of them is surprising. In particular, the apparent lack of understanding and awareness of, as well as concern for, the derivation, construction, and proper application of two of the most commonly used oscillators (i.e., the Relative Strength Index (RSI) and Stochastics) are greatly disturbing. These two indicators were introduced to the charting and trading communities in the late 1970s and were featured at that time in two popular weekly chart publications, as well as on the first real-time electronic chart and quote service. Due to their widespread exposure to trading audiences, these indicators became instantly popular and have been widely used even to this day. Surprisingly, it appears that the momentum generated by their auspicious beginnings has been sufficient to propel interest in and use of these indicators to levels far greater than anyone's most optimistic expectations. At that time, I was a subscriber to both these services. However, most of the providers and other users, when questioned regarding the formulas, the indicators, and their proper interpretation, were unable to explain their composition and supportive logic and to provide a consistent and objective approach to their correct application and proper interpretation. Particularly annoying, however, is the fact that traders have neither objected to these perceived shortcomings nor even questioned basic facts, such as the indicators' monikers, since both are obviously misnamed—the RSI is not a true relative strength indicator, and Stochastics is not a stochastic process by any stretch of the imagination. Furthermore, the label "Stochastics" was not acquired until many years after the originator of the indicator, Ralph Dystant, had died. For reference purposes, he had called the oscillators %D and %K. According to Rick Redmont, a cofounder of Computrac, the name Stochastics arose from a description of the indicators prepared by Mr. Dystant for his subscribers. When Computrac first included this indicator in its database in 1978, the company selected this name because of its simplicity rather than its suitability and appropriateness. In order to confirm my belief that most traders have a tendency to be gullible, when delivering speeches I occasionally quiz audiences regarding the formulas for both RSI and Stochastics. On only one occasion has an individual been able to correctly recite the formula for one indicator, and in no instance has anyone been able to provide both. Given the degree of reliance upon these and other widely used market timing oscillators by many traders, as well as the size of the market positions some traders assume based upon their casual interpretation of these indicators, this lack of understanding is mind-boggling. For reference purposes, the formulas for the RSI and Stochastics indicators can be found in most books on technical analysis.

In addition to the general lack of understanding of the construction and composition of many popular market timing indicators, as well as their mislabeling, another criticism that can be leveled against most conventional, widely followed overbought/oversold oscillators is the methodology used to derive them. Most indicator values are calculated using a series of exponential formulas. Consequently, extraordinary events, such as a presidential assassination, an electrical or computer failure, a declaration of war, or a suspension of trading, introduce aberrant price data that may distort an oscillator's value. Although the impact of these market-unrelated events may diminish over time, the influence exerted upon an indicator by these calamities nevertheless affects an exponential oscillator until the underlying security's trading activity is either suspended or terminated. Of most concern is that this fatal flaw is inherent in all exponential mathematical formulas, and it is impossible to eradicate the oscillator distortions they might cause. On the other hand, by applying a simple arithmetic formula to calculate an indicator value, the problems caused by these external developments are systematically and mathematically eliminated over a period of time. Furthermore, these arithmetic oscillators appear to be more sensitive to short-term price swings than those exponentially derived, which tend to mute volatility. As a result, all of the overbought/oversold oscillators you will find in this book have been arithmetically derived.

There are as many interpretations assigned to an indicator as there are traders using it. Most traders who use oscillators to arrive at trading decisions, however, apply a form of divergence analysis. For example, (1) at a suspected market low, they compare the price of a security with the indicator value at a comparable point in time and then relate both these values to the price and the indicator level at a subsequent lower price level, and (2) at a suspected market high, they compare the price of a security with the indicator value at a comparable point in time and then relate both these values to the price and the indicator level at a subsequent higher price level. Specifically, in the first instance, if price declines to a lower level and the indicator fails to confirm this weakness and records a higher low, then they argue this price-indicator divergence that is recorded implies an imminent upside price reversal; in the second case, if price advances to a higher level and the indicator fails to confirm this strength and records a lower high, then they maintain this price-indicator divergence that is recorded implies an imminent downside price reversal. My research suggests this widely followed practice of divergence analysis is merely a symptom of a condition that may appear at impending market tops or bottoms, and *duration*, or the amount of time an indicator exceeds a defined oscillator band, is the cause and is consequently more important. Therefore, in the following discussion, the utility of conventional divergence analysis techniques will be challenged. As an alternative, traders will benefit by applying a concept called TD Duration Analysis™.

Whereas at perceived market bottoms and tops most traders focus upon the interrelationship between successive price levels and indicator values at comparable points in time, TD Duration Analysis avoids such a comparison and concentrates solely upon the length of time an indicator remains in an oversold or an overbought zone. In other words, TD Duration Analysis counts the number of consecutive trading days in which an indicator is either below or above an indicator band and makes a distinction between "mild" and "severe" oversold or overbought readings dependent upon the length of this series of trading days. The advantage of this form of analysis is that it precludes stubborn adherence to an unprofitable trading position merely because successive indicator and price readings indicate a price/indicator divergence and imply market action. Such interpretive shortcomings have proven to be the bane of conventional indicator analysis and are particularly pronounced in the case of an uninterrupted series of oscillator readings at successively higher low levels or lower high levels outside the oscillator band, with price activity simultaneously failing to confirm by recording divergences. Rather than resisting participation in the prevailing market trend whenever an oscillator records a "severe" reading by exceeding either the upper or the lower indicator band for more than five consecutive trading days, for example, because of an apparent divergence, TD Duration Analysis, on the other hand, forces a trader to either accede to the market trend or to step aside and do nothing. Conversely, on those occasions when an indicator records a "mild" reading by remaining in either an overbought or an oversold zone for less than six consecutive trading days, for example, TD Duration Analysis forewarns of potential price reversals provided they are perfected or qualified (see discussion of TD Price Oscillator Qualifier™ later in this chapter). The examples should demonstrate more clearly the tendencies of market price activity to behave in a manner consistent with my concept of TD Duration Analysis rather than conforming to the tenets of the widely followed and popular approach of divergence analysis. Note in Figure 1.1 how the price of IBM continued lower despite the fact that the TD Range Expansion Index™ (TD REI) low in June 1995, was above the indi-

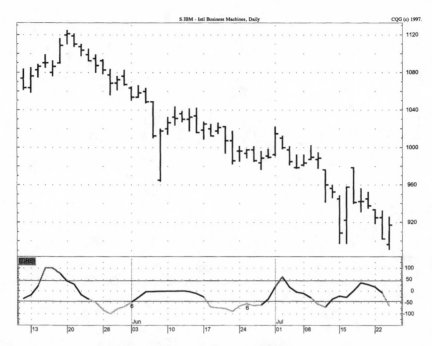

**Figure 1.1**  In this example, a higher indicator low in late June versus late May did not translate into a meaningful advance and definitely did not approach the price level of late May. The fact that the TD REI indicator remained oversold in June for more than the TD Duration limitation of five days implied inherent weakness. Note that between the late May and June oversold oscillator readings, the highest level the indicator reached was 0. Although its usage is not recommended, for those traders who apply divergence analysis, the fact that the oscillator did not record an intervening overbought reading permits this comparison. Note the TD REI indicator reading on July 24. It was followed by an up close. This suggested the potential for an imminent rally.

cator low a month earlier in May. Fortunately, TD REI is sufficiently sensitive that it was able to record an overbought reading coincident with the early July peak that preceded the subsequent price decline. Furthermore, Figure 1.2 illustrates a price/indicator divergence that was not resolved to the downside as divergence analysis practitioners might suggest should have occurred. In any case, once again TD Duration Analysis implies that the amount of time the TD REI indicator remains outside its indicator band is excessive and, consequently, the trend is expected to continue until this extreme indicator reading dissipates, retreats into the neutral zone, and then records a modest—less than six days—overbought reading. Furthermore, if you are inclined to apply divergence analysis, you should introduce a filter that will improve this technique's accuracy and efficacy. In particular, before you act upon a perceived price-indicator divergence, the price move should be confirmed by the TD Price Oscillator Qualifier (TDPOQ), which is described later in this chapter.

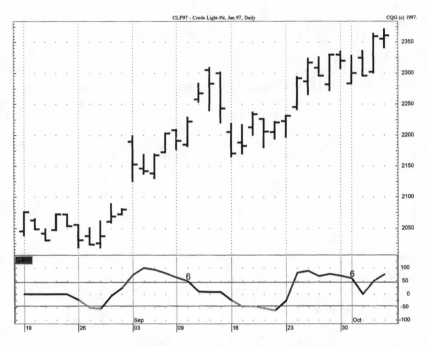

**Figure 1.2** Lower indicator highs and complementary higher price highs in September were accompanied by TD Duration of six or more days. This suggested internal price strength and the likely continuation of the price advance despite this indicator divergence. Although its usage is not recommended, if you are inclined to apply divergence analysis, the fact that the successive overbought and oversold levels are preceded by an oversold and an overbought reading precludes the application of divergence analysis and the introduction of indicator comparisons.

One major difference exists between Figures 1.1 and 1.2, and this applies specifically to the interpretation assigned by those traders using divergence analysis to arrive at their market forecasts. Please review the indicator levels displayed on the two charts. Other than the fact that the extreme indicator level for Figure 1.1 reads oversold on two occasions for a period of at least six days each and for Figure 1.2 the indicator levels display overbought on two occasions for a period of at least six days each, thereby both exceeding the maximum allowable time to expect a potential trend reversal according to my oscillator interpretation discipline (TD Duration Analysis applied to the TD REI indicator), there is one noteworthy distinction between the two examples. Whereas in both Figures 1.1 and 1.2 the two extreme readings occur approximately one month apart, it is what occurs between these two periods that is significant. In example 1, the indicator level between these two extreme oversold readings fails to exceed 0 upside, and in this instance divergence analysis could be applied, although it is not necessarily recommended. On the other hand, in example 2, the oscillator activity behaves quite differently since between the two extreme overbought readings, the indicator moved into the oversold zone. Because this intervening extreme oscillator movement occurred, no reasonable basis exists for the application of divergence analysis, since the intermediate oversold reading effectively nullified any reasonable connection between the two overbought indicator levels. In other words, if you were interested in applying divergence analysis and relating a series of comparable indicator and price levels to draw conclusions regarding a market's price activity, then the period between two successive oversold readings should not include a recording of overbought, and, conversely, the period between two successive overbought readings should not include a recording of oversold. Once again, although the practice of divergence analysis is not recommended, a similar interpretation to the one just described will enable a user of this approach to operate more effectively and profitably.

Among the many other arithmetic oscillators I have developed over the years, five key indicators are particularly helpful in the identification of both price tops and bottoms, as well as in the establishment of the overall trend of markets: TD Rate of Change™ (TD ROC I, TD ROC II), TD Range Expansion Index (TD REI—alternate and standard), TD DeMarker I and II, and TD Plurality. In addition to these original trading indicators, this book will reveal additional proprietary techniques, including trading devices that serve not only to confirm price reversals, but also to define the inception of a price trend after one of these oscillators has generated a potential low-risk entry indication. The features of the indicators presented here, as well as the confirmation techniques that accompany them, are both the objective and the mechanistic processes that should be installed to facilitate their application and interpretation. In this regard, these methods do not possess the handicaps and shortcomings commonly identified or associated with many widely followed conventional indicators, such as the following:

1. The exponential distortions caused by non-market-related influences
2. The arbitrary reliance upon closing prices rather than other meaningful price data
3. The subjective interpretations assigned to oscillator movements
4. The inclusion of irrelevant price activity and price relationships
5. The improper focus upon day-to-day price activity rather than other time period relationships
6. The application of divergence analysis rather than TD Duration Analysis

Furthermore, providing a checklist of procedures to follow will allow the process of indicator application, implementation, and interpretation to become a more simplified, logical, practical, and rewarding experience for both analysts and traders alike.

# TD ROC I™ and TD ROC II™

## *TD ROC I*

*Observation:* It is not uncommon for traders to calculate the rate of change of price movement in order to formulate conclusions regarding future market price behavior. Two common methods used to compute momentum-based oscillators can be employed to accomplish this goal. One approach calculates the ratio between the market's current price and that same price *x* days, weeks, months, and so forth, earlier. The other technique determines the difference between the market's current closing price and the closing price *x* days earlier. The former method is preferable, and my uniquely constructed and interpreted oscillator is called *TD Rate of Change* (TD ROC). Typically, the time span used by most market timers between the comparative reference prices to calculate the rate of change is a long period of time, such as month-to-month or year-to-year. The specific process performed and the time period selected to arrive at the rate of change values, however, may vary from one analyst or trader to another. Many years ago, while conducting momentum research and calculating ratios to illustrate graphically the rate of change of month-end closing prices for various markets compared with the same markets' month-end closes one year earlier, I inadvertently compared the daily closing prices 12 days apart instead of my intended selection of 12 months. Quite by accident, I uncovered a rate-of-change indicator that possesses remarkable predictive value in identifying prospective price-reversal levels. In particular, when applying this methodology to high-priced markets, such as Treasury bond futures, government securities, S&P futures, and stock market indices, this specific version of rate-of-change analysis (TD ROC I) typically fluctuated within a wide band defined by 102.5 and 97.5 percent of the closing price 12 trading days earlier. Further research indicated that coincident with the TD ROC I indicator value exceeding either the upper or the lower band for 15 or fewer price periods (price bars), a potential price top or bottom was identified. Whereas in most instances in which my concept of TD Duration Analysis is applied to market timing indicators, a meter of five or fewer price periods is assigned to distinguish between a mild and a severe indicator reading, in the case of TD ROC I and TD ROC II, 15 or fewer price bars are used, and for the TD DeMarker indicator (see following), a duration of 8 price bars or fewer are applied to qualify as a mild reading. For example, in those instances in which TD ROC I remains above or below the upper or the lower band for 16 or more price bars, there is a tendency for price to continue its trend until this severe overbought/oversold condition is dissipated, TD ROC I returns to neutral (the zone between the two bands), and another attempt to record a "mild overbought/oversold reading" (a period of less than 16 price bars) is realized.

With one exception (see following discussion regarding TD Alternative Oscillator™ method), this conclusion is consistent with my theory of TD Duration Analysis of oscillator behavior. Figure 1.3 illustrates how price for the S&P December futures contract and the TD ROC I indicator align themselves at prospective trend reversal levels. There was only one instance in which the oscillator remained above the overbought threshold for more than 15 trading days (see the late January through mid-February period on the chart). All other observations were for less than 15 trading days and all, with the exception of late September 1996, coincided with price reversals. Furthermore, whereas the early May price low was not identified by TD ROC I, it was correctly accomplished by applying TD ROC II (compare the two TD ROC oscillator charts of the S&P that appear in Figure 1.6), and that is why you should use both.

**TD ROC Indicator Band Settings:**   Extensive research showed that the trading band for TD ROC I can be adapted to accommodate the vagaries associated with different types of markets and time periods by simply introducing minor adjustments to the basic TD ROC settings, such as expanding

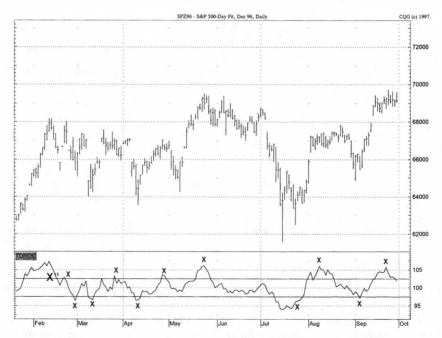

**Figure 1.3**   TD ROC I indicator readings in overbought and oversold zones for more than 15 days (big *X*) constitute a severe or an extreme intensity of buying or selling pressure, and the indicator must therefore recycle by moving back into the neutral zone and then returning into the overbought or the oversold zone for a shorter period of time, thereby recording a mild oscillator indication, which is more consistent with a market top or bottom.

or contracting the trading band parameters. Just such an adaptation will serve you well for both lower-priced securities and less volatile markets, as well as for intraday analysis and trading. For example, both short-term interest rate futures, such as Eurodollars, T-bills, short sterling, Euroyen and Euromarks, and intraday trading, such as 1-, 5-, and 10-minute intervals, often require a narrower oscillator band be constructed and applied in order to produce effective results. In these instances, the tighter band is created by multiplying the standard parameter settings of plus and minus 2.5 percent (102.5 and 97.5 percent) by 10 percent each, thereby reducing the band width to 100.25 and 99.75 percent. This revised oscillator band is more sensitive and exact when applied to markets operating within a trading environment characterized by similar circumstances and conditions. By using a computer, this adjustment, as well as many other variations, can be simply tested, manipulated, and applied. Figure 1.4 demonstrates how this variation can be introduced to a daily chart of the German mark December 1996

**Figure 1.4** When the TD ROC I level is in an overbought or oversold zone for more than 15 days, a severe or extreme reading is recorded and the indicator must recycle by moving back into the neutral area and then back into overbought or oversold for a shorter period of time to register a modest reading. Intraday, inactive, and markets trading in decimals can use an adapted version of TD ROC with settings 10% of the standard parameter settings. In other words, 100.25% and 99.75% can be substituted for the standard 102.5% and 97.5%. In this example, the deutsche mark future can be expressed either way, but as you can see, the smaller band generates more overbought and oversold indications and the wider oscillator band is exceeded upside in late July and downside in December (large *X*s).

futures contract. Due to the fact that the deutsche mark is priced in decimals and it is a relatively volatile market, a dichotomy exists. It is possible to apply the standard TD ROC I oscillator thresholds of 102.5 and 97.5 percent, as well as the adjusted and contracted band of 100.25 and 99.75 percent, even though a daily chart and not a short-term intraday chart is displayed. Once again, a duration of 15 days is installed for this narrower band to delineate between extreme (or severe) and mild overbought and oversold readings for TD ROC I. Furthermore, by applying the TD Price Oscillator Qualifier (TDPOQ) described next, the entry level can be refined and defined further.

### TD Price Oscillator Qualifier (TDPOQ) and TD Alternative Oscillator Method

Although this discussion of the TD Price Oscillator Qualifier (TDPOQ) and the TD Alternative Oscillator method relates specifically to TD ROC, they are equally applicable to the other indicators presented in this book. Furthermore, don't be surprised if both techniques have application to various indicators you may currently be using as well. Both will be presented at this time.

Extensive research has identified a price pattern that generally develops subsequent to, or coincident with, an overbought or oversold condition and that serves as a simple and conservative method to confirm the inception of a potential trend reversal. An effective technique, called the TD Price Oscillator Qualifier (TDPOQ), has been designed specifically to evaluate the price behavior of the underlying security once a market oscillator has indicated a potential low-risk entry opportunity at a suspected market bottom or top. The movement of this market oscillator relates only to the price behavior of the underlying security once an indicator has recorded an oversold or an overbought reading. To apply TDPOQ to confirm an anticipated upside move, you should make certain that the oscillator's current position is, or most recently has been, below the lower oscillator band and not above the upper band. Conversely, to apply TDPOQ to confirm an anticipated downside move, you should make certain that the oscillator's current position is, or most recently has been, above the upper oscillator band and not below the lower band. In each instance, it is important that the indicator not remain below the lower band for more than the prescribed number of days at a price bottom in order to conform to the requirements of TD Duration Analysis or above the upper band for more than the prescribed number of days at a market top in order to conform to the requirements of TD Duration Analysis— the TD Alternative Oscillator method notwithstanding. However, this time requirement can be adjusted depending upon the indicator and the band thresholds selected. Furthermore, the TDPOQ opportunity extinguishes itself upside once the oscillator advances above a specified level and downside once the oscillator declines below a predetermined level: for example, in the case of TD REI plus 10 for an upside move and minus 10 for a downside move; in the case of TD DeMarker I, 50 for an upside move and 50 for a downside move; and in the case of TD ROC I and II, 101.0 for an upside move and 99.0 for a downside move. In those instances in which the narrower price band for TD ROC is applied, for example, the upside cancellation becomes 100.10, and the downside cancellation level is 99.90.

Here are the required steps for a low-risk buy entry:

1. A mild oversold condition.
2. A closing price that is greater than the previous trading day's closing price.
3. The opening price on the trading day immediately following the up close day is less than or equal to the previous trading day's high (the up close day's high).
4. The high that same trading day must exceed upside the previous trading day's true high (a *true high* is the trading day's high or the previous day's close, whichever is greater).

Conversely, the required sequence of events for a low-risk sell entry is:

1. A mild overbought condition.
2. A closing price that is less than the previous trading day's closing price.
3. The opening price on the trading day immediately following the down close day is greater than or equal to the previous trading day's low (the down close day's low).
4. The low that same trading day must exceed downside the previous trading day's true low (a *true low* is the trading day's low or the previous day's close, whichever is less).

This evaluation is ongoing until the indicator moves from the oversold zone and exceeds an oscillator level approaching overbought for an upside move or until the indicator moves from the overbought zone and exceeds an oscillator level approaching oversold for a downside move. If this pattern fails to occur at a prospective bottom or top, then a trigger mechanism crucial to the confirmation process of the breakout is lacking. The requirement that the opening price on the day after the up close or down close day be contained by the previous day's price range is a critical component since it indicates a degree of trading skepticism regarding the prospects for a breakout. This methodology does present an element of risk since the indicator can remain within the overbought or oversold zone for a period of time exceeding the maximum allowable limit defined under TD Duration Analysis to be acceptable to classify the indicator reading as mild or modest oversold or overbought, and when that occurs, trading prudence dictates that the position be exited or, at a minimum, a close stop loss be installed. The only exception would be if the TD Alternative Oscillator method applies to that specific indicator activity (see following).

**Advanced TDPOQ:** Other enhancements to the basic TDPOQ process can be simply introduced. However, each additional condition serves to reduce the frequency of trend-reversal confirmations. Figure 1.5 illustrates the standard TDPOQ and the TD Alternative Oscillator Method (see following). One enhancement to TDPOQ that has been applied with a high degree of success requires that from an oversold indicator reading, the first up close day must be preceded the previous trading day by a low that is less than the low one trading day earlier, and an oversold indicator reading must be recorded either prior to or on that same day. Conversely, from an overbought condition, the first down close day must be preceded the previous trading day by a high that is greater than the high one trading day earlier, and an overbought indicator reading must be recorded either prior to or on that same day. Furthermore, you should be warned that the following can occur

**Figure 1.5**   If the TD Alternative Oscillator is applied to the Dow Jones Industrial Average in August 1987, despite the fact that the TD ROC I was extremely overbought since it remained above 102.5 for more than 15 days (large *X*), the indication of a market top was confirmed once TD ROC I declined below 102.5 and the close the same day was above the close two trading days earlier (*a* and *a′* on chart). Note the other mild overbought and oversold trend-reversal indications generated by TDPOQ, which are marked with a small *x*.

when applying TDPOQ: If either the market's open on the trading day suc-ceeding the up close day is above the previous day's high, it often coincides with a short-term price peak, despite the fact that the indicator has only recently recorded an oversold reading, or if the market's open on the trading day succeeding the down close day is below the previous day's low, it often-times coincides with a short-term low, despite the fact that the indicator has only recently recorded an overbought reading (see Figure 1.6). A prudent trader should be alert to both those markets that record a gap opening upside above the previous trading day's high on the trading day immediately follow-ing the up close after an oversold oscillator reading and those markets that register a gap opening downside below the previous trading day's low on the trading day immediately following the down close after an overbought oscil-lator reading, since such abrupt and exaggerated openings suggest the mar-ket has become prematurely short-term overbought or oversold, and as a result, price oftentimes reacts, at least over the very short term, contradic-tory to standard TDPOQ expectations. Consequently, the TDPOQ prereq-uisite to open less than or equal to the previous day's high for an upside move and greater than or equal to the previous day's low for a downside move, as

**Figure 1.6**   Note the sign of a bottom at the May 1996 S&P low generated by TD ROC II (*X*) and, at the same time, the inability of TD ROC I to confirm this low (*X'*). The TDPOQ indication of a low-risk entry occurred one day after the price bottom *a*. TDPOQ identified a top for both indicators subsequent to the May high *b*. However, TDPOQ was not activated on day *c* given its weak opening beneath the previous day's low, thereby presenting a short-term low-risk buy opportunity.

well as the requirement that the breakout exceeding these levels occur subsequent to the market's opening price, are critical variables. Not only should
a trader make certain that the opening price be contained by the previous
day's high or low, depending upon whether it is an upside or downside move,
but he or she should also be aware that an exception or alternative option to
this TDPOQ opening-gap disqualification rule exists. Specifically, if the
closing price on the trading day succeeding the up close after an oversold
oscillator reading is greater than that same day's opening price, or the closing price on the trading day succeeding the down close after an overbought
oscillator reading is less than that same day's opening price, then despite the
fact that an aggressive opening price gap exceeding the previous day's price
range may have occurred, entry can still be qualified. In other words, if the
opening price on the trading day succeeding the up close day is above the
previous day's high, and the close that day is above the open, the concern that
the open gap may have been overzealous is offset by the fact that the close is
above the open, indicating potential price follow-through. Conversely, if the
opening price on the trading day succeeding the down close day is below the
previous day's low, and the close that day is below the open, the concern that
the open gap may have been extremely weak is offset by the fact that the close
is below the open, indicating potential price follow-through. The only additional consideration to ensure low-risk entry for this particular price pattern
is that often the price gap created by the aggressive buying or selling at the
market's opening be filled at some point prior to the close of trading that same
day. In summary, an indication that the upside gap above the up close day's
high will produce a short-term high rather than a continuation of the opening breakout is a failure to perpetuate the price movement upside by effecting
a close above the open price level that same trading day or, on occasion, the
failure to fill the opening price gap. By the same token, an indication that the
downside gap below the down close day's low will produce a short-term low
rather than a continuation of the opening breakout is a failure to perpetuate
the price movement downside by recording a close below the open price level
that same trading day or, on occasion, the failure to fill the opening price gap.

What is valuable about TDPOQ, as well as the many other qualifiers
and refinements to the various indicators presented throughout this book, is
the fact that these techniques will likely have application to many of the
methods and indicators you may currently be using in the markets. At the
very least, some of my trading filters and qualifiers, when applied to the indicators and systems you currently use, could enhance your potential for trading success.

## TD Alternative Oscillator Method

Although its occurrence is rare, in exceptionally strong or weak markets,
an extreme or severe oscillator reading may coincide with a market top or

bottom. In those instances, you should apply an interpretation called the TD Alternative Oscillator method to the oscillator and to the underlying security price. Specifically, this technique refers to the price and indicator relationship that may exist just after the indicator has recorded an extreme or severe reading for a period of over 15 trading days. This relates primarily to the TD ROC I, TD ROC II, and TD DeMarker I and II indicators. For example, once the TD ROC I indicator has recorded an extreme or severe indicator reading, if the closing price of the underlying security on the first day the TD ROC I indicator advances above its lower oversold band into "neutral" territory, after being below the band for 16 or more days, is less than the close two trading days earlier, or if the intraday low that same day is less than the intraday low two trading days earlier, then a low-risk buy entry exists, *provided* the TD Price Oscillator Qualifier (TDPOQ) subsequently confirms. Conversely, once the TD ROC I indicator has recorded an extreme or severe indicator reading, if the closing price of the underlying security on the first day the TD ROC I indicator declines below its upper overbought band into "neutral" territory, after being above the band for 16 or more days, is greater than the close two trading days earlier, or if the intraday high that same day is greater than the intraday high two trading days earlier, then a low-risk sell entry exists, provided once again the TD Price Oscillator Qualifier (TDPOQ) subsequently confirms. Figure 1.5 displays just such an occurrence. As you can readily see, during almost the entire month of August 1987, the TD ROC I oscillator remained above 102.5 percent (large $X$ on oscillator chart). Coincident with the oscillator downside penetration through 102.5 percent, the price closed greater than the close two days earlier, and the intraday high was greater than the intraday high two trading days earlier (*a* on the price chart and *a′* on the indicator chart). Subsequently, TDPOQ was fulfilled. Two additional upside and one downside TDPOQ indications from mild oversold and overbought conditions are shown on the chart with small *x*'s as well. Note in early October the oscillator was mildly overbought, and two days after the high, TDPOQ was triggered, indicating a low-risk sell entry level and an impending market decline. In any case, whenever extreme or severe oscillator readings coincide with a potential market top or bottom, you should use the interpretation assigned to the TD Alternative Oscillator method or avoid trading.

In conclusion, the formula for TD ROC I is simple. To arrive at the indicator value, merely divide the market's closing price by the closing price 12 trading days earlier and then plot that value on an indicator chart beneath the price activity of that market over the same time period. Define the overbought and the oversold band levels. Typically, recommended levels are 102.5 for the upper band and 97.5 for the lower band for most high-priced futures markets. You may want to select a narrower oscillator band of 99.75

and 100.25 for inactively traded, lower-priced markets, as well as markets traded over very short term time intervals, such as 30 minutes or less. Additionally, when operating in the market on a time frame of microscopic proportion, such as one-minute price bars, you may see favorable results by combining TD Sequential and TD ROC I. However, some markets must be analyzed and reviewed to determine their ideal parameter settings. For example, you might apply an oscillator band of 89 and 111 for most actively traded equities. Furthermore, if a market is in an uptrend, you may decide to elevate the lower level of the band, and if a market is in a downtrend, you may elect to lower the upper band threshold somewhat to accommodate for the trend and level of buying or selling pressure. TDPOQ should be applied to fine-tune low-risk entry zones and market entries associated with exceptionally strong or weak opening prices, either above the previous trading day's high for an upside move or below the previous day's low for a downside move, should be avoided unless the close the same trading day is above the open for an upside move or the close the same trading day is below the open for a downside move and, in most instances, the price gap caused by the aggressive market opening is filled before the close. If the oscillator resides in the oversold or overbought zone for an extended period of time—more than 16 trading days—it's recommended that either the application of the TD Alternative Oscillator method, confirmed subsequently by TDPOQ, be applied or that no trading whatsoever take place at that time. In addition, you can occasionally apply other indicators to the oscillator itself to anticipate and establish a trading edge. Specifically, you can draw a TD Line on the oscillator to determine when the oscillator is breaking out of its trend, or you can calculate the rate of change of the oscillator. Both techniques generally lead the price movement and are early warning indications of a trend reversal. In conclusion, any indicator should be combined with other indicators or series of indicators for best results. For example, you could apply TD Sequential and TD Combo (see following chapters) to the S&P futures on a one-minute chart and simultaneously plot a one-minute TD ROC oscillator band of 99.75 to 100.25 as well because by combining these two indicators, both Setup and Countdown completions become more discernible. In addition, by applying TD REI with a narrower oscillator band as well, the successful identification process for low- and high-risk possibilities is enhanced considerably.

The various components and parameter option settings, as well as the suggested default settings, for TD ROC I follow.

*Basic ROC I*

1. *Price* comparisons to be used to calculate TD ROC I: Refers to the reference prices selected and compared to calculate TD ROC I. Additional

price options include open, high, low, midpoint, average, high plus low plus close divided by three, true high, and true low, as well as various combinations of these prices. Default is Close.

2. *Period* to be used to calculate TD ROC I: Refers to the number of price bars between the current bar and the reference bar. Default is 12.

3. Number of bars to be used for *Duration* Analysis: Refers to the minimum number of consecutive bars in which TD ROC I must remain above (or below) the oscillator band in order to display the duration count on the indicator chart. This option is provided to highlight the event for purposes of TD Duration Analysis and to forewarn that the current price move is excessive and will require the oscillator to return to the neutral zone and back to overbought or oversold to record a mild as opposed to a severe oversold reading. Default is 16.

4. Upper oscillator band *level:* Refers to the minimum TD ROC I oscillator level that can be defined as overbought. This definition is critical in determining the condition and risk associated with the market and for the application of TD Duration Analysis. Adjustments or modifications made to this setting control the frequency, degree, and threshold for overbought indicator readings. Default is 102.5 (100.25).

5. Lower oscillator band *level:* Refers to the maximum TD ROC I oscillator level that can be defined as oversold. This definition is critical in determining the condition and risk associated with the market and for the application of TD Duration Analysis. Adjustments or modifications made to this setting control the frequency, degree, and threshold for oversold indicator readings. Default is 97.5 (99.75).

*Advanced TD ROC I*

6. *Display:* Refers to the type of oscillator presentation provided. This option allows the user to select the presentation of the rate of change either as a chart or a histogram. Default is Chart.

7. *Type* of moving average to be used: Refers to the various types of moving averages that can be introduced to the individual calculations to smooth the TD ROC I indicator. Options include simple, exponential, and centered. Default is None.

8. *Period* to be used in calculating the moving average: Refers to the length of the series of bar values averaged to create the TD ROC I value. Default is 0.

9. Number of bars (*period*) to be used for moving-average smoothing: Refers to those instances when a moving average is applied and additional indicator smoothing is desired. Default is 0.

Regardless of which level you select for the overbought/oversold indicator band, you should apply TDPOQ to confirm price and oscillator movement. The TD Alternative Oscillator method can be applied to those extended periods of time in which the TD ROC I indicator is severely overbought or oversold. However, the indication of a low-risk entry does not exist until the TD Price Oscillator Qualifier has spoken and confirmed a potential inception of a price trend.

## TD ROC II

Although TD ROC I is generally derived by calculating ratios of closing prices, other price comparisons can be easily substituted, such as highs, lows, opens, combinations or averages of opens, highs, lows, closes, and price range midpoints. However, one serious deficiency exists when using any of these price selections. All these rate-of-change oscillators are constructed by a method similar to the one used to calculate the standard, traditional, or classic closing basis TD ROC I in the respect that they are one-dimensionally price-driven. They relate a specific closing price with the closing price $x$ periods earlier, and they perform an identical, repetitive process to make this series of calculations. In other words, the entire exercise is redundant and static. TD ROC II, on the other hand, is a price momentum hybrid in the sense that both the methodology applied and the reference price used vary according to the relative position of the underlying TD ROC I indicator. That is, the specific level of TD ROC I determines which price comparisons to install for the calculation of TD ROC II.

Due to its dynamic construction, TD ROC II is generally more sensitive to impending price reversals than TD ROC I. Whereas the formula for TD ROC I requires the calculation of the ratio of the current period's close and the close 12 trading bars earlier, TD ROC II divides the current high by the high 12 trading bars earlier whenever the TD ROC I value at the same point in time is above 100, and TD ROC II divides the current low by the low 12 trading bars earlier whenever the TD ROC I value at the same point in time is below 100. In other words, TD ROC II is designed so that the value calculated for TD ROC I will serve as the price rudder that determines the specific components and relationships to install to calculate the TD ROC II indicator by dictating whether a comparison of either price highs or price lows should be made rather than merely using closing price levels for each comparison, as TD ROC I does. The S&P June contract shown in Figure 1.6 displays the difference in indicator results between TD ROC I and TD ROC II, which is a result of this revision or variation in the rate-of-change analysis formula. Note in this example how much more sensitive and accurate TD ROC II was at the May 1996 low. Numerous variations of this approach can also simply be applied, and you can use them as ideas for your own research and analysis:

1. The selection of highs and lows can be substituted with other price combinations.
2. The periodicity can be adjusted from 12 trading bars to other time intervals.
3. The threshold level of 1.00 established to differentiate between which price variables to use can be changed to other values.
4. The threshold level can be revised to a range, such as less than or equal to 99.5 and greater than or equal to 100.5, and when TD ROC I is between this zone, the TD ROC I close calculation can be applied.
5. The overbought/oversold indicator band can be expanded or contracted to accommodate the peculiarities and vagaries associated with specific markets and time intervals.

The introduction of variable indicator calculations is a unique contribution to the library of market timing methodologies, since it provides a dynamic approach to indicator analysis. Furthermore, this approach is at the cusp of a new generation of market analytics, since it is designed to adapt the selection of variables for an indicator formula, as well as the calculation process of the indicator itself, based upon the changes recorded in oscillator activity of a primary or underlying oscillator. The successful results attained using this approach are comparable to the earlier research success from my studies on breakout indicators and models back in the 1970s, a long time prior to their subsequent widespread acceptance and usage by traders and most all Commodity Trading Advisors (CTAs). Exploration of other applications of this methodology to many of my other market timing indicators is ongoing, and this same concept is being applied to the creation of a master indicator that is a composite of a series of my market timing oscillators, each possessing unique sensitivities and properties. This indicator is constructed somewhat similarly to the TD Plurality indicator described subsequently, but on a grander scale. In other words, the relative position of a key indicator along an overbought/oversold indicator spectrum will determine which other unrelated indicators you should rely upon to arrive at trading decisions, depending upon the condition and the position of the central indicator. Although at first glance, this may appear to be similar to a diffusion index, it is different, since the critical indicator that controls the selection of the indicator (or indicators) applied at any particular time is not necessarily a component of the indicator formula, and the specific indicator (or indicators) selected for usage depends upon the specific oscillator level of this key indicator.

The formula for TD ROC II is slightly more complex than TD ROC I. To determine which variables to use to arrive at the TD ROC I indicator value, merely divide the market's current closing price by the closing price 12 trading days earlier. If the value is above 100.00, then divide the current day's price high by the price high 12 days earlier. If the value is below 100.00, then divide the current day's price low by the price low 12 days earlier. Next, plot each value on an indicator chart beneath the price activity of that market over the same time period. Define the overbought and oversold band levels. Just as with TD ROC I, typically I recommend 102.5 for the upper band and 97.5 for the lower band for most high-priced markets. However, some markets must be analyzed and reviewed to determine their ideal parameter settings. For example, I apply an oscillator band of 89 and 111 for most actively traded equities. Over the short term, for periods less than 30 minutes, as well as for lower-priced and inactive markets, the oscillator band should be adjusted to 99.75 and 100.25. Furthermore, if a market is in an uptrend, you may elevate the lower level of the band, and if a market is in a downtrend, you may lower the upper band threshold somewhat to be assured that you accommodate for the trend and level of buying or selling pressure.

In conclusion, it is strongly recommended that both TD ROC I and TD ROC II be used when evaluating a market. Sometimes one may speak while the other is silent and, consequently, as a trader it will behoove you to follow both religiously. Additionally, experience suggests that it is always wise to combine this form of indicator analysis with other indicators such as TD Sequential, TD Combo, or TD REI, to perfect low-risk entry opportunities.

The various components and parameter option settings, as well as suggested default settings, for TD ROC II are as follows:

*Basic TD ROC II*

1. *Price* comparisons to be used to calculate TD ROC II:  Refers to the reference prices selected and compared to calculate TD ROC I, which in turn dictates the *price* levels to be applied to arrive at a value for TD ROC II. Additional options include open, high, low, midpoint, average, high plus low plus close divided by three, true high, true low, or various combinations of these prices. Default is Close.
2. *Period* to be used to calculate TD ROC II: Refers to the number of price bars between the current bar and the reference bar. Default is 12.
3. Number of bars to be used for *Duration* Analysis: Refers to the minimum number of consecutive bars in which TD ROC II must remain above (or below) the oscillator band in order to display the duration count on the indicator chart. This option is provided to highlight the event for purposes of TD Duration Analysis and to forewarn that the

current price move is excessive and will require the oscillator to return to the neutral zone and back to overbought or oversold to record a mild as opposed to a severe overbought or oversold reading. Default is 16.

4. Upper oscillator band *level:* Refers to the minimum TD ROC II oscillator level that can be defined as overbought. This definition is critical in distinguishing the condition and risk associated with the market and for the application of TD Duration Analysis. Adjustments or modifications made to this setting control the frequency, degree, and threshold for overbought indicator readings. Default is 102.5 (100.25).

5. Lower oscillator band *level:* Refers to the maximum TD ROC II oscillator level that can be defined as oversold. This definition is critical in distinguishing the condition and risk associated with the market and for the application of TD Duration Analysis. Adjustments or modifications made to this setting control the frequency, degree, and threshold for oversold indicator readings. Default is 97.5 (99.75).

*Advanced TD ROC II*

6. *Display:* Refers to the type of oscillator presentation provided. This option allows the user to select the presentation of the rate of change either as a chart or a histogram. Default is Chart.

7. *Type* of moving average to be used: Refers to the various types of moving averages that can be introduced to the individual calculations to smooth the TD ROC II indicator. Options include simple, exponential, and centered. Default is None.

8. *Period* to be used in calculating the moving average: Refers to the length of the series of values averaged to create the TD ROC II value. Default is 0.

9. Number of bars (*period*) to be used for moving average smoothing: Refers to those instances when a moving average is applied and additional indicator smoothing is desired. Default is 0.

10. *Price* value of TD ROC I to be used when substituting alternate prices—upper threshold: Refers to the minimum band value recorded for TD ROC I that causes the price relationship to shift from TD ROC I to TD ROC II. Default is 100.

11. *Price* value of TD ROC I to be used when substituting alternate prices—lower threshold: Refers to the maximum band value recorded for TD ROC I that causes the price relationship to shift from TD ROC I to TD ROC II. Default is 100.

12. *Price* "alternate" to be applied when upper threshold is exceeded: Refers to the converted price to be applied when TD ROC I exceeds the maximum band value. Default is High.

13. *Price* "alternate" to be applied when upper threshold is exceeded: Refers to the converted price to be applied when TD ROC I exceeds the minimum band value. Default is Low.

Regardless of which level you select for the overbought/oversold indicator band, you should apply TDPOQ to confirm price and oscillator movement. The TD Alternative Oscillator method can be applied to those extended periods of time in which the TD ROC II indicator is severely overbought or oversold. However, the indication of a low-risk entry does not exist until the TD Price Oscillator Qualifier has spoken and confirmed a potential price move.

## TD REI™—Standard and Alternate

Throughout my professional career in the investment business, I have been disturbed by the apparent unwillingness or disinterest of traders to challenge either the construction or the application of various market timing oscillators that appear either on an electronic network or in a chart book. Whenever an indicator appears on one of these services, it seems that most traders are inclined to accept and apply it to markets they follow without any questions whatsoever. It would not be surprising to know that some do not care what the composition and the recommended interpretation of this indicator might be. This criticism is no doubt well deserved. Of greater concern, however, is the fact that most indicators are constructed with little variation from one another. Although consecutive closing prices are generally used in calculating most indicators, my own research indicates the high or the low price, or any series of other prices, produces similar or better results than a simple comparison of consecutive closing prices. Furthermore, as stressed in the introduction to this chapter, exponential calculations possess obvious shortcomings that do not exist with arithmetic formulas. The TD Range Expansion Index (REI) attempts to circumvent both these deficiencies. Additionally, my method of identifying potential oscillator breakouts by qualifying the underlying price activity of the market analyzed subsequent to recording indicator readings in "mild" low-risk buy or sell zones perfects the process of confirming pending trend reversals. This technique provides traders with a disciplined, mechanical process whereby they are able to interpret presumably random oscillator and price activity. Finally, the TD Price Oscillator Qualifier (TDPOQ) evaluates the ensuing price activity to determine a prudent low-risk price entry level. This method of oscillator interpretation can be applied simply and successfully to many other indicators as well. The benefits derived from this form of analysis extend much further than those described solely by applying TD REI. In fact, this methodology applies as well to most of the other indicators discussed throughout this book.

Collectively, business and political news events, fundamental and economic forecasts, portfolio management decisions, hedging activities, as well as many other factors influence daily securities' price movements. The impact of these various items, however, is usually discounted and reflected in prices quickly. To circumvent these price disruptions and misleading short-term trend movements, TD REI has been created specifically to relate the price movement of a particular day to that of two trading days earlier. This comparison can be changed or modified easily from the default setting of two trading days to other trading days' comparisons as well, such as 1, 3, 4, or 5 days earlier. The influence upon an indicator as a result of volatile day-to-day price swings caused by short-lived events and news releases is diminished significantly. By requiring current or recent price activity to overlap with the trading range $x$ days earlier, the shortcoming of most trading oscillators of prematurely recording overbought or oversold readings is reduced as well. At those times, when the oscillator should be most valuable to a trader—in trading range markets—the oscillator effectively accomplishes the goal of anticipating prospective reversal points, since price overlap will occur in that environment.

There are two methods to deal with the issue of price overlap: One is to maintain the price intersection relationship regardless of how many days the REI is calculated, and the other is to "adjust" the comparison to compensate for oscillator time periods longer or shorter than the defaulted five- or eight-day TD REI series calculation. The TD REI oscillator originally was designed many years ago to be an eight-trading-day calculation, and the price intersection rule was developed with that time period in mind. Instead of the previously recommended eight-day TD REI calculation, I now find that a five-day price series for TD REI is more effective. Traders should have the capability to adjust the price period and series to their preferences and that they should be able to change the price intersection requirement to accommodate for this revision as well. For example, the original eight-trading-day calculation for TD REI requires that the current day's price activity intersect the price range either five or six trading days earlier or that the price range two trading days ago intersect the closing price either seven or eight trading days ago. If the price series is reduced to any value less than eight trading days down to four trading days, the price comparison can be reduced according to the number of trading days in which the indicator series deviates from the standard comparison of eight trading days. In any case, for any TD REI calculation of four trading days or less, the intersection rule remains the same.

The formula for an "unadjusted" five-day TD REI is as follows:

*Step one.*    Compare the current day's intraday high with the intraday high two trading days earlier and the current day's intraday low with the intraday low two trading days earlier. By making this two-day price range comparison rather than relating the current trading day's close to the previous trading day's close, the potential impact of price distortions to the indicator values caused by short-term events is reduced, and the likelihood is increased that a discernible price trend has been established. Next, add together the differences between the current day's high and the high two days ago and the current day's low and the low two days ago. Obviously, this sum can be both positive or negative, depending upon whether the current day's high is greater or less than the high two trading days earlier, and the current day's low is greater than or less than the low two trading days earlier. Note the two-bar comparison can be replaced with other price periods as well, such as 3, 4, or 5 bars.

*Step two.*    Either (*a*) the current day's high must be greater than or equal to the low five or six trading days earlier *and* the current day's low must be less than or equal to the high five or six trading days ago, *or* (*b*) the high two trading days ago must be greater than or equal to the close seven or eight trading days ago and the low two trading days ago must be less than or equal to the close seven or eight trading days ago. If *neither a nor b* occur, then either of two options can be selected: (1) the "standard" method assigns a value of zero (0) to that specific day, or (2) the "alternate" method assigns a value of zero (0) to both that specific trading day as well as the prior trading day. In either case, the price comparison between highs and lows is not calculated, since it is likely that because a period of price overlap or intersection did not occur, the market is about to break out, or already has broken out, and consequently, by postponing or suppressing the indicator calculation for that trading day, the indicator is silent and the risk of recording premature overbought or oversold oscillator readings is reduced.

*Step three.*    If either condition *a* or *b* of step two is met, then the differences between the current day's high and the high two trading days ago, as well as the current day's low and the low two trading days ago, are calculated and summed. For those days in which conditions *a* and *b* are not fulfilled, then either a value of zero is assigned to that trading day, *or* both that day, as well as the previous trading day's oscillator value, are assigned values of "0," depending on whether the standard or the alternate method is applied.

*Step four.*    Next, for the standard method, add all the daily values, including zeros, over the current five- or eight-day trading period (or any period you desire). Then divide this value by the absolute value of the sum of the price movement of the daily values over that same time period—the *absolute value* is the calculated price movement or difference either up or down regardless of whether any trading day's value may be positive or negative, and each calculated price movement is treated as if it were a positive value. Consequently, whereas the numerator can be a positive, negative, or zero value since each daily value over the selected number of trading days is summed, the denominator can only be positive, since the price movement traversed over that same time period, either up or down, is added together, regardless of whether it is positive or negative. Next, this ratio is multiplied by 100 to create a percentage. Conduct the same procedure for the alternate method, with the one exception: that the previous day's indicator value is also assigned the value of zero (0), instead of assigning a value of zero (0) for only the current trading day as with the standard method, if intersection fails to occur.

*Step five.* Define an indicator band to establish when the market is potentially overbought or oversold. Typically, for a five- or eight-day TD REI, you might apply an indicator band of −45 to +45. However, if you wish to operate more aggressively, you can from time to time modify the band to −35 to +35 or −40 to +40. Additionally, for short-term interval charts, such as 1, 5, or 10 minutes, or inactively traded markets, the trading band can be contracted further.

*Step six.* Apply the TD Price Oscillator Qualifier to ensure that the underlying price activity confirms the oscillator behavior (see both REI oscillators presented in Figure 1.7). Note that the large $X$ identifies those occasions in which TD Duration Analysis correctly postponed any premature selling and forewarned of a continuation of the advance due to the amount of time the indicator remained in the overbought area— more than five days. Also see how well TDPOQ confirmed the inception of the various price trend reversals (see series of small $x$'s and $y$'s) for both the five- ($x$) and the eight- ($y$) trading-day TD REI (standard method). For additional information and explanation regarding TDPOQ, refer to the previous discussion.

The various components and parameter option settings, as well as suggested default settings, for TD REI (both standard and alternate) follow.

*Basic TD REI*

1. *Period* to be used to calculate TD REI: Refers to the number of trading bars to be compared and then summed to calculate the TD REI indicator values. Default is 5 (possibly 8).

2. Number of bars to be used for *Duration* Analysis: Refers to the minimum number of consecutive bars in which TD REI must remain above (or below) the oscillator band in order to display the duration count on the indicator chart. This option is provided to highlight the event for purposes of TD Duration Analysis and to forewarn that the current price move is excessive and will usually require the oscillator to return to the neutral zone and back to overbought or oversold to record a mild as opposed to a severe oversold reading. Default is 6.

**Figure 1.7**   Note that this chart displays both a five-day TD REI (upper) and an eight-day TD REI (lower). Each is the Standard Method, and intersection is "unadjusted". The upper chart includes two instances in which extreme overbought readings for the TD REI indicator for the Italian bond December 1996 were given—September and November 1996 (*X*). The other occasions in which the oscillator recorded a mild reading either below or above the oscillator band, price responded once TDPOQ was triggered (*x*). The extreme overbought reading for the eight-day TD REI is likewise marked with a large *X*, and the TDPOQ indications are marked on the chart with the letter *Y*.

3.  Upper oscillator band *level:* Refers to the minimum TD REI oscillator level which can be defined as overbought. This definition is critical in distinguishing the condition and risk associated with the market and for the application of TD Duration Analysis. Adjustments or modifications made to this setting control the frequency, degree, and threshold for overbought indicator readings. Default is 45.

4.  Lower oscillator band *level:* Refers to the maximum TD REI oscillator level that can be defined as oversold. This definition is critical in distinguishing the condition and risk associated with the market and for the application of TD Duration Analysis. Adjustments or modifications made to this setting control the frequency, degree, and threshold for oversold indicator readings. Default is –45.

5.  *Price* to be used when comparing highs: Refers to the prices that are compared and summed to calculate the TD REI value for the highs. Additional options include open, high, low, midpoint, average, high plus

low plus close divided by three, true high, true low, or various combinations of these prices. Default is High.

6. *Price* to be used when comparing lows: Refers to the prices that are compared and summed to calculate the TD REI value for the lows. Additional options include open, high, low, midpoint, average, high plus low plus close divided by three, true high, true low, or various combinations of these prices. Default is Low.

7. *Display:* Refers to the type of oscillator presentation provided. This option allows the user to select the presentation of the rate of change either as a chart or a histogram. Default is Chart.

8. Number of bars back (*ago*) to be used when comparing highs: Refers to the price bars that are compared and summed to calculate the TD REI value for the highs. Default is 2.

9. Number of bars back (*ago*) to be used when comparing lows: Refers to the price bars that are compared and summed to calculate the TD REI value for the lows. Default is 2.

10. *Version:* Refers to whether the standard or the alternate method is applied on that specific trading day. In other words, if no intersection occurs, the standard method assigns a zero (0) value to that trading day only and the alternate method assigns a zero (0) value to both that trading day and the prior trading day.

*Advanced TD REI*

11. Should *equal* be used when comparing prices for lookback intersection? Refers to whether "equal" conditions apply when comparing highs or lows to previous highs, lows, or closes for intersection qualification purposes. Default is Yes; use *equal* when comparing.

12. *Type* of moving average to be used: Refers to the various types of moving averages that can be introduced to the individual calculations to smooth the TD REI indicator. Options include simple, exponential, and centered. Default is None.

13. *Period* to be used in calculating the moving average: Refers to the size of the series of values averaged to create the TD REI value. Default is 0.

14. Number of bars (*period*) to be used for moving average smoothing: Refers to those instances when a moving average is applied and additional indicator smoothing is desired. Default is 0.

15. Should an *adjustment* be made if the period for the calculations is less than eight bars? Refers to whether the basic TD REI formula should be revised to accommodate those instances when a TD REI period of less than eight trading bars is selected. In other words, the basic formula requires a comparison of the current price bar's high and low and the

high and low five or six trading days earlier or the high and low two trading bars earlier with the close seven or eight trading bars earlier. If the TD REI period is less than eight trading bars, and if this option is selected, then each trading day less than eight trading bars reduces the comparison by one day as well. For example, if six trading days are selected and the *adjustment* selection is made, then the current bar's high and low comparisons are made with the price bars three and four trading days earlier, and the comparisons for the high and low two trading bars ago are the closes five and six trading days ago. The *adjustment* is made only down to TD REI of four trading bars and it is not increased above the maximum setting, which is for eight days. Default is No; don't adjust.

Finally, regardless of which level you select for the overbought/oversold indicator band, you should apply TDPOQ to confirm price and oscillator movement (see Figure 1.7). Although it rarely occurs, the TD Alternative Oscillator method can be applied to those extended periods of time in which the TD REI indicator is severely overbought/oversold as well. However, the oscillator must record a severe overbought or oversold reading if the TD Alternative Oscillator method is applied, and once activated, this technique is applicable only to the first trading day in which the oscillator advances out of oversold or declines from overbought. In either situation, the indication of a low-risk entry alone is generally considered insufficient, and it is preferable to await confirmation of the TD Price Oscillator Qualifier. Once it has spoken, a price move usually ensues.

# TD DeMarker I and II™

TD DeMarker I and II are trading oscillators developed to anticipate potential price trend reversals and to define and confirm the underlying direction or trend of the market once it has been established. Just as with the other indicators presented, they are arithmetically, rather than exponentially, calculated; they utilize intraday prices as opposed to closing prices; their interpretation is more objective and mechanized than widely used conventional market timing indicators; and they apply price relationships and patterns to identify likely trend breakouts.

The formula for the TD DeMarker I indicator is simple and straightforward. The current and previous trading days' price highs are compared. If the current trading day's high is greater than the previous trading day's high, then the difference is calculated and recorded, but if the difference is either negative or equal, then zero is assigned to that day's value. A similar exercise is repeated over a series of $x$ consecutive trading days, and the sum of these respective values becomes the numerator of the TD DeMarker I equation. At the same time, the denominator is the numerator value plus the difference between the previous trading day's low and the current trading day's low summed over the specified series of $x$ consecutive trading days as well and, if the previous trading day's low is less than or equal to the current trading day's low, then a zero is assigned to that day's value. Next, an overbought/oversold oscillator band from 79 to 21 for a typical eight-day TD DeMarker I indicator is constructed, followed by an interpretation of the oscillator movement similar to the one applied to TD REI using TDPOQ and TD Duration Analysis of five days, provided the DeMarker I indicator is 13 or more price periods. For DeMarker I indicator periods of less than 13 days, such as this eight-day TD DeMarker I, it's preferable to use a duration of 16, just as with TD ROC I and TD ROC II. Also, apply the TD Alternative Oscillator method whenever extreme oscillator readings of 16 days or more occur, and then generally await confirmation of the TD Price Oscillator Qualifier. Once it has spoken, a potential price move generally ensues.

The formula for the TD DeMarker II indicator is markedly different than the one for the TD DeMarker I indicator. The numerator value is composed of two values summed together, which represent buying pressure: (1) the difference between the current trading day's high and the previous trading day's close over a series of $x$ consecutive trading days *plus* (2) the difference between the current trading day's close and the current trading day's low over an identical series of $x$ consecutive trading days. If the calculation of the difference between the current trading day's high and the previous trading day's close is negative, then a zero (0) value is assigned to that portion of the dual component for that day. The denominator value is the identical value calculated for the numerator, *plus* it is composed of two values summed together, which represent the selling pressure: (1) the difference between the previous trading day's close and the current trading day's low over a series of $x$ consecutive trading days *plus* (2) the difference between the current trading day's high and the current trading day's close summed over an identical series of $x$ consecutive trading days. If the calculation of the difference between the previous trading day's close and the current trading day's low is negative, then a zero (0) value is assigned to that portion of the dual component for that day. In other words, TD DeMarker II divides the buying pressure by the sum of the buying pressure *plus* the selling pressure over a specified number of trading days. An oscillator band is constructed, and TD Duration Analysis, TDPOQ, and the TD Alternative Oscillator method can be applied as well.

Figure 1.8 illustrates how TD DeMarker I can be applied. Specifically, it is preferable to generate low-risk entries using TDPOQ. However, other interpretations can be invoked as well, and they are described next. In this example, an eight-day TD DeMarker I is used. The overbought/oversold zones are defined as 79 and 21, and TDPOQ is used to generate low-risk

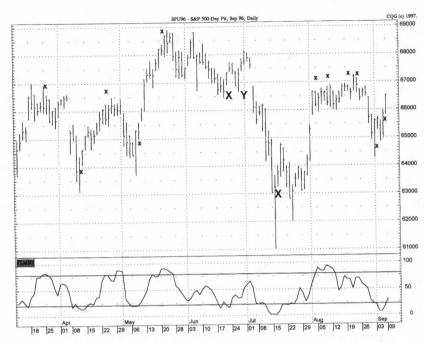

**Figure 1.8**  The series of small *x*'s on the chart identify the TDPOQ qualified low-risk entries. The large *X*'s identify those instances in which the opening price was not contained by the previous trading day's price range and thereby did not fulfill the the requirements of TDPOQ, and the opening price gap versus the previous day's close was not filled by that day's close. Furthermore, in one instance (*Y*) the oscillator was already above 50.00, and consequently, TDPOQ was no longer qualified for a low-risk entry indication.

entries. To apply TDPOQ, it is recommended that for an upside move the opening price on the trading day following an up close versus the previous day's close be contained by the up close day's high. Conversely, for a downside move, it is equally important that the opening price on the trading day following a down close versus the previous day's close be greater than or equal to the down close day's low. Furthermore, the window of opportunity to generate a TDPOQ low-risk entry upside expires once the oscillator advances above 50 and, conversely, for a downside move once the indicator declines below 50. Note that on this chart, the series of small *x*'s identifies low-risk TD DeMarker I entries and the large *X* defines the instance in which the opening price occurred outside the previous trading day's price range or the oscillator was above 50 for an upside move or was below 50 for a downside move.

Clues regarding the underlying market trend are often revealed by the amount of time TD DeMarker I spends in either overbought or oversold territory. For example, if the most recent experience for an eight-day TD DeMarker I oscillator has been for the indicator to remain in the overbought zone for more than five trading bars, then the overall market trend is likely to be up, and if the oscillator has been positioned most recently in oversold territory for more than five trading bars, then the overall market direction is likely to be down. Counting and comparing the number of trading bars or time in which the TD DeMarker I indicator remains either overbought or oversold also provides hints as to the underlying trend of the market.

Furthermore, by integrating both TD DeMarker I and TD DeMarker II with other indicators, such as TD REI, TD ROC I and II, TD Plurality, TD Trap, and TD Open, your success in identifying potential price trend reversals should be enhanced. Additionally, to realize better results, you should experiment and introduce time series other than those discussed here and also apply more than one chart of the same indicator but with varied periodicities to draw your conclusions regarding market behavior.

The various components and parameter option settings, as well as suggested default settings, for TD DeMarker I follow.

### Basic TD DeMarker I

1. *Period* to be used to calculate TD DeMarker I: Refers to the number of trading bars to be compared and then summed to calculate the TD DeMarker I indicator values. Default is 8.

2. Number of bars to be used for *Duration* Analysis: Refers to the minimum number of consecutive bars in which TD REI must remain above (or below) the oscillator band in order to display the duration count on the indicator chart. This option is provided to highlight the event for purposes of TD Duration Analysis and to forewarn that the current price move is excessive and will usually require the oscillator to return to the neutral zone and back to overbought or oversold to record a mild as opposed to a severe oversold reading. Default is 16.

3. Upper oscillator band *level:* Refers to the minimum TD DeMarker I oscillator level that can be defined as overbought. This definition is critical in distinguishing the condition and risk associated with the market and for the application of TD Duration Analysis. Adjustments or modifications made to this setting control the frequency, degree, and threshold for overbought indicator readings. Default is 60.

4. Lower oscillator band *level:* Refers to the maximum TD DeMarker I oscillator level that can be defined as oversold. This definition is critical in distinguishing the condition and risk associated with the market and for the application of TD Duration Analysis. Adjustments or modifications made to this setting control the frequency, degree, and threshold for oversold indicator readings. Default is 40.

5. *Price* to be used when comparing highs: Refers to the prices that are compared and summed to calculate the TD DeMarker I value for the

highs. Additional options include open, high, low, midpoint, average, high plus low plus close divided by three, true high, true low, or various combinations of these prices. Default is High.

6. *Price* to be used when comparing lows: Refers to the prices that are compared and summed to calculate the TD DeMarker I value for the lows. Additional options include open, high, low, midpoint, average, high plus low plus close divided by three, true high, true low, or various combinations of these prices. Default is Low.

7. Number of bars back (*ago*) to be used when comparing highs: Refers to the price bars that are compared and summed to calculate the TD DeMarker I value for the highs. Default is 1.

8. Number of bars back (*ago*) to be used when comparing lows: Refers to the price bars that are compared and summed to calculate the TD DeMarker I value for the lows. Default is 1.

9. *Display:* Refers to the type of oscillator presentation provided. This option allows the user to select the presentation of the rate of change either as a chart or a histogram. Default is Chart.

*Advanced TD DeMarker I*

10. *Type* of moving average to be used: Refers to the various types of moving averages that can be introduced to the individual calculations to construct the TD DeMarker I indicator. Options include simple, exponential, and centered. Default is None.

11. *Period* to be used in calculating the moving average: Refers to the number of variables averaged to create the TD DeMarker I value. Default is 0.

12. Number of bars (*period*) to be used for moving average smoothing: Refers to those instances when a moving average is applied and additional indicator smoothing is desired. Default is 0.

The selections for TD DeMarker II are identical to TD DeMarker I, with the exception of the price bar comparisons. In the case of TD DeMarker I, the respective highs and the lows are compared. In the case of TD DeMarker II for the buying pressure calculation (numerator), the high is compared with the previous trading day's close, and the current trading day's close is compared with the current trading day's low; for the selling pressure calculation (the other denominator component), the low is compared with the previous trading day's close, and the current trading day's high and close are compared. Improvement of the proper settings for this new and enhanced indicator is in the works.

Finally, regardless of which level is selected for the overbought/oversold indicator band, you should apply TDPOQ to confirm price and oscillator movement. The TD Alternative Oscillator method can be applied to those extended periods of time in which either the TD DeMarker I indicator or TD DeMarker II indicator is severely overbought/oversold. However, the indication of a low-risk entry does not exist until the TD Price Oscillator Qualifier has spoken and confirmed a potential price move.

## TD Plurality™

TD Plurality is an indicator shell or template developed to enable a trader to create and display a composite indicator that represents a combination of a series of dissimilar price or pattern relationships. Whenever TD Plurality becomes excessive, it can be described as either overbought or oversold, and at that time a trader is alerted to market timing opportunities. The advantage or value of TD Plurality versus most conventional or traditional market timing indicators, or even some individual indicators presented elsewhere in this book, is its ability to combine a group of totally different and unrelated price or pattern comparisons and then to produce a single oscillator reading much like a diffusion index, representing the summation of a series of generally unrelated and dissimilar price relationships.

It is preferable to make simple price and pattern comparisons and calculations to create a general indicator capable of defining zones of high and low risk. Although the structure provided by TD Plurality can accommodate many other variations and combinations of price relationships, only two simple examples are displayed (see Figure 1.9a and b). Keep in mind that because TD Plurality is designed to be a dynamic indicator matrix shell capable of accommodating and presenting various price comparisons, or series of price relationships, at any particular time, just like TD Range Expansion Break-Out™ (TD REBO) discussed in Chapter 6, any example presented may not necessarily be the optimal selection. You should create and experiment with other variations of your own and include them within this structure. These two examples illustrate two possibilities of price relationships that are used in my own research and analysis of the markets.

Figure 1.9a is basic and two-dimensional in the sense that only two price relationships are evaluated to identify potential trend change turning points. Specifically, this example shows a comparison of the current trading day's close versus the current trading day's open and the current trading day's close versus the close one trading day earlier. If the current close is less than the open, then a −1 is counted. Conversely, if the current close is greater than the open, then a +1 is counted. Additionally, if the current day's close is less than the previous trading day's close, then a −1 is counted. Conversely, if the current day's close is greater than the previous trading day's close, then a +1 is counted. Over a period of five trading days, the net sum of all days in which

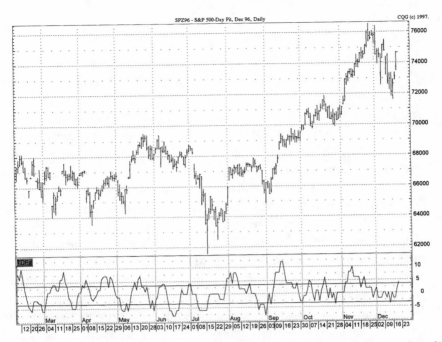

**Figure 1.9(a)** This chart illustrates one version of TD Plurality, which relates a trading day's close and open, as well as a trading day's close and the previous trading day's close. The trading band is defined from 3.5 to −3.5.

**Figure 1.9(b)** The interpretation of TD Plurality assigned to this example is somewhat more complex than that used for Figure 9a. Specifically, once the oscillator exceeds either 2.5 upside or −2.5 downside, the closing price must be above the close three trading days earlier for a low-risk buy indication and less than the close three trading days earlier for a low-risk sell indication. Additionally, for an upside move TD Plurality must be below zero, and for a downside move, it must be above zero. *x* identifies those instances in which these prerequisites have been met. Note that close *Y* is invalid, since TD Plurality was below zero.

the current close is greater than the current open is added to the net sum of all the days in which the current close is less than the current open; this sum is in turn added to the cumulative net sum of all the days in which the current close is greater than the previous trading day's close; and this sum is added to the cumulative net sum of all the days in which the current close is less than the previous trading day's close. If this cumulative total of these relationships over the entire time period is either less than −3.5 or greater than 3.5, generally short-term market lows and highs occur. Although there is nothing extraordinary about these comparisons, and more ideal ones can be selected, you can still appreciate the potential of such an indicator as TD Plurality by examining Figure 1.9a. It is impossible, given the set of conditions set forth in this example, to record an indicator value in increments of exactly one-half (0.5); the oscillator swings within this oscillator band move only in whole numbers. However, by defining the band as −3.5 and 3.5, it is easier to display and identify oscillator readings that are extreme. In most instances, the price lows and highs coincide with this oscillator activity. By introducing other components to TD Plurality, as well as other price decision rules, better results can be achieved. Once again, remember that nothing is perfect; if trading were this simple, no challenge to success would exist. However, such is not the case in life or likewise in trading. In order to perfect this basic approach further, Figure 1.9b introduces two refinements to this relationship. Specifically, not only must the oscillator move below −2.5 and above 2.5, but also a closing price must be recorded coincidentally or subsequently that is greater than the close three trading days earlier for an upside move and a closing price must be recorded coincidentally or subsequently that is less than the close three trading days earlier for a downside move. Additionally, you should employ the following filter for both upside and downside indicator qualifications: If the TD Plurality oscillator is above zero, then the upside comparison of close versus close three trading days earlier is canceled; if the TD Plurality indicator value is below zero, then the downside comparison of close versus close three trading days earlier is canceled as well. The letter Y identifies a disqualified downside opportunity in Figure 1.9b, since the indicator value is below zero.

The previous two chart examples (Figure 1.9a and b) illustrate TD Plurality, but the scope and the coverage of the indicator was limited to only two price and pattern comparisons. Suppose a trader wanted to develop a number of relationships and then merge them into one master composite indicator. This is simply accomplished since TD Plurality permits a trader to define a price relationship on each separate line or row. Furthermore, it enables the user to allocate as many as eight unique and unrelated conditions. Some of the comparisons typically used include the following: the current day's close is less than the close one trading day ago; the current day's close is less than the current day's open; the current day's close is less than the close three trading days ago; the current day's low is less than the low two days ago; the current day's high is less than the close two trading days earlier; the current day's low is greater than the close two trading days earlier; the current day's low is less than the previous day's high; the current day's high is greater than the previous day's low; the current day's price range is less than the previous day's price range as well as the inverse of these relationships. The only limitation to this litany of comparisons is your imagination. Heretofore, no one has provided a structure whereby a trader can insert various components and comparisons or statements and arrive at a composite indicator based upon all these factors operating coincidentally and which can be evaluated, weighted, and rated. TD Plurality provides this facility and capability.

Figure 1.10 presents the TD Plurality indicator, which in this instance is an amalgam of an assortment of price comparisons. Although the specific components that created this example were chosen from a universe of other possibilities, it illustrates the types of variables that can be combined to create an index. In this instance, a value of −1 is assigned to each of the following four statements: The current day's close is less than the previous trading day's close; the current day's close is less than the current day's open; the current day's close is less than the close three trading

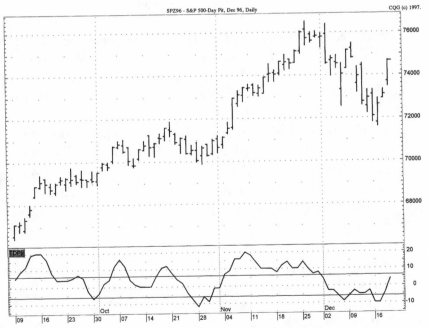

**Figure 1.10**  This version of TD Plurality includes eight variables (see text). Note how the overbought and the oversold zones identified potential low- and high-risk opportunities. One method to apply to the oscillator to identify potential price reversals is to identify the first instance in which the oscillator upticks from oversold to neutral or from overbought to neutral.

days ago; and the current day's low is less than the low two days ago. At the same time, a +1 value is assigned to the reverse propositions expressed in the following statements: The current day's close is greater than the previous trading day's close; the current day's close is greater than the current day's open; the current day's close is greater than the close three trading days ago; and the current day's high is greater than the high two days ago. If traders wish to assign a greater weighting to any one comparison over another comparison, they may elect to do so easily within the matrix designed for TD Plurality.

By applying TD Duration Analysis, as well as various techniques to fine-tune the entry, such as the one described previously, which requires that a closing price exceed a prior close upside to confirm an upside breakout or that a closing price exceed a prior close downside to confirm a downside breakout or even using TDPOQ, many trading opportunities are highlighted. Another effective method is to identify a possible trend change as the first uptick in TD Plurality from oversold or the first downtick in the indicator from overbought. In order to make TD Plurality a more effective and productive tool, you should use it in conjunction with other indicators presented throughout this book, such as applying TD Lines to the underlying price and to the TD Plurality indicator itself.

Following are the various components and parameter option settings, as well as suggested default settings, for TD Plurality.

1. Price 1 column: Refers to the first *price* to be compared to a second *price* (Price 2) to calculate each component comprising the TD Plurality oscillator. This comparison can consist of one row or a group of rows of *price* comparisons. Default for rows 1 through 6 is Close, for row 7 is Low, and for row 8 is High.

2. Number of bars back for Price 1 (Ago 1) column: Refers to the day of the Price 1 value(s). Default is Current day (0) for all eight rows.

3. Relationship comparison: Refers to the type of comparison that exists between the variables in the Price 1 column and the Price 2 column. Default is Less than for rows 1, 3, 5, and 7 and Greater than for rows 2, 4, 6, and 8.

4. Price 2 column: Refers to the second *price* (Price 2), which is compared to the first *price* (Price 1) to calculate each component comprising the TD Plurality oscillator. This comparison can consist of one row or a group of rows. Default for rows 1 through 6 is Close, for row 7 is Low, and for row 8 is High.

5. Number of bars back for Price 2 (Ago 2) column: Refers to the day of the Price 2 value(s). Default is 1 Ago for rows 1 and 2, Current day (0) for rows 3 and 4, 3 Ago for rows 5 and 6, and 2 Ago for rows 7 and 8.

6. True column: Refers to the value assigned to the statement if the comparison between Price 1 and Price 2 is *true*. Default is −1 for rows 1, 3, 5, and 7 and 1 for rows 2, 4, 6, and 8.

7. False column: Refers to the value assigned to the statement if the comparison between Price 1 and Price 2 is *false*. Default is 0 for all.

8. Period column and box: Refers to the number of consecutive trading days for which the comparison(s) is (are) made and summed. Default is 5.

9. Upper oscillator band *level:* Refers to the minimum TD Plurality oscillator level that can be defined as overbought. Default is 6.

10. Lower oscillator band *level:* Refers to the maximum TD Plurality oscillator level that can be defined as oversold. Default is −6.

# Chapter

# 2

# TD Sequential™

*Observation:* Many years ago, conducting extensive research on the markets convinced me that a predictable, natural rhythm dominated the price movements of markets and that, once properly identified and decoded, a trader could use this rhythm to anticipate potential price trend reversals. To accomplish this goal initially, I experimented with conventional market cycles; however, my frustration grew with each attempt to apply them profitably. Most irritating was the fact that classical cycles' analysts selected arbitrary time periods to forecast tops and bottoms, and when they did not occur as they had projected and the actual price movement unfolded precisely opposite, they would dismiss this unexpected event as a cycle "inversion" and continue to argue the value of cycles analysis. Their steadfast adherence to this methodology was admirable, but at the same time, this tenacity failed to explain the unpredictable and seemingly random price moves that occurred, and that was a rather serious shortcoming. The goal was to research and develop a rigid, mechanical methodology of my own to forecast market movements instead of relying upon such a seemingly arbitrary technique. The result of this research is TD Sequential. Although developed over two decades ago, this indicator's composition has changed only modestly throughout the years. Subsequent to its public release a couple of years ago, its variations and applications have taken on a life of their own. Numerous enhancements have been developed for this market timing tool. These will be explained, clarified, and shared with you in this chapter. TD Sequential's accuracy is often uncanny and the diversity and zealousness of its followers is flattering. Only recently, a well-known market commentator and market letter writer called to ask if I knew an individual who appeared regularly on national television, was a well-known publisher, and served in the administrations of two presidents as undersecretary of both Treasury and Commerce, as well as ambassador to the European Common Market. When I responded in the negative, he informed me that this individual was trading and making his interest rate forecasts based upon TD Sequential.

Each day a fierce battle is being waged between buyers and sellers in every publicly traded marketplace. As is the case with countries engaged in a war, the victor is not necessarily decided by a single battle, but rather by a series of them. Economics 101 teaches that prices move up when there are more buyers than sellers and prices move down when there are more sellers than buyers. This theory is certainly valid, but trading experience and logic show that it is far better to participate in a price move in its infancy than once it has matured and is about to reverse trend. By identifying the particular inflection point occurring just prior to the exhaustion of supply or demand, an alert trader is able to participate in a larger portion of the market's subsequent trend.

During the mid 1970s, I observed a powerful, natural price rhythm pervasive throughout all markets at all levels of time. Study and research led to the conclusion that price activity behaved in a predictable fashion. The goal was to create an indicator capable of identifying price exhaustion areas that coincided with the collective capitulation of traders exiting their losing market positions. A psychologist would no doubt attribute my intention to depart from the traditional and conventional trend-following techniques used and promoted by most other traders (entering a market after a top or a bottom has been formed) and my stubborn effort to identify the market top or bottom to the precise price tick as an attempt to assert my masculinity or some other obtuse manifestation of my psyche. On the contrary, this obsession to develop anticipatory market timing techniques is a lifelong ambition to create research that introduces precision and objectivity into the market timing profession by identifying market tops and bottoms mechanically. TD Sequential accomplishes this goal. This indicator is designed to evaluate the condition of a market at any particular point in time based upon price patterns, price relationships, and price movement. A comprehensive presentation of TD Sequential requires a lengthy discussion to ensure that all aspects of the timing concept and approach are discussed and described in sufficient detail. Although such an objective could be the topic of an entire book unto itself, discussion of the salient elements of TD Sequential and its various by-products should enable you to acquire a complete understanding of the TD Sequential process, as well as of its various components. Only then will you appreciate its robust design, massive composition, versatile application, and variability.

Ideally, TD Sequential is designed to describe the relative attractive-ness of a market at any particular point in time along its price continuum from low to high risk and vice versa. In general terms, the following discussion describes the basic TD Sequential indicator and the methodology it employs to accomplish this goal by separating price activity into three distinct phases: Setup, Intersection, and Countdown. The TD Sequential Setup phase is composed of a series of consecutive price relationships that, upon completion, serve to define the underlying market environment by identifying *either* of the following:

1. A series of consecutive price relationships precedent to the Countdown phase of TD Sequential that, upon Countdown's completion, usually identifies a price trend's likely exhaustion area.
2. The termination of a corrective phase in the market and the pending resumption of the underlying price trend.

Intersection, the intermediate stage of TD Sequential, evaluates price relationships in order to identify and confirm a slowdown or deceleration in a price trend's intensity and qualify the inception of Countdown. Countdown, the third stage of TD Sequential, consists of a series of price relationships that need not necessarily be consecutive and that generally, upon completion of Countdown, identifies the level at which price reverses trend. On those occasions in which Countdown fails to successfully identify a turning point and price fails to reverse trend and a stop loss is activated, oftentimes the trend will intensify, thereby affording a trader an opportunity to reverse his or her premature incorrect entry. If at any time prior to the last day of buy Countdown, a closing price exceeds the highest true high of the most recent buy Setup (a *true high* is the high that appears on the chart or on the previous day's close, whichever is greater) or if at any time prior to the last day of sell Countdown, a closing price exceeds the lowest true low of the most recent sell Setup (a *true low* is the low that appears on the chart or on the previous day's close, whichever is less), then the active Setup is canceled. Furthermore, if a previous Setup is exceeded on a closing basis prior to the completion of the current Setup in the other direction, generally a reversal of trend has been signaled and a continuation of this current, newly established price trend is likely to continue through the completion of Countdown, provided there is immediate price follow-through the day after the breakout. TD Setup Trend (TDST) is an effective trend-following indicator developed to identify just such trend-reversal occurrences, and it is described and discussed in a later section of this chapter. On the other hand, if subsequent to the completion of a buy Setup and Countdown, all closes of the current sell Setup fail to exceed the extreme intraday true high of the most recent buy Setup or, if subsequent to the completion of a sell Setup and

Countdown, all closes of the current buy Setup fail to exceed the extreme intraday true low of the most recent sell Setup, generally this failure suggests the completion of a market correction or reaction and is a harbinger that the prevailing or preexisting price trend is likely to resume. In other words, the recent market move constituted a contratrend short-term rally in a bear market or a short-term decline in a bull market.

The initial research to develop TD Sequential was conducted upon stock charts using simple visual inspection, a time-consuming process. Lack of sufficient access to an extensive computer network and software staff produced only sketchy, incomplete results. Consequently, I resorted to using a magnifying glass, diligently poring over price relationships that existed in chart books such as Trendline and Daily Graph stock charts to identify a series of common denominators occurring at market tops and bottoms. Once these relationships were uncovered, this same technique was applied to Victoria Feed, CRB, and Commodity Perspective futures price charts. Experimenting with 8-day Setups and 13-day Countdowns, both Fibonacci-based numbers eventually led to a better combination using a 9-day Setup and a 13-day Countdown. I used a series of 9 consecutive closing price comparisons and a lookback of 4 trading days prior to each to identify Setups, but I was disappointed that neither number was Fibonacci-derived. Subsequently, however, one observant Fibonacci student pointed out that the sum of 4 and 9 is 13, which *is* a Fibonacci number. In any case, looking back now, the surprising fact is that although my original research encompassed an exhausting, time-consuming process of trial and error many years ago, my attempts in recent years to improve upon these parameter settings by means of sophisticated computer software and high-speed computers have failed to produce any significant enhancements, with the exception of the favorable results generated by the TD Sequential Recycle Qualifiers, TDST, and TD Combo (see next chapter).

## Setup

A *buy Setup* is defined as a series of nine *or more* consecutive closes less than the close four trading days earlier, and a *sell Setup* is defined as a series of nine *or more* consecutive closes greater than the close four trading days earlier. The Setup period could, and often does, extend past the minimum number of nine consecutive closes less than or greater than the close four trading days earlier. Although this extension of the Setup period past the minimum of nine days may not be important in regard to the TD Sequential Countdown process, it is critical to both the interpretation and application of TD Setup Trend (TDST), which is a TD Sequential derivative indicator, since it often determines the durability of a price trend, and it is critical for determining which subsequent Setups are recycled and which are not. In any case, it is essential that both a buy and a sell Setup be composed of *at least* nine consecutive closes that are *each* less than the close four trading days earlier for a buy or greater than the close four trading days earlier for a sell. Should a close *equal* to the close four trading days earlier be recorded prior to the completion of the minimum Setup series requirement of *at least* nine consecutive closes less than or greater than the close four trading days earlier, this would invalidate the ongoing Setup process, and consequently, the Setup search process must begin anew. Further, in order to "initialize" the buy Setup phase, the day prior to the commencement of buy Setup day 1 must be greater than or equal to the close four trading days earlier; and in order to "initialize" the sell Setup phase, the day prior to the commencement of sell Setup day 1 must be less than or equal to the close four trading days earlier. This requirement ensures the correct identification of the inception of the Setup process and thereby assures an accurate accounting for the Setup series as well. To make certain that the Setup days are properly identified and accounted for, each buy Setup day on a chart should be numbered sequentially beneath each price bar and each sell Setup day on a chart should be numbered sequentially above each price bar and that, ideally, they should be numbered with the same color to distinguish them from the numbers assigned to the Countdown series, which should be of a different color and which should appear below and above the price bars as well, depending on whether it is a buy or a sell Countdown.

Although it is preferable to use closing price comparisons to identify qualified Setup days, other comparisons can be substituted as well. For example, open, high, low, midpoint, average of various prices, low/high (low for buy Setup and high for sell Setup) or high/low (high for buy Setup and low for sell Setup) can be inserted, and all authorized Sequential indicator study packages included over the various data vendor networks include these options, as well as many other variable selections. This feature allows the user to customize the comparisons, and this selection process extends as well to the choice of the specific days that are compared. Although a four-day comparison is preferred, other time periods may be chosen just as easily (2, 3, 5, etc.). As you can readily see when establishing the buy or the sell Setup parameters, numerous price and time comparisons and combinations can be selected. Since an assortment of comparisons can be introduced for Countdown, recycling, condition qualifiers, cancellation for both Countdown and Setup as well, the likelihood of traders competing with one another and applying identical parameter settings, is diminished significantly. As with the many other indicators presented in this book, my goal is to provide a template or structure for you to customize and develop your own set of indicators or systems using the various parameter options presented. The ones provided here are not necessarily the optimal selections, and it is likely that your choices may, in fact, prove to be more effective.

## TD "Power of Nine"™

Although Setup requires a minimum of nine consecutive closes less than or greater than the close four trading days earlier, the Setup series could conceivably extend much further (see Figure 2.1 of the British pound and Figure 2.2 of IBM). Once the minimum requirement for a price Setup is fulfilled—nine consecutive closes either less than or greater than the close four trading days earlier—typically, the market experiences either a trend reversal or a price "hiccup" or consolidation period commencing either the day before, the day of, or the day following the completion of the ninth day. The market's propensity to behave in this manner is appropriately described as the TD "Power of Nine." Often this tendency is camouflaged due to the fact that subsequent intraday price movements may give the chart reader the impression and the perception of the continuation of a trend after day 9 of Setup is recorded when in actuality merely the intraday price movement (not a subsequent closing price) exceeds day 9's close. Figure 2.3 illustrates the ten-

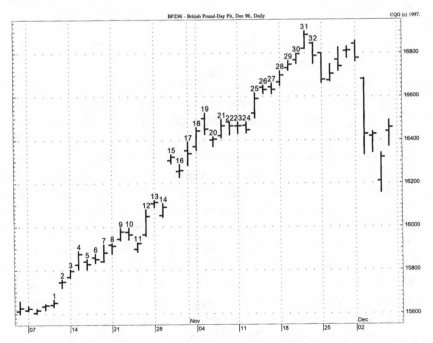

**Figure 2.1**  This chart displays a series of Setup days. Instead of terminating the sell Setup at the minimum number of consecutive closes greater than the close four trading days earlier which is 9, extend the sell Setup through sell Setup completion. In this example, this series of consecutive closes greater than the close four days earlier continued for 32 days. Although such a long series is exceptional, it is not uncommon.

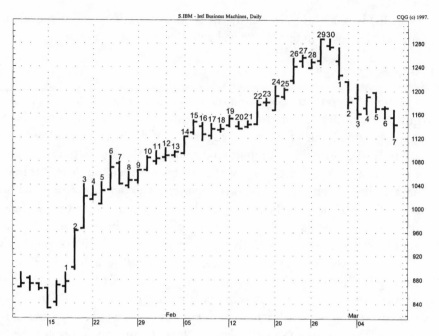

**Figure 2.2** Just as Figure 2.1 registered a series of consecutive Setup days, so, too, does this chart display an uninterrupted 30 consecutive closes greater than the close four trading days earlier.

dency for short-term price trends to exhaust themselves upon completion of the minimum number of consecutive closes required to fulfill TD Sequential Setup, which is either nine consecutive closes greater than or less than the close four trading days earlier. On the other hand, in exceptional, runaway upside or downside markets, price activity may not hesitate at all upon the completion of the series of nine consecutive closes less than or greater than the close four trading days earlier. Those instances in which the market fails to even stall at these likely support and resistance levels usually become apparent either prior to or upon completion of the nine consecutive series of closes either up or down, since by that time at least one closing price will probably have exceeded the extreme intraday high or low recorded by the most recent price Setup in the other direction—see TD Setup Trend (TDST) following. Regardless of how the Setup period develops and the price movement unfolds, a number of critical elements must be constantly monitored and evaluated. They include Setup Cancellation, Intersection, Recycling, TD Sequential Qualifiers, and TDST.

A series of nine consecutive closes less than or greater than the close four trading days earlier is the minimum number of days required for either a buy or sell Setup. Because it is common for price to experience a hesitation, correction, or reversal in trend at that point, if you were to entertain trading

**Figure 2.3**  This chart illustrates the tendency of Ascend Computer to interrupt its short-term trends once the minimum requirement for a sell or a buy Setup is fulfilled—nine consecutive closes less than or greater than the close four trading days earlier. Note that the one instance in which price failed to respond occurred in September and was accompanied by a price close that was above the true high of the highest day of the buy Setup that appeared in August. Otherwise, the close of the ninth day of Setup coincided with the short-term highs and lows. x's identify the 9s.

these "9s," as I refer to them, you should require, at a suspected short-term bottom, that the intraday low of day 9 be below the intraday low of day 6 and, at a suspected short-term top, that the intraday high of day 9 be above the intraday high of day 6. If this particular pattern does not exist, then generally, one of the ensuing two trading days or the third trading day's opening hour will usually exceed downside the intraday low of day 6 or the intraday high of day 6 upside, depending on whether a buy or sell Setup has been formed.

Additionally, to ensure that the extreme high or low price is identified coincident with the recording of the minimum Setup requirement of nine consecutive closes, you should evaluate a lower-level TD Sequential relationship to synchronize the completion of the lower-level TD Sequential Countdown to effect a trade. In other words, the higher-level Setup series defines the overall market environment, but the shorter-term Countdown refines the specific time period of execution. For example, if the daily chart is displaying the ninth day of Setup, the one-minute or five-minute interval should produce a 13 Countdown at the same time in order to fine-tune your entry on that day. In a sense, this process is similar to the procedure that should be followed when applying a high-level TD Line to arrive at a long-term price objective for the market, but you use a lower-level TD Line to activate entry and to make certain that the price objective of the short-term TD Line breakout is contained within the long-term TD Line objective.

Finally, for those traders who do not wish to await the completion of TD Sequential Countdown or spend the time counting, you may experience success by applying TD Lines to markets that have completed buy or sell Setups and are positioned for retracement rallies or declines. Provided the TD Line Qualifiers are fulfilled and at least one of the oscillators (TD REI, TD DeMarker I or II, TD Plurality, TD ROC I or II) records a simultaneous overbought or oversold oscillator reading, the TD Line breakouts subsequent to TD Sequential Setup completions are potential candidates for low-risk entry trades. By introducing similar combinations of indicators operating concurrently to confirm potential low-risk opportunities, a prudent low-risk method of trading has been developed.

## Setup Cancellations

### Contratrend Moves

One type of Setup cancellation relates to the extent to which price experiences a contratrend move prior to the completion of Countdown. Specifically, there are five different ways to cancel an outstanding buy or sell Setup. Depending upon which option is selected, prior to completion of a buy Countdown and beginning the day following the ninth consecutive close less than the close four trading days earlier, any one of the following events can take place and produce a cancellation of an active buy Setup:

1. An intraday high may occur that exceeds the highest close recorded during the entire buy Setup period.
2. An intraday high may occur that exceeds the highest high recorded during the entire buy Setup period.
3. A close may occur that exceeds the highest close recorded during the entire buy Setup period.
4. A close may occur that exceeds the highest high of the entire buy Setup period.
5. A close may occur that exceeds the highest true high recorded throughout the entire buy Setup period (a *true high* is the high that appears on the chart or the previous day's close, whichever is greater).

Obviously, the most conservative buy Setup cancellation is item 1, since it merely requires an intraday price high above the highest close of the entire buy Setup period to negate a buy Setup. Conversely, the most liberal option is cancellation 5, since it requires a close exceeding the highest intraday true high of the entire buy Setup period. It is preferable to use the latter (item 5) for buy Setup cancellation purposes. Therefore, even if subsequent to a minimum buy Setup completion of nine consecutive closes less than the close four trading days earlier, an intraday price high occurs that is greater than the highest true high of the entire buy Setup period or a closing price is recorded that is greater than the highest close of the entire buy Setup sequence unless the closing price is also greater than the true high of the highest buy Setup day, you should not cancel Countdown. However, you would cancel the Countdown process if any close occurs that is greater than the highest true high of the entire buy Setup period.

Similarly, there are five ways to cancel an outstanding sell Setup. Depending upon which option is selected, prior to completion of sell Countdown and beginning the day following the ninth consecutive close greater than the close four trading days earlier, any one of the following events can take place and cause cancellation of an active sell Setup:

1. An intraday low may occur that exceeds the lowest close recorded during the entire sell Setup period.

2. An intraday low may occur that exceeds the lowest low recorded during the entire sell Setup period.

3. A close may occur that exceeds the lowest close recorded during the entire sell Setup period.

4. A close may occur that exceeds the lowest low recorded during the entire sell Setup period.

5. A close may occur that exceeds the lowest true low recorded throughout the entire sell Setup period (a *true low* is the low that appears on the chart or the previous day's close, whichever is less).

Once again option 1 is the most conservative sell Setup cancellation, since an intraday price low below the lowest close of the entire sell Setup period is all that is required to negate a sell Setup. Further, the most liberal option is cancellation 5 since it requires a close exceeding the lowest intraday true low of the entire sell Setup period. It is preferable to use the latter (option 5) for cancellation purposes. Consequently, even if subsequent to a minimum sell Setup completion of nine consecutive closes greater than the close four trading days earlier, an intraday price low occurs that is less than the lowest true low of the entire sell Setup period or a closing price is recorded that is less than the lowest close of the entire sell Setup sequence unless the closing price is also less than the true low of the lowest sell Setup day, you should not cancel Countdown. However, you would cancel the Countdown process if any close occurs that is less than the lowest true low of the entire sell Setup.

Typically, the various Setup cancellation options appear as anagrams on most authorized system vendor software offering the DeMark Indicator software package in the Cancel category or column:

1. HaHC/LbLC indicates a High above the Highest Close of the entire buy Setup period for a Setup cancellation and a Low below the Lowest Close of the entire sell Setup period for a Setup cancellation.

2. HaHH/LbLL indicates a High above the Highest High of the entire buy Setup period for a Setup cancellation and a Low below the Lowest Low of the entire sell Setup period for a Setup cancellation.

3. CaHC/CbLC indicates a Close above the Highest Close of the entire buy Setup period for a Setup cancellation and a Close below the Lowest Close of the entire sell Setup period for a Setup cancellation.

4. CaHH/CbLL indicates a Close above the Highest High of the entire buy Setup period for a Setup cancellation and a Close below the Lowest Low of the entire sell Setup period for a Setup cancellation.

5. CaHTH/CbLTL indicates a Close above the Highest True High of the entire buy Setup period for a Setup cancellation and a Close below the Lowest True Low of the entire buy Setup period for Setup cancellation.

Any of these options may be selected. The most conservative of the group is item 1, and the most liberal of the series is item 5. My preference is option 5. Please note that you should always be conscious of the level of the following trading day's opening price and, if you desire to be "technical" about the treatment of Setup disqualification as described in items 1 through 5, you would not only consider the closing price and its relationship to the specific Setup levels, but would also monitor the following trading day's price activity to ensure that the Setup cancellation is confirmed. In other words, research indicates that if the opening price on the trading day after the Setup cancellation opens below the buy Setup cancellation level (above the sell Setup cancellation level) *or* if the opening price on the trading day after the Setup cancellation opens below the buy Setup cancellation day's closing price and the high that same day fails to exceed the high of the previous trading day (opens above the sell Setup cancellation day's closing price and the low that same day fails to exceed the low of the previous trading day), then the cancellation may be ignored. The charts of March 1995 silver (see Figure 2.4a and b) illustrate one example with the cancellation and one with the TD Critical Qualifier™ exception. The relationship between the current trading day's opening price and the previous trading day's closing price is described in my discussion of the TD Critical Qualifier (see discussion of retracements in Chapter 6 for further information). I am bending the Setup cancellation rules by introducing the following trading day's

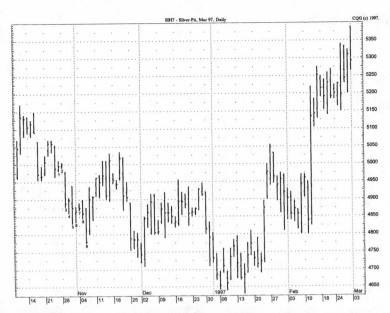

**Figure 2.4(a)** This chart displays the March 1996 silver futures contract. A buy Setup was completed the first week of November. Ten trading days after the ninth day of Setup, a close exceeded the intraday true high of the highest trading day of the Setup period and canceled the active Setup. Figure 2.4b displays the same chart, but in this case the TD Critical Qualifier is introduced and as a result the buy Setup is not canceled and the price action unfolds into a low-risk buy Countdown 13 at the bottom of the market. The discussion of TD Sequential Countdown appears later in this chapter.

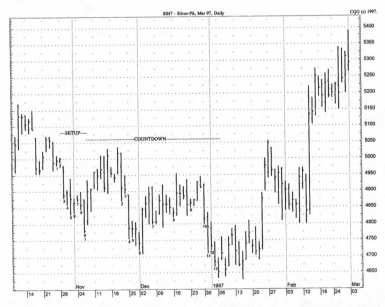

**Figure 2.4(b)** This chart demonstrates how the application of the TD Critical Qualifier enables TD Sequential to continue from buy Setup through Countdown and a low-risk buy entry. By not introducing the TD Critical Qualifier, Figure 2.4a becomes the dominant TD Sequential outcome, since Setup cancellation was activated. The periods of TD Sequential Setup and Countdown are identified on the chart. A discussion of TD Sequential Countdown is presented later in this chapter.

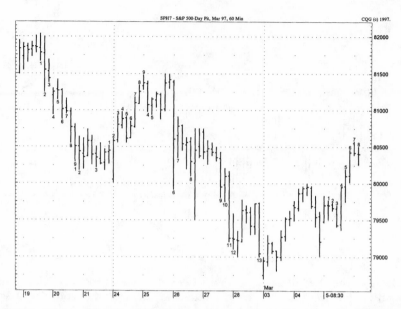

**Figure 2.4(c)** The hourly chart of S&P March 1997 presents a "reverse Setup" situation on February 25. In disregarding this contradictory Setup and not recognizing this option in the Cancellation selections, an ideal low-risk entry was presented on March 3. A similar situation on a daily basis appears in Figure 2.4d.

**Figure 2.4(d)** Just as in the case of Figure 2.4c, the low-risk TD Sequential buy zone is correctly identified on the daily chart of May 1995 silver if the "reverse Setup" cancellation selection is ignored. Either the length of the consecutive "reverse Setup" series or the degree of price penetration of the original Setup is critical in determining whether to activate the "reverse Setup" cancellation.

open, as well as the standard previous trading day's closing price, to cancel a Setup, but the TD Critical Qualifier is an important element in confirming all sorts of breakouts, as well as confirming Setup cancellations. In fact, I plan to add this additional criterion to the Setup cancel selection options that appear in the indicator software, as well as to the Recycle rules and options.

## Reverse Setup

Another form of Setup cancellation is the occurrence of a reverse Setup—a series of nine or more closes greater than or less than the close four trading days earlier—which contradicts the direction of the current Setup. For example, if a buy Setup is currently active and a sell Setup develops before buy Countdown is completed, then the buy Setup is canceled and is replaced by the sell Setup, which then becomes active. In other words, the sell Setup becomes the dominant or controlling Setup and sell Countdown is commenced. Conversely, if a sell Setup is currently active and a buy Setup develops before sell Countdown is completed, then the sell Setup is canceled and replaced by the buy Setup and the buy Countdown is begun. In addition, this reverse cancellation selection can be turned "on" or "off" in the Cancel column. This particular cancellation process can be perfected and used to successfully identify price trend reversals by introducing an indicator called TD Setup Trend (TDST), which will be discussed shortly. My research in regard to reverse Setups is not complete, since there are instances when Setups are canceled by contradictory Setups when it would have been prudent to ignore this option (see Figure 2.4c and d). Although it is not common, you can see that by disregarding the cancellation, ideal low-risk entry zones would have appeared.

### Setup Contained within Previous Setup

On occasion, there are instances when a Setup is completed—nine or more consecutive closes less than or greater than the close four trading days earlier—and, subsequently, another Setup formation in the same direction occurs, and the extreme high and the extreme low of the second Setup is contained by the extreme high and the extreme low of the original setup. Initially, similar occurrences seemed like a Setup Recycle. Upon further inspection, it became apparent that a Setup succeeded by a second Setup in the same direction that does not exceed the extreme intraday high or low price levels established by the first Setup may be disregarded and, consequently, the original Setup remains active and the second Setup fails to qualify as a valid Recycle. The research that led to this conclusion served as the catalyst for the introduction of various Recycle options, which subsequently superseded this option—see following. The "Setup Within" cancellation feature can be turned on or off in the Cancel column.

### Setup Recycle

A third method of Setup cancellation is the appearance of a Setup in the same direction as the previously active Setup prior to the completion and perfection of Countdown. Such an event occurs often and merely indicates a renewed interest and intensity in the underlying market trend and therefore precedes or accompanies the perpetuation of a market move. This event is called a standard "Setup Recycle" or simply "Recycle." I have developed various Recycle option selections to deal with this event whenever it occurs. When TD Sequential was developed many years ago, Recycles occurred infrequently and were the exception rather than the rule. The frequency of their appearance has increased significantly in recent years, especially in the stock market, and this can be attributed to an intense, unrelenting urgency to either enter or exit the market. By including these Setup Recycle options, a trader can refine this Recycle selection process by evaluating each of them individually and then selecting the specific setting he or she is most comfortable with (see Parameter options presented on page 94, item 13). In other words, with this feature, traders can simply ignore specific variations of Setup Recycles, since they are not limited merely to the standard, single Recycle cancellation option described previously ("Setup Contained within Previous Setup"). Obviously, a trader can be conservative and opt to recycle whenever a renewed Setup occurs, but oftentimes he or she forfeits a trading opportunity that would have existed had the Setup Recycle been "ignored."

## Setup Qualifiers

Although Setup Qualifiers can be helpful in perfecting the Setup phase, they are not frequently applied. However, the option of having Setup Qualifiers is important in the sense that some traders may elect to concentrate solely upon Setup research, TDST (see following), or other aspects of TD Sequential and totally disregard Countdown and the complete TD Sequential indicator. For example, as described in the discussion of TD Sequential Setup and the TD "Power of 9," if a trader wishes to become proficient solely in the application and interpretation of price Setups, my research and experience indicates that generally, for a buy Setup, the ninth day's low of Setup should be less than the sixth day's low and, if it is not, oftentimes a subsequent low within the next one to three trading days will eventually exceed the low of day 6. Conversely, for a sell Setup, typically, the ninth day's high of Setup should be greater than the sixth day's high. Once again, if it is not, then within the ensuing three trading days a subsequent high will oftentimes exceed day 6's high. In either case, you should *never* cancel or postpone a Setup because this pattern is absent if you are following TD Sequential and

Countdown, although there are Setup Qualifiers to accomplish this objective when performing research and analysis devoted exclusively to Setups. This option is offered only in order to perfect entry for those traders interested in techniques that enhance precision timing and relationships when applying price Setups. Additionally, in those instances in which it appears that a Setup will fail to close above the true high or below the true low of the contradictory Setup, such as with TDST (see following discussion), the Setup Qualifiers will serve the purpose of postponing or deferring this requirement, thereby enabling an ideal price entry that may not have existed otherwise. In other words, by introducing Setup Qualifiers, the Setup can be postponed until prescribed criteria are fulfilled without the risk of an interruption to, or a disqualification of, the Setup requirement of consecutive trading days. Figures 2.5a, b, and c display three daily Setup charts of IBM from August 1995 through late 1996. As you can see, in each instance in which either the low of day 9 of the buy Setup is greater than the low of day 6 of the same buy Setup or the high of day 9 of the sell Setup is less than the high of day 6 of the same sell Setup, one of the subsequent three trading days' intraday lows exceeds downside day 6's low for the buy Setup or one of the ensuing three trading days' highs exceeds upside day 6's high for the sell Setup. There are occasions in which one stock market index conforms to the conventional price Setup

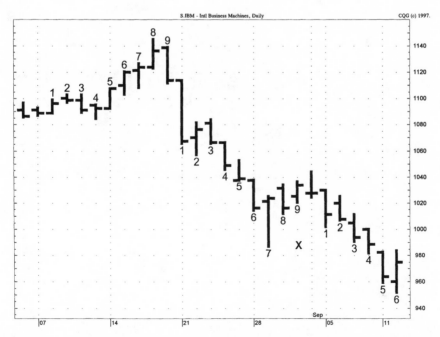

**Figure 2.5(a)**  Note that the low of day 9 of the buy Setup was greater than day 6 of the buy Setup (x on chart). Usually, within three trading days, the low of day 6 is exceeded downside, at least intraday. Figure 2.5b and c illustrate the same phenomenon for IBM.

**Figure 2.5(b)**   This chart is the reverse of Figure 2.5a, since a sell Setup appears and the high of day 9 is below the high of day 6 of Setup. Nevertheless, the market responds similarly by recording a higher high than day 6 within three days after day 9 of Setup.

**Figure 2.5(c)**   Once again, a failure of the high of day 9 of sell Setup to exceed the high of day 6 of Setup suggested that a subsequent high within the next three trading days would exceed day 6's high.

configuration and, at the same time, another stock market index deviates and fails to conform and perform likewise. For example, if the low of day 9 of a buy Setup is above the low of day 6 or if the high of day 9 of a sell Setup is below the high of day 6, then the market usually adjusts to exceed day 6 of Setup within a few trading days. Such a dichotomy was apparent in the price behavior of two seemingly similar markets in January 1996. Figures 2.6a and b display the price activity of the New York Composite March 1996 future and the S&P March 1996 future subsequent to day 9 of the sell Setup on January 6, 1996. Not all market price patterns fulfill the precise specifications I have described all of the time. Whereas the New York Stock Exchange Composite futures contract posted a high equal to or greater than the high of day 6 of the sell Setup within three days after day nine of the Setup, the S&P future failed to do likewise. For that reason, not only should related markets be followed and monitored closely but also, in the case of the futures markets, numerous expirations of the same market should be reviewed continuously to protect against similar events.

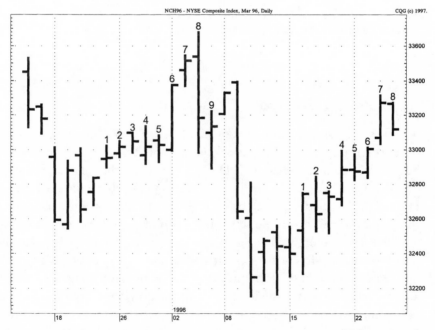

**Figure 2.6(a)**   Note that the minimum sell Setup period was completed when nine consecutive closes greater than the close four trading days earlier was recorded on January 5, 1996. The high of Setup day 9 was less than the high of Setup day 6, and the market subsequently corrected this anomaly by rallying two trading days after Setup day 9 to exceed the intraday high of day 6. This event occurred in contrast to the S&P March 1996 future, which failed to accomplish a similar rally. For this reason, it is recommended that a trader follow more than one market or additional contract expirations to confirm indications (see Figure 2.6b).

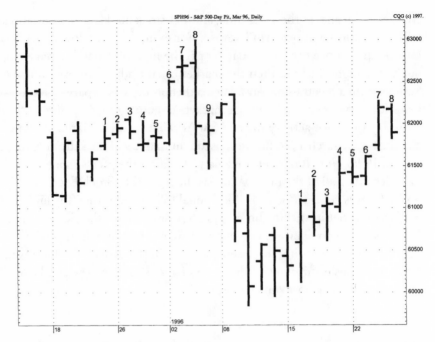

**Figure 2.6(b)** Although the high of Setup day 9 failed to exceed the high of Setup 6 within three trading days after day 9, the New York Composite future did as shown on Figure 2.6a.

## TD Setup Trend (TDST)

TDST serves as an effective tool in identifying and defining important trend-reversal price levels. It is a key indicator that is a derivative of TD Sequential Setup cancellation. TDST is essentially the same as Setup cancellation CaHTH CbLTL, which indicates a Close above the Highest True High of the buy Setup period for a buy Setup cancellation and a Close below the Lowest True Low of the sell Setup period for a sell Setup cancellation. TDST is much more valuable as a trend indicator than many conventional, widely used trend-following approaches, such as buying when a high exceeds upside the highest high of the previous 40 trading days, going neutral when a low exceeds downside the lowest low of the previous 20 trading days, and selling short when a low exceeds downside the lowest low of the previous 40 trading days. TDST is dynamic and not rigid like other trend-following techniques in the sense that it is designed to adapt and to adjust to the dynamics of the market's continuously changing supply and demand landscape. Previous price Setup highs and lows define key price levels as important reference points, and by exceeding these barriers an alert trader is able to anticipate trend reversals. Specifically, TDST becomes active whenever dramatic shifts in supply or demand occur that are sufficient to cancel an ongoing Countdown phase by closing above the extreme intraday true high of the buy Setup or by closing below the extreme intraday true low of the sell Setup. Such breakouts warrant immediate attention and action, since the expectation is for the continuation and extension of this newly established price trend through the completion of TD Sequential Countdown. Typically, by comparing the current closing price and its relationship to the previous Setup intraday true high for an upside breakout and intraday true low for a downside breakout, TDST is able to identify whether a current price trend will continue through Countdown or is more likely to expire upon the completion of Setup and resume its previous trend. Furthermore, although TDST breakouts generally occur prior to the completion of Setup, in exceptionally strong markets, look for TDST to alert you to imminent and unexpected trend reversals that could occur at any time within the Setup process and occasionally even subsequent to the completion of either a buy or sell Setup when a renewed burst of strength or weakness becomes apparent.

There are two situations that could invalidate a TDST breakout: (1) a failure to follow through in the direction of the TDST breakout by recording a higher high (or lower low) than the TDST breakout day's high (or low) within the next three trading days or (2) a downside opening gap the day following an upside TDST breakout day or an upside opening gap the day following a downside TDST breakout that is not filled that same trading day. The TD Critical Qualifier, discussed in Chapter 5, accomplishes the same goal in the case of similar types of analysis that require breakouts to be qualified, validated, or confirmed, such as TD Line breakouts, price retracement levels, REBO indications, and other indicators presented in this book. In those instances, you should evaluate the price activity by focusing upon and evaluating what you believe to be the most important price level of the trading day subsequent to any type of indicator breakout—namely, the following trading day's opening price. Not only is the closing price a critical component of validation of a price breakout, but even more important is the following trading day's opening price relative to the breakout level. Consequently, even though a market may record a breakout due to short-term buying or selling pressure, such activity can be canceled or reversed depending upon the next trading day's opening price, if that price retraces the breakout level by recording a price gap. Experience suggests short-term price distortions create price activity that occasionally causes closing prices to record breakouts. This price behavior is often caused by extraordinary events, such as unexpected political or economic news, short covering, option expiration, major buy or sell programs, or quarter-end or month-end window dressing. If this price dislocation does occur at the time of the market's close and it is of a short-term variety, price equilibrium is generally restored upon the opening the following trading day. That is why the opening price is the most critical price level of the day and frequently labeled the "king price" or the critical price. The discussion of price retracements addresses the TD Critical Qualifier in more detail. In other words, any artificial price factors that may have contributed to the previous trading day's price breakout are often corrected at the following trading day's opening price. The significance of the opening price level is particularly apparent when applying TDST, TD Retracements, TD Sequential and TD Combo, TD Line breakouts, TD Diff™ and so on.

TDST is a valuable contribution to the library of trend-following tools and an important consideration when deciding whether to continue to hold a market position acquired as a result of another market timing indicator or when determining whether price movement can be expected to continue after Setup through TD Sequential or TD Combo Countdown. Almost every chart in this chapter regardless of which market or time period is studied, will include a series of TDST indications. The following charts will provide numerous examples to ensure your understanding of this important trend-following concept. In each case, I have removed TD Sequential Countdown and have displayed only TD Sequential Setup. Figure 2.7 displays the daily price activity for the German Bund in December 1996. Note that the horizontal line originates at the price level of the highest intraday

QDZ96 - German BUND-Pit Only, Dec 96, Daily          CQG (c) 1997.

**Figure 2.7**  The close above the horizontal line that appears on the German Bund chart, beginning in August 1996 and extending to day 6 of sell Setup, indicates that the trend has likely reversed upside. TD Setup Trend (TDST) uses as a reference the highest true high of the buy Setup, and once price closes above this level and follows through by recording a higher high, the upside move should continue through sell Setup and Countdown or until the trend is reversed by recording a close below the lowest true low of a subsequent sell Setup.

true high of the buy Setup period, which began on August 21 and was completed on September 4, 1996, since the close on September 5 was greater than the close four trading days earlier. That same horizontal line intersects day 6 of the sell Setup on September 12. Upon the close that day, TDST was activated, and a TDST trend reversal was confirmed the following trading day when a higher intraday price high was recorded. Even if a trader preferred to trade more conservatively, the close on that day exceeded the TDST level. Figure 2.8 shows the various TDST indicator levels at numerous times in March 1997 for crude oil. As you can readily see, not only is "what TDST is saying" important, but also "what it is not saying." By exceeding the intraday true highs of the respective buy Setups in both early August and early December and by failing to exceed the intraday true lows of the respective sell Setups in both late July and early November, the crude oil future's contract was announcing in no uncertain terms its intention to trade higher, which it did throughout this entire period.

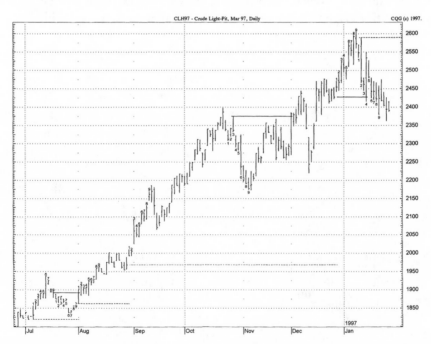

**Figure 2.8**   Note that the horizontal line identifying the lowest true low of the sell Setup formed in July was not exceeded on a closing basis in late July. In fact, once price closed greater than the close four days earlier on August 4, it indicated that the downside potential had likely been exhausted, and this indication was confirmed when day 1 of the sell Setup exceeded the highest intraday true high of the buy Setup formed in late August—identified with a solid horizontal line. A similar situation occurred in December, when price closed above the highest true high of the previous buy Setup. Furthermore, in November, when price failed to close below the horizontal line extended from the late August sell Setup intraday true low, the indication of a rally was confirmed.

Figure 2.9 (Treasury bonds in December 1996) from July through October shows a sell Setup that was completed in mid-July. Subsequently, price declined into early September and evolved into a buy Setup that was completed after recording 15 consecutive closes less than the close four trading days earlier, on September 10. Note that the lowest true low of the entire sell Setup period was $106^{13}/_{32}$ and occurred on July 11. Although that price level may have been violated intraday during the formation of the subsequent buy Setup in early September, the lowest closing price recorded throughout the entire buy Setup period was precisely $106^{13}/_{32}$ on September 6. Since a closing price was unable to close less than the close four trading days earlier, and the TDST level, the expectation of the continuation of the decline was virtually nullified, and the downside pressure quickly dissipated as soon as a close was recorded that was greater than or equal to the close four trading days earlier. Since a TDST downside breakout requires a close below the lowest intraday true low of the most recent sell Setup and then a confirmation of a price follow-through, the chance of a continuation of the decline through buy Countdown, as well as the possibility for a downside trend being established at that time, is reduced. This does not imply that such an event will not occur;

**Figure 2.9**  Often the precision associated with TDST is amazing. The intraday true low on July 11, the lowest low of the sell Setup, was $106^{13}/_{32}$, and the lowest closing low of the subsequent buy Setup was on August 5 at exactly $106^{13}/_{32}$. Once the first close greater than or equal to the close four trading days earlier occurred and canceled the active buy Setup, an assumption can be made that the trend has reversed upside.

however, the probability of it developing diminishes significantly. In this case, price did reverse upside within three trading days of the buy Setup completion—15 consecutive closes less than the close four trading days earlier. Subsequently, on October 4 price closed above the intraday high of $110^{21}\!/_{31}$ recorded on August 20, and this TDST breakout suggested a reversal of the price trend, which did in fact occur a few weeks later. However this breakout was suspect since it was not confirmed the following day. Occasionally, similar situations arise in which not just one, but multiple breakouts fail to get confirmed, such as is shown in Figure 2.10. Both closes in August and October exceeded the intraday true high of the previous buy Setups, and the only prerequisite preventing TDST breakouts was confirmation, which never appeared in either instance. Furthermore, although the intraday high in November hit "precisely" the highest intraday true high, this rally failed to muster enough strength to even close above that level.

The two exceptions just described arise occasionally and, consequently, until TDST breakouts are confirmed they remain suspect. Once again, to confirm a TDST upside breakout indication, first of all, the opening price on

**Figure 2.10** Although price closed above the highest true high of the buy Setups two times and traded above the intraday true high of the buy Setup on another occasion as well, none were confirmed and price continued to decline. The highest intraday true high is identified by an extended line. Note that the August close was followed by an opening price gap downside and the high of the October close was not followed by a higher high or close within the following three trading days and the November intraday upside high rallied exactly to the solid TDST line but failed to close above it.

the trading day following a TDST upside breakout must not record a gap downside (open below the previous trading day's close), and the opening price on the trading day after a TDST downside breakout must not record a gap upside (open above the previous trading day's close) *and* the high on the day following the TDST breakout must be succeeded by a higher high in the case of a TDST upside breakout or the low on the day following a downside TDST breakout must be succeeded by a lower low in the case of a downside breakout. Often this rule is adapted by allowing price to exceed the intraday high of the TDST upside breakout day or the intraday low of the downside TDST breakout day over a longer period of time, such as within three trading days. Using these specific techniques as well as a series of others will confirm that these breakouts are not price aberrations. It is possible that the forces of supply and demand may have been in disequilibrium the previous trading day and, as a result, the closing price may have misrepresented the true dynamics of the market at the time of the market's close, and the current trading day's opening price will likely attempt to compensate and adjust for this disequilibrium. However, should either exception occur and TDST is not confirmed, it may be regenerated subsequently provided price does record a close above the intraday high of the upside TDST breakout day or a close below the intraday low of the downside TDST breakout day. Most TDST breakouts occur before the Setup process has been completed, and if a TDST breakout is unable to occur during that period, then you should presume that the original trend is intact and about ready to reassert itself. But in those exceptional instances in which the TDST breakout fails to occur prior to Setup completion and then is subsequently able to accomplish the TDST breakout level it had originally failed to exceed, you may generally perceive this breakout as powerful, with implications of a strong, impending market move. This is in fact what did occur in the Treasury bond example in October in Figure 2.9. As described previously, Figure 2.10 illustrates both exception conditions. The early August rally exceeded on a closing basis the highest high of the buy Setup, but the opening price the next day was lower, and the close that same day was below the TDST breakout price exceeded the previous trading day. Furthermore, the next 14 trading days failed to record a high above the TDST breakout price, and on August 26 it closed exactly on the TDST breakout price level, but the next trading day the opening price was lower and the market declined—once again failing to confirm the TDST breakout. The September 25 buy Setup intraday true high was exceeded on a closing basis on October 22, but the next trading day price gapped lower on the opening, and all the subsequent trading days displayed on the chart failed to record a TDST breakout as well, but the intraday high of November 13 did trade to the precise level intraday. Another buy Setup occurred on November 27 when the ninth day of Setup was recorded. This new Setup resulted in a lower intraday true high Setup level, which is the closing price of November 14, the day before day 1 of the buy Setup, since a downside gap occurred on Setup day 1, the succeeding trading day.

Figures 2.11 and 2.12 illustrate two more examples of TDST. Figure 2.11 (IBM) identifies both TDST upside and downside breakout levels. On June 20, 1995, IBM closed above the TDST breakout level, which was the intraday true high recorded on May 26, and on August 21 the stock closed below the intraday low of August 11, which was day 4 of Setup and also the lowest true low of sell Setup. Figure 2.12 displays a TD Sequential 9-13 low-risk buy indication followed by a TDST closing upside breakout above the highest intraday true high realized during the entire buy Setup period. The horizontal line defines where the TDST breakout occurs. Note the subsequent confirmation and, consequently, the potential of the market not only reversing trend upside, but also the forewarning of the price move continuing through TD Sequential Countdown by the TDST upside breakout.

Accurate market forecasts have been made in the past by applying a market timing derivative of TDST, which is consistent with my practice of identifying and taking advantage of price exhaustion areas by selling into market strength and buying into market weakness. This unorthodox approach includes a simple process of identifying the TDST levels, and as price approaches these breakout points, assume that the current closing price will fail to exceed the TDST level and, if by chance it does, then the break-

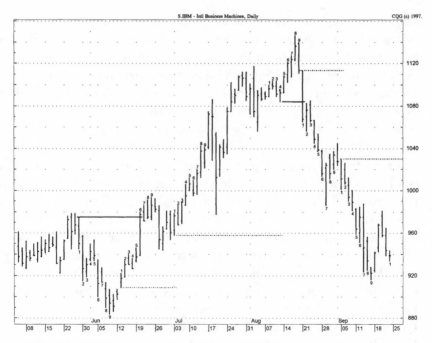

**Figure 2.11**  The TDST breakouts for IBM in mid-1995 occurred in June upside and in August downside.

**Figure 2.12** Rather than just display the Setup period, a TD Sequential Countdown is included on this chart as well. Note that the high of the buy Setup completed in February defines the reference level for TDST—an extended line across the chart identifies this price level. Once exceeded in late April, a trader is alerted to the fact that sell Countdown will likely be fulfilled. Similarly, a TDST support was broken downside in mid-March, which indicated TD Sequential would probably continue through Countdown completion.

out will fail to get confirmed. Although this might appear difficult to do, it is very simple to understand and execute. Specifically, since days 1 through 4 of Setup most often coincide with the intraday true high of a buy Setup or the intraday true low of a sell Setup, it is easy to prepare yourself psychologically for the movement of price to the breakout zone, which a trader can identify in advance. Then, as price approaches this reference level, traders can define their entry area and calculate their risk exposure. One positive aspect of this approach is the ability to operate against the trend and to anticipate various scenarios that might carry price movement to those levels. Typically, you can identify the various TDST levels as they unfold; Setup occurs, and as price eventually approaches or even exceeds the TDST level intraday—intraminute, intrahour, or whatever the trading time period selection might be—a trade can be initiated in opposition to the current trend, with the expectation that the important TDST level will *not* be exceeded on a closing basis. However, a stop loss should be placed in the event that price exceeds the TDST level on a closing basis and has been confirmed the following price bar with an opening price exceeding the stop loss as well (TD Critical Qualifier see page 195). In other words, the assumption of a trader who follows this methodology is that the TDST level on a closing basis will provide support downside and resistance upside, and the intraday movement exceeding that level presents an opportunity to buy weakness and to sell strength.

Once again, this approach contradicts the trend-following application of TDST described previously and is most similar to the logic applied to one of the low-risk alternative entry techniques for TD Sequential; for example, a low-risk entry opportunity presents itself as price approaches a stop-loss level, and by adding positions at more advantageous entry levels, as the stop loss approaches, in order to lower the entry price for a buy and to raise the entry price for a sell, and since most of my stop losses require activation on a closing basis only, intraday TDST breakouts can be faded against the short-term trend. In conclusion, TDST is designed to identify a key reference price level along the spectrum of the previous TD Sequential Setup, which, when exceeded, suggests a trend change. By closing above and then confirming this breakout, a trader is forewarned of a trend change. TDST may be described this way: If a gardener wanted to remove a weed growing in the yard or if a doctor wanted to remove a tumor, he or she would remove the entire weed by its roots or the tumor and surrounding cells by their core just to be certain neither would regenerate, and then a series of tests would be conducted to verify success. So also, to confirm that a trend has reversed, it is critical that its origin be exceeded on a closing basis and subsequently confirmed by the following price bar's opening price (TD Critical Qualifier page 195).

## Recycling

Historically, it was not uncommon for markets to progress from TD Sequential Setup through Countdown completion without recording a *price flip*—a close that interrupts one or more of a series of consecutive closes less than the close four trading days earlier by registering a close greater than or equal to the close four trading days earlier in the case of a buy Setup or, conversely, a close that interrupts one or more of a series of consecutive closes greater than the close four trading days earlier by recording a close less than or equal to the close four trading days earlier in the case of a sell Setup. The number of consecutive closes less than the close four trading days earlier could extend past the minimum number of nine consecutive closes less than the close four days earlier, which is required for a buy Setup, or past the minimum number of nine consecutive closes greater than the close four trading days earlier, which is required for a sell Setup, and continue through the entire completion of Countdown without being interrupted by at least one price flip. Figure 2.13 (December 1996 British pound) displays a series of 32 consecutive sell Setup days in which the closing price was greater than the close four trading days earlier. The thirteenth day of Countdown is identified with an X on the same chart—although the 13 appears that day, the specific low-risk sell activation can be generated a number of ways, such as the first close subsequent to sell Countdown day 13, which is less than that same day's opening price, and also

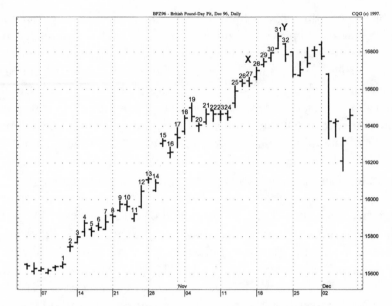

**Figure 2.13** The sell Setup series of consecutive closes greater than close four trading days earlier continued uninterrupted for a period of 32 trading days. The thirteenth trading day of TD Sequential Countdown occurred on day *X* and the first close less than the same day's open with a low less than the previous day's close occurred on the Setup day 32 (*Y*).

a low that same day less than the previous day's closing price, which incidentally occurred the day after the price peak in this example. Since there was not even one instance in which price closed less than or equal to the closing price four trading days earlier prior to Countdown day 13, there was no possibility of a sell Setup recycle. Similar nonrecyclable TD Sequential situations were common when I developed TD Sequential over two decades ago. In fact, even when a price flip did occur that contradicted a series of consecutive closes greater than or less than the close four trading days earlier, it was not necessarily a condition precedent to a Setup Recycle. Figure 2.14 illustrates a similar occurrence in late February 1996 during the IBM rally, since the consecutive series of closes greater than the close four trading days earlier was unimpeded by any close less than or equal to the close four trading days earlier. In fact, the series of consecutive sell Setup closes greater than the close four trading days earlier was 30, and no risk of a recycle arose throughout the entire move from inception of sell Setup through Countdown. On the other hand, the decline of IBM in late 1995 into early 1996 was punctuated by numerous price flips—closes greater than or equal to the close four trading days earlier—which posed the potential problem of recycling. Given the option to select dealing with unknown elements such as price flips and the attendant risks associated with them (e.g., Setup Recycles) or given the opportunity to select and apply TD Sequential Countdown to price activity with no price flips (and no potential of Setup Recycling), gladly I would

**Figure 2.14** The rally into the late February 1996 price peak was uninterrupted in the sense that the sell Setup continued for 30 consecutive days, at which time price peaked. Noteworthy is the fact that throughout this entire advance not once did a close occur that was less than or equal to the close four trading days earlier. Such uninterrupted moves prevent the occurrence of recycles, and consequently make the Countdown process less cumbersome and ambiguous. By awaiting the first close less than the open the same day and, at the same time, low less than the previous day's close (or low), a low-risk entry level can be established. Observe also that at the early January 1996 low, a TD Sequential low-risk indication was generated, but the decline into this low was not uninterrupted, having been punctuated by numerous closes greater than the close four trading days earlier, thereby elevating the risk of Setup recycles. Both the TD Sequential thirteenth day of buy and sell Countdown are identified with Xs.

choose the nonrecyclable option. In recent years, there have been many more instances of price interruptions or price flips. This phenomenon reflects the tendency of markets to regenerate and sustain the underlying, established price trend due to the intensity of the buying or the selling pressure, which is interrupted only intermittently by recording sporadic price flips. It would be ideal to have the forces of buying and selling remain static for purposes of identifying price tops and bottoms; however, news reports, portfolio considerations, market perceptions, weather, statistical information, interest rates, money supply, and so forth are dynamic factors and cause changes continuously in the supply/demand equation and mix. The culmination of all these factors is reflected in one bottom-line measurement: *price movement.* In other words, investors' expectations, hopes, fears, and greed alone cannot move prices. Only one factor can, and that is money flow into and out of the market, and this activity is determined by two forces: supply and demand. The process that I refer to as Recycling regenerates a Setup whenever the forces of supply or demand reassert themselves. Since these price imbalances occur, depending upon the definition of Recycling selected, the Setup period is able to begin anew and perpetuate a price trend. This influx of supply or demand enables a long-term market trend to remain intact by interjecting occasional periods of contratrend price movement to relieve short-term overbought or oversold conditions. Recycling relates only to the reestablishment of a new Setup in the same direction as the previous Setup due to the revitalization of the market's trend and intensity. When TD Sequential was developed, my research work indicated instances in which recycling occurred. However, its incidence was infrequent and it was the exception rather than the rule to experience more than one Setup Recycle before Countdown completion. In recent years, there have been many more occurrences in which recycling has taken place, not just one time but a series of consecutive recycles. In fact, the stock market rally from late 1994 through the middle of 1996 was propelled higher with no less than 14 consecutive sell Setups and subsequent Recycles being recorded without even one completion of a sell Countdown (see Figure 2.15, S&P cash). This is unprecedented and bespeaks the intensity of that market advance. Prior to that record series, there was an instance in 1985 in which the currency markets recycled five or six times, but that was at their secular lows and at the U.S. dollar secular peak. There are numerous Recycle and Countdown options and variations that deal with potential market Recycles, and they will be addressed shortly in discussions of both TD Sequential Countdown and TD Sequential Recycle setting options. Obviously, if no risk of a Recycle exists, the identification of a TD Sequential low- or high-risk price zone is straightforward and simple. However, if the Setup is interrupted at any time by a price flip, then the potential of Recycle looms large and is an important consideration. The former proposition of no chance of Recycle is preferable since it is simpler to follow, but in one respect it is lacking. By definition, the fact that the Setup was not interrupted indicates that in order to reverse the Setup trend using the TDST indicator, it is a longer distance than if a Recycled Setup closer to the thirteenth day of Countdown had occurred. In other words, by installing Recycle provisions to recalculate Countdown and to ignore them on occasion whenever a renewed Setup occurs, the possibility of exceeding the extreme price recorded during the most recent Setup on a closing basis is enhanced considerably, since the renewed Setup can be ignored for the purpose of Countdown but not in the case of TDST (see IBM, Figure 2.16, for an example). In other words, TDST disregards the existence of Countdown subsequent to the original Setup and evaluates the relationship only between the prior Setup and the subsequent completion of the Setup in the other price direction to determine whether a price trend has in fact reversed or whether the price move has merely been a market correction prior to the resumption of the previous market trend.

Depending upon the specific option selected, Recycling can take place at any time after the original Setup has occurred and has been subsequently interrupted by a price flip (a close greater than or equal to the close four

**Figure 2.15** From the December 1994 low through May of 1996, the S&P Cash Index recorded 14 consecutive sell Setups without recording a single sell Countdown completion. Each sell Setup recycled the prior TD Sequential Countdown. Previously, the most consecutive Setups and recycles was five, recorded at the secular U.S. dollar peak and concommitant continental and Japanese currency lows in 1985. The series of consecutive sell Setups and recycles are numbered.

trading days earlier in the case of a buy Setup or a close less than or equal to the close four trading days earlier in the case of a sell Setup) until Countdown has been completed and confirmed or perfected by a price flip. The various Setup Recycling options that would require Countdown to be restarted include the following:

1. A new Setup occurs "before, on, or after" completion of Countdown and prior to the price flip.

2. A new Setup occurs "before or on" completion of Countdown and prior to the price flip.

3. A new Setup occurs "on or after" completion of Countdown and prior to the price flip.

4. A new Setup occurs "only after" Countdown is complete and prior to the price flip.

5. A new Setup occurs "only before" Countdown is complete.

If any of the following options occur, then Setup Recycle will *not* occur:

6. The most recent (current) Recycle that occurs prior to the price flip is ignored.

**Figure 2.16** By ignoring the Recycled sell Setup one day after the price peak in August, TD Sequential sell Countdown of 13 occurred at the high. Additionally, TDST was activated two trading days after the high when day 1 of the buy Setup closed below the lowest true low of the sell Setup—see horizontal line.

7. All Recycles that occur are ignored.

8. A current Recycle that occurs prior to the price flip whose entire Setup period from highest intraday high to the lowest intraday low encompasses less price movement than the entire original (prior) Setup period is ignored.

9. A current Recycle that occurs prior to the price flip whose entire Setup period from the highest intraday true high to the lowest intraday true low encompasses less price movement than the entire original (prior) Setup period is ignored.

10. A current Recycle that occurs prior to the price flip whose entire Setup period from the highest close to the lowest close encompasses less price movement than the entire original (prior) Setup period is ignored.

Finally, this additional option can be used in conjunction with options 8 through 11.

11. Any Recycle Setup that occurs prior to the price flip, provided the entire price movement of the Setup from intraday true high to intraday true low encompasses greater than $x$ times the price movement covered by the entire original (prior) Setup period, is ignored.

My preferences are option 1, which is the original, basic vanilla Recycle option "before, on, or after" and which is the most conservative, *and* a combination of options 9 and 11, which are more liberal and sensitive to the identification of prospective trend reversals. Additionally, TD Combo, TDST, and TD ROC I and II, and others are good choices to confirm trading opportunities presented by TD Sequential, both short and long term.

Many options for Recycle consideration have been presented for the sake of completeness and to allow you to experiment with a variety of selections that may satisfy your own special needs for the treatment of Recycling. Examining the possibilities will instill a level of comfort and confidence in your trading abilities. Furthermore, should you have these selections programmed on any authorized data vendor network, for example, you can apply these or similar techniques to your own research and analysis of other market timing techniques. Figure 2.17 illustrates both the buy Setup and Countdown for U.S. Treasury bonds in March 1995. The controlling Recycle option is the most basic and conservative—namely, "on, before, or after." In other words, if at any time prior to the completion of buy Countdown and the day of the first subsequent price flip (close greater than or equal to the close four trading days earlier) another buy Setup is formed (nine or more consecutive closes less than the close four days earlier), then the original buy Setup is replaced with the new Setup and buy Countdown begins anew. This feature prevents buying prematurely in the face of another onslaught of selling pressure. In this example, you can see that no subsequent buy Setup occurred after the Setup of early October through the trading day after the Countdown day 13, when the close exceeded the close four trading days earlier (price flip upside occurred). Once again, this is the traditional, standard, conventional, and most elementary form of TD Sequential because its treatment of Recycling is the simplest. For instructional purposes, all other options for Recycling described previously would also have qualified the Countdown 13 as well, since if the recycle prerequisites of "before, on, or after" are met and this selection is the most conservative, then all other Recycle options that are more liberal will be satisfied as well.

Rather than present examples of each Recycle option, I present the two versions I rely upon at this time for my trading decisions—as well as the Multiplier option. Figure 2.18, on the other hand, applies the recycle option "ignore smaller true high/true low," which calculates the true high minus true low price difference between the current Setup and compares it to the true high minus true low price difference of the previous Setup, and this relationship dictates which Setup precedes Countdown. By applying the standard Recycle option "before, on, or after," a new Setup will always replace the previous Setup in the same direction, provided Countdown has not been completed and perfected by a price flip. This chart, however, displays a Countdown of 13 at the 1993 weekly high as well as late 1994 weekly low for

**Figure 2.17** TD Sequential Countdown generated a low-risk buy Countdown 13 on the close of trading November 11, 1994, at 95¹⁵⁄₃₂ for the March 1995 Treasury bond. The buy Setup was completed by fulfilling the minimum requirement for Setup of nine consecutive closes less than the close four trading days earlier. The buy Countdown commenced that same day, since Intersection had occurred, and the subsequent Countdown days were punctuated with a series of price flips (closes greater than or equal to the close four trading days earlier), any one of which could have easily been succeeded by a buy Setup recycle. In this instance, no recycle took place, and the close the trading day succeeding the buy Countdown closed greater than the close four trading days earlier, thereby precluding a recycle. By selecting the recycle option to the most conservative option of "before, on, or after," often a recycle will occur at market bottoms and tops and opportunities will be forfeited. At the same time, the "before, on, or after" recycle approach may appear less frequently, but the ambiguity associated with the other Recycle options is not a factor. The horizontal line identifies the TDST breakout level.

Treasury bonds. This chart also shows a Setup just prior to the high and just after the low. These ongoing Setups could have recycled TD Sequential Countdown at the high and at the low had they encompassed a distance greater than the original Setup. The fact that each Setup price difference from true high to true low covered less price movement than the immediately prior Setup justified the continuation of Countdown into the respective 1993 price peak and late 1994 price low. The distance traversed by both Setup periods includes the lowest intraday true low and the highest intraday true high from day 1 of each Setup through the completion of the Setup. Keep in mind that the Setup distance is not completed and, consequently, not defined at day 9 of Setup, which is merely the minimum period required to establish a Setup. Rather, it continues through the day preceding the price flip. Figure 2.16 (IBM) illustrates another example of "ignore smaller true high/true low," in

**Figure 2.18** This weekly chart of U.S. Treasury bonds uses the recycle option "ignore smaller true high-low" and compares the price difference between the highest intraday high and the lowest intraday low of the current buy Setup and the most recent previous buy Setup (same process for the Sell Setup). If the recycle option "before, on, or after" had been selected instead of the "ignore smaller true high low," the 1993 high and the late 1994 low would not have produced 13 low-risk Countdowns and would have recycled. Obviously, in these two examples, it was prudent to "ignore" the potential recycles.

which Setup continues through the Countdown period and is completed one day after the high. By ignoring these two instances of Setup Recycles, both the weekly Treasury bond top and bottom low-risk zones were defined precisely. A similar situation exists with IBM. You may not experience this degree of accuracy in the future, but this adaptation enables a TD Sequential user to deploy subtle interpretations to capitalize upon these market anomalies and to expand the opportunities that exist and may be camouflaged or suppressed by using the traditional "before, on, or after" recycle option.

The generic "ignore" ("ignore smaller true high/true low") recycle option includes a multiplier feature. Specifically, by electing any option that requires a measurement and price comparison of the current Setup low to high and the previous Setup low to high for Recycle determination, it is possible to improperly exclude a potential TD Sequential Countdown indication that spans a greater price distance from Setup high to Setup low than the previous Setup's difference. Initially, this seemed most perplexing. Much time, energy, and research were required to resolve this matter. Applying my theory of price exhaustion demonstrates that if the current Setup period is nominally larger from Setup true high to true low than the prior Setup distance from true high to true low, it is correct to Recycle. *However,* in those instances in which the Setup is significantly, rather than marginally, greater, an exception exists that suppresses the Recycle option. In order to quantify this requirement, experiments were conducted with numerous multipliers designed to supersede the impact of a greater price difference for the current Setup period versus the previous Setup's price difference and that may, in retrospect, incorrectly cause a Recycle to occur. This alternative option has enabled me to take advantage of opportunities that may have been canceled due to Recycling. The multiplier used varies from 1.618 to 3 times the previous Setup true high to true low price difference. Figure 2.19a (the cash Mid-Cap 400), for example, demonstrates how the recycle option "ignore smaller true high/low" can be integrated with the Multiplier option, which requires the difference between the true high and true low of the current Setup to be at least two times the difference between the previous Setup's true high and true low to override the Setup Recycle and continue the current or ongoing Countdown without interruption. In fact, in this case the difference of the current Setup from true high to true low is practically three times greater than the prior one. Consequently, despite the fact that the Setup difference was greater than the previous Setup difference and the Recycle should have occurred, the introduction of the Multiplier option or feature provided that if the difference were greater than two times the previous Setup's difference, then the potential Recycle should be suppressed or ignored.

Originally, years ago, I developed another effective process to handle the issue of Recycling. However, I typically elect to apply the "ignore" option with the Multiplier override. A trader may elect to qualify a Recycle by requiring that a new Setup record a specified or qualified minimum number of consecutive closes less than the close four trading days earlier for a buy Setup Recycle and a minimum number of consecutive closes greater than the close four trading days earlier for a sell Setup Recycle above the standard minimum Setup series selected—a minimum of nine consecutive closes less than or greater than the close four trading days earlier. In other words, to establish Setup, a certain number of minimum consecutive comparisons must be met; but to satisfy a subsequent Recycling, another more stringent minimum Setup series greater than the original Setup must be fulfilled—a consecutive series greater than the number required for the original Setup. For example, while the usual Setup requires a minimum of nine consecutive closes—either less than the close four trading days earlier for a buy Setup or greater than the close four trading days earlier for a sell Setup—to qualify as a potential Recycle candidate, the series of consecutive closes greater than or less than the close four trading days earlier can be increased to a larger number series of consecutive closes, such as 10, 11, or 12, or even less likely, decreased to a lower number to justify Recycling. Although this option initially appeared reasonable and provided adequate results, due to the increasing incidence of

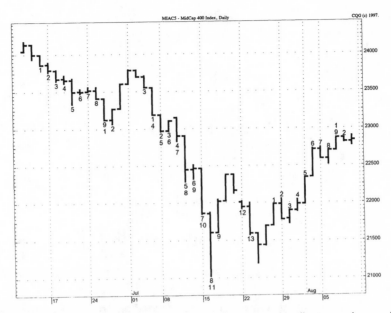

**Figure 2.19(a)**   This chart of the cash MidCap 400 Stock Index illustrates the combination of TD Sequential and the recycle option "ignore smaller true high low," as well as a multiplier of two or more times the difference of the previous Setup price distance. If either option occurs, then the recycle is disregarded. In other words, despite the fact that the difference between the more recent buy Setup's true high and true low is greater than the previous buy Setup's difference, the fact that it is more than two times greater disallows the Recycle.

Recycling in recent years, I prefer to use the various Recycle options described in the previous paragraphs.

One final consideration dealing with the issue of Recycling pertains to the relationship of the opening price the day following the final day of Recycle Setup versus the close five trading days earlier. In other words, although a Setup Recycle may have occurred the prior day *unless* the opening price the following trading day confirms, the Recycle is ignored. Once again, TD Critical Qualifier must be present. Figure 2.19b illustrates such an occurrence.

## Intersection

Countdown is the comparison process that begins on day 9 of Setup or the first subsequent day, whichever occurs last, provided Intersection has taken place. The Intersection requirement is designed to protect against premature entries into markets that were experiencing either blowoffs upside or blowouts downside. In the early 1970s I had been monitoring two stocks closely—Equity Funding and W. T. Grant—to determine whether TD

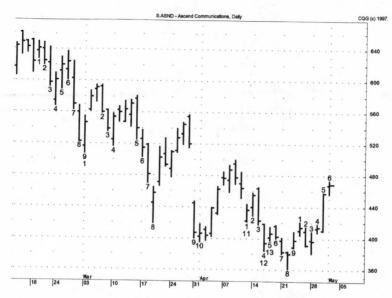

**Figure 2.19(b)**    Note that an apparent Recycle occurred on April 23. However, the open the following trading day failed to confirm the Recycle, and as a result the Recycle was ignored. In other words, not only must the close of Setup day 9 be less than the close four trading days earlier, but also the opening price the trading day following the ninth day of Setup must be less than the close of Setup day 5 as well, or no Recycle exists.

Sequential had successfully identified potential low-risk buy entry zones. Both had been declining precipitously. I identified what I believed to be low-risk buy entry areas and, subsequently, was surprised to witness trading suspended in both, their stocks deleted from the stock exchange, and, ultimately, their values become worthless since both companies filed for bankruptcy. Carefully, I evaluated the characteristics of similar situations and uncovered a common denominator that would have prevented premature purchase in these instances as well as in similar ones. As the price declines accelerated and the daily price ranges failed to overlap one another, a sense of urgency to liquidate apparently dominated the trading psyche of the stock sellers. Conversely, a comparable mood of aggressive buying mania can result in those markets steeply advancing in price almost vertically. Often the reason for this accelerated upside movement can be attributed to either a significant fundamental development and pending news announcement, a short squeeze, or more likely a buyout. Obviously, whereas the possibility of a company filing for bankruptcy, with its underlying stock declining to zero, or the likelihood of a company's stock being bought out are realistic trading concerns, the chance of either a futures contract, a market index, or commodity declining to zero or being bought out (or the market being cornered) is virtually nonexistent. Nevertheless, the concept of Intersection can be applied to all markets for the sake of consistency and simplicity. Since the rate of decline or advance may be unusually steep, implying investors' urgency to exit or enter the market, research suggests that this acceleration must subside or diminish in order to qualify for Countdown. Intersection accomplishes this goal by requiring that the advance or the decline be sufficiently retarded to allow price activity to consolidate, or at least overlap, for a period of time. Consequently, in the case of a buy Setup, Intersection requires that the high of day 8 of Setup or the first subsequent day be greater than or equal to the low three or more trading days earlier, up to and including the first day of Setup. On the other hand, in the case of a sell Setup, Intersection requires that the low of day 8 of Setup or the first subsequent day be less than or equal to the high three or more trading days earlier, up to and including the first day of Setup. If this period of price Intersection occurs on either day 8 or day 9 of Setup, then Countdown commences on day 9 of Setup, and if Intersection does not occur until after the Setup is complete, then Countdown is deferred until that time. In conclusion, although it is necessary to apply Intersection to individual stocks, other markets that are not susceptible to buyouts or bankruptcies, such as financial futures, indices, or commodities, do not necessarily require this consideration.

## Countdown

Countdown is a stage of TD Sequential consisting of a series of price relationships, not necessarily consecutive, that upon completion generally identifies the termination or exhaustion of a price trend. Once Setup has been completed and Intersection has been perfected, the inception of Countdown takes place. Although other comparisons may be substituted, my research suggests that depending on whether a buy or sell Setup has been defined, either the current day's close is compared with the low two days earlier (for buy Countdown) or the current day's close is compared with the high two days earlier (for sell Countdown). Just as both the Setup price and time selections are variable, so, too, can the Countdown price and time selections and relationships be substituted with various other options, such as open, high, low, midpoint, average and 1, 3, 4, 5. My preference for the number of closes less than or equal to the low two trading days earlier for a buy Countdown and for the number of closes greater than or equal to the high two days earlier for a sell Countdown is 13, but other time periods and price relationships can be introduced or substituted as well. For very short time intervals (e.g., one-minute price bars) applied to inactive markets, a trader may wish to require that the close be less than or greater than the low or high two bars earlier and disallow "equal to." Furthermore, in order to liberalize Countdown, I have occasionally introduced a variable called TD Termination Count,™ which applies only to the last day of Countdown (the thirteenth day, in most cases) by merely requiring that the close, open, *or* intraday low be less than the low two trading days earlier in the case of the last day of a buy Countdown series or, conversely, that the close, open, *or* intraday high be greater than the high two trading days ago in the case of the last day of a sell Countdown series. The variables for the TD Termination Count can be substituted, and whichever one is selected becomes the counterpart to the selected default comparison, which is close versus low or high two trading days earlier, depending whether it is buy or sell Countdown.

The parameter settings throughout this book are merely suggestions. Various other price comparisons and time periods can be substituted for the ones supplied and could produce comparable if not better results. For example, if you were to compare the current day's low with the low two trading days earlier for a buy Countdown and the current day's high with the high two trading days earlier for a sell Countdown rather than comparing the current day's close with the low and high, the Countdown 13 low-risk entry level and high-risk entry level would not necessarily be the same. But this does not imply that the revised comparison is any better or worse than the conventional TD Sequential Countdown approach; rather, it suggests only that numerous options are possible. I encourage you to research them for TD Sequential and for the many other indicators presented in this book.

You should not be misled by including the intraday price movements in your market perspective, since the critical components of conventional Countdown are the closing prices, and TD Sequential must be viewed in that context. Consequently, when studying low-risk TD Sequential entries, it is important to disregard sharp and exaggerated intraday price swings since the reference point for conventional Countdown is the closing price level.

*Countdown Qualifier:* When Sequential was developed, most 9-13 buy and sell indications were what could be described as orthodox. Low-risk buy zones (high-risk sell zones) occurred at extreme lows and were stretched to oversold, and high-risk buy zones (low-risk sell zones) occurred at extreme highs and were characterized as overbought. In recent years, I have witnessed what I call "high-level buy 13s" and "low-level sell 13s." By their very structure, these patterns are deficient and weak, since they suggest entry at less than ideal price levels. To address and counteract this negative development and to avoid the risk of these unfavorable price patterns and relationships affecting ideal TD Sequential Countdown entries, at least one general TD Sequential Countdown qualifier should be introduced to perfect low-risk buy and low-risk sell Countdowns. One such prerequisite recommended as a standard Countdown qualifier default to circumvent the hazard of high-risk level 13 buys and low-risk level 13 sells is to require the close of day 13 of buy Countdown to be less than or equal to the close of day 8 of Countdown and, conversely, the close of day 13 of sell Countdown to be greater than or equal to the close of day 8 of Countdown. At a minimum, you should (1) replace the requirement that the close of day 13 of the buy Countdown be less than or equal to the close of day 8 of buy Countdown with the low of day 13 of the buy Countdown less than or equal to the close of day 8 of the buy Countdown *and* (2) replace the requirement that the close of day 13 of the sell Countdown be greater than or equal to the close of day 8 of the sell Countdown with the high of day 13 of the sell Countdown greater than or equal to the close of day 8 of the sell Countdown. Other possible qualifier relationships might include the following:

The close of day 8 of buy Countdown must be below the close of day 5 of buy Countdown (reverse for sell Countdown).

The close of day 8 of buy Countdown must also be below the close of day 3 of buy Countdown (reverse for sell Countdown).

The close of day 8 of sell Countdown must be above the close of day 3 of sell Countdown as well (reverse for sell Countdown).

However, it is obvious that the more Countdown qualifiers that are introduced, the less likely that 13s will appear, the more likely Recycles will occur, and more important, the greater the potential risk of optimizing market behavior and creating unrealistic market conditions and expectations. Certainly, many other combinations can be introduced to perfect the Countdown process and to reduce the risk of buying a high-level 13 or of selling a low-level 13 Countdown. There exist a number of possible relationships that are equally helpful in perfecting the Countdown process and you should experiment with your own. My suggestion is to keep this artificial barrier to Countdown completion simple so as not to contaminate the Countdown process and thereby taint TD Sequential. Such an effort would be similar to an individual attempting to reduce obesity through the use of drugs alone, without diet or exercise. Such interference with nature may be helpful, but to rely upon it to the exclusion of other natural remedies could be harmful or even fatal in the long run. So also can excessive tampering with an indicator—often referred to as *optimization modeling techniques*—result in unrealistic expectations and trading results, which can in turn lead to the death of your personal trading portfolio. Figures 2.20 and 2.21 demonstrate the value of at least applying the requirement that day 13 of TD Sequential buy Countdown be below day 8 of Countdown and that day 13 of TD Sequential sell Countdown be above day 8 of Countdown. As you can readily see, this qualifier defers the low-risk buy indication, prevents high-level 13 low-risk buys, postpones the high-risk sell indication, and avoids low-level 13 high-risk sells. This qualifier has been used for well over 10 years, and it has been an integral component of the TD Sequential indicator process. It has prevented many costly high-level buy and low-level sell indications throughout the years. Figure 2.22 illustrates a similar experience, only in reverse. Obviously, exceptions exist, such as the one in Figure 2.23, which helps to deter-

**Figure 2.20**  At the January 1996 high a 13 Countdown was recorded. Had the Qualifier that required the close of day 13 of sell Countdown to be greater than or equal to day 8 of Countdown not been present, the 13 would have been recorded the day after Countdown 12. Note the asterisks identify possible Countdown days that were disqualified. As you can see, by deferring Countdown, a more accurate identification of the high-risk zone was made. Also review the 13 buy Countdown day at the April low, which was less than or equal to day 8 of Countdown.

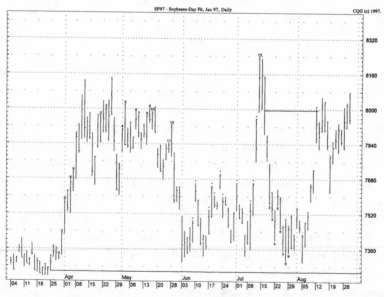

**Figure 2.21**  The last day of TD Sequential Countdown was deferred until the close of 13 exceeded the close of day 8 of Countdown. This Qualifier has been used for over 10 years and is a simple filter to ensure high-level sell and low-level buy Countdown completions. This is not an attempt to optimize, but rather a way to ensure the market is stretched. Consequently, the 13 was registered at the high of the entire move. Note how TDST was not violated at the low and the market subsequently rallied.

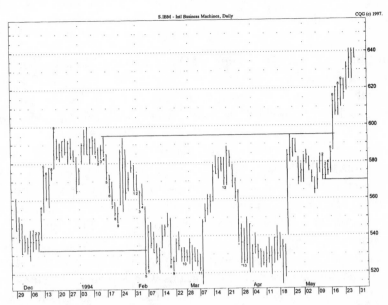

**Figure 2.22** The IBM decline was narrow in the spring of 1994. TD Sequential identified the low-risk buy area, and the precision was improved by introducing the buy Countdown Qualifier, which required that Countdown day 13 be less than or equal to the close of Countdown day 8. This deferred the ultimate low identification, which proved timely. Note how well the TDST breakout downside in February forecast the completion of the TD Sequential Countdown. See also how TDST stopped the April rally precisely and in May how price exceeded the TDST and rallied steeply higher.

**Figure 2.23** This example identifies a TD Sequential Countdown situation, which does not include the Qualifier day 13 close less than or equal to Countdown day 8 close. Because no Qualifier is active until day 13 of Countdown, be aware of the potential of the market to rally but do not necessarily rate its outlook as low-risk buy until the close of day 13 is less than or equal to day 8 of Countdown. Note also that the solid horizontal line identifies an optimal TDST indication, and given the fact that TD Sequential recorded a 12 buy Countdown, you should be inclined to recognize this potential breakout.

mine what is required to qualify a TD Sequential 9-13 indication. Forfeited trades are offset, however, by many more that are postponed by failing to meet this requirement. Consequently, it is recommended that this qualifier be applied in most if not all situations. You should review the series of sample charts from various markets illustrating all aspects of TD Sequential, including Setup, Intersection, and Countdown, as well as TDST indications (see Figures 2.24 through 2.37).

Certainly, you should experiment with other qualifiers for both Countdown and Setup, as well as combine qualifiers for Setup and Countdown and then introduce any qualifiers of your own into the TD Sequential matrix. Typically, you might want to install six qualifier groups, and within each group have subgroupings from *a* to *d* to enable the user to introduce both "and" and "or" statements or conditions within groups as well as between groups. All authorized indicator vendor packages include this feature. Additionally, I recommend that any authorized software prepared to present the DeMark indicators and that might include qualifiers excluding a specific Setup or Countdown day(s) for any reason whatsoever—and, as a result, produce results different than those generated by the standard or default setting for either Setup or Countdown days—include asterisks (or some other designation) to represent whichever day(s) may have been excluded. By

**Figure 2.24** A TD Sequential 9-13 was generated at the August 1987 DJIA high. Additionally, TDST indicated a downside breakout in October 1987, just prior to the market crash, which is identified by the horizontal line.

**Figure 2.25** TD Sequential buy Countdown identified precisely the S&P Cash Index clos-ing low on December 4, 1987. TDST established a downside breakout level just prior to the October price decline. The horizontal line defines the point at which price was expected to reverse trend to the downside.

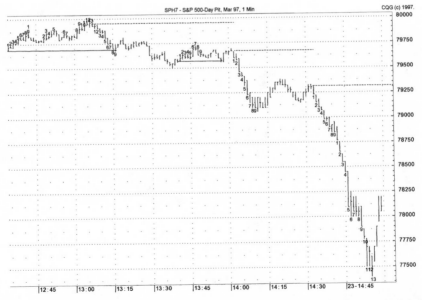

**Figure 2.26** On January 23, 1997, TD Sequential on a "one-minute" basis correctly iden-tified the precise closing high at 13:06 CST and the exact "one minute" closing low at 14:55 CST. Note that at approximately 13:30 and 14:05, two TDST levels were exceeded downside, suggesting continued market weakness and a strong likelihood of TD Sequential proceeding through Setup and into buy Countdown. Other than the fact that the chart des-ignates "one minute," these comments could have been applicable to any other time frame as well.

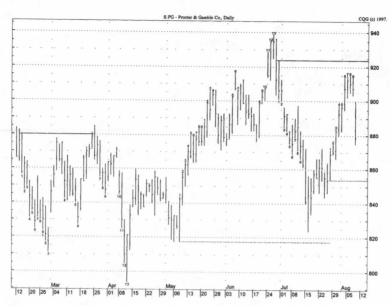

**Figure 2.27** TD Sequential successfully identified both the precise low and high with 13 Countdown indications from April to late June 1996. Note that the market was unable to exceed the TDST level in March to the upside on a closing basis but subsequently did in May and was unable to exceed the TDST downside level in July—the horizontal lines define these breakout points.

**Figure 2.28** TD Sequential has been successful and sensitive to the identification of exhaustion bottoms and tops in the currency markets. The British pound June 1996 contract made its low coincident with Countdown 13.

**Figure 2.29** The Japanese Government Bond (JGB) high was correctly identified by TD Sequential. The market's ability to withstand the subsequent decline and its reluctance to decline below the TDST level defined by the low of sell Setup day 1 was noteworthy. The horizontal line indicates the TDST breakout level.

**Figure 2.30** The collapse in copper in 1996 was well publicized. At the time the market bottomed, TD Sequential identified a low-risk entry point. The May decline was characterized by a TDST downside breakout, which is identified with a horizontal line on the chart. In fact a price gap downside occurred at the TDST breakout level, and such gap movements are not uncommon with TDST breakouts.

**Figure 2.31**  The Canadian dollar peak coincided with a TD Sequential 13 Countdown day.

**Figure 2.32**  The May 1995 price high was identified as a high-risk buy (low-risk sell) opportunity by TD Sequential.

**Figure 2.33** The sugar 1996 high and subsequent low were identified by TD Sequential: Note that the TDST breakout downside indicated TD Sequential buy Countdown would extend through completion.

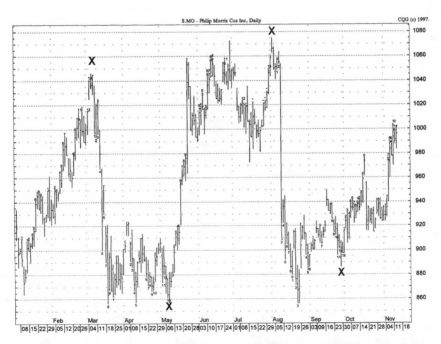

**Figure 2.34** Numerous trend reversals in Philip Morris were identified by TD Sequential with precision (see *X*s on chart). The one occasion in which TD Sequential was silent was in August, *but* that high-risk zone was correctly identified if "ignore smaller true high/true low" Recycle option was selected.

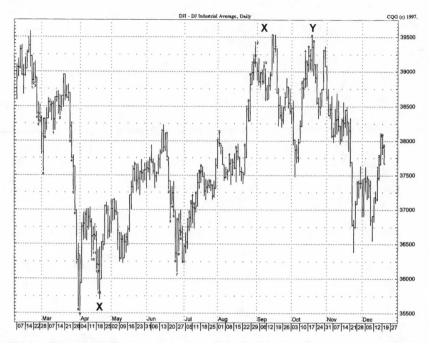

**Figure 2.35** TD Sequential correctly identified both the April 1994 low and the September 1994 high. These indications are identified with an *X* on the chart. In fact a TD Sequential Reinforcement low-risk sell indication was given in October (*Y*) when the market recorded a secondary sell Setup. Such indications are generally powerful when they occur.

**Figure 2.36** TD Sequential correctly identified the April 1996 price peak in wheat and remained silent for close to seven months, at which time TD Sequential identified a low-risk buy entry zone—see *X*s on chart.

**Figure 2.37**   Together with the other TD Sequential examples, hopefully you will appreciate the fact that TD Sequential has universal application to all markets and no optimization or customization need be introduced.

denoting the deletion of either Setup or Countdown days, the trader is provided with a perspective of how the Setup or Countdown process would have proceeded had the qualifiers not existed. The qualifiers presented here are merely suggestions emanating from many years of experience designing and applying TD Sequential. In fact, over 14 years ago, creating my own series of qualifiers and applying the same conditions to all markets produced enormous success in identifying the extreme terminal points of many market moves. This exercise evolved ultimately into TD Combo (see Chapter 3). My goal was to create an anticipatory indicator that did not possess the shortcomings of TD Sequential by generating high-level 13s at bottom areas and low-level 13s at tops. In order to combat this occasional shortcoming of TD Sequential, as well as to acquire a greater level of confidence in identifying market bottoms and tops, I established the following requirement: that prices for buy Countdown become progressively more strained as they move lower by recording successively lower closes and that prices for sell Countdown become successively more extreme as they move higher by registering successively higher closes. Other concerns with TD Sequential were the requirement of Intersection for TD Sequential and the increasing incidence of frequent Recycles. TD Combo ignores the issue of Intersection, and by commencing Countdown during the Setup period and requiring successively lower closes for buy Countdown or successively higher closes for sell Count-down, the likelihood of Recycling is diminished somewhat. As you can read-ily see, the three perceived handicaps of TD Sequential are either eliminated or reduced significantly by this relative indicator to TD Sequential. TD Combo is presented in Chapter 3, and the resolution of these concerns regarding TD Sequential are addressed there in more detail.

## Execution Settings

It is not my intention to provide you with fixed settings for any of the indi-cators. Hopefully, you will experiment and customize the following selec-tions to fit your specific trading style, expectations, and needs. Although I recommend these selections since they are the ones that have proven most effective and those with which I am most comfortable at this time, they are not necessarily the optimal settings. The specific selection grid presented here is a version of the standard design that is implemented on most autho-rized vendor networks.

   1. To establish Setup, I recommend the comparison of the close of the current price bar with the close four trading bars earlier. (This setting for the "close" appears in the Price column, which defines the price to be compared with a previous price level, and "4" appears in the Period column since it defines the number of price bars back to make the comparison and both are situated in the row identified as Setup.) Default for Setup completion is a series of nine consecutive closing price bars less than or greater than the close four trading bars earlier, depending on whether it is a buy or a sell Setup. (This selection appears in the Signal column and also in the row enti-tled Setup.)
   2. To establish Countdown, compare the close of the current bar with the low or high two trading bars earlier, depending upon whether it is a buy or a sell Setup. (This setting for the "close" typically appears in the Price col-umn, the "2" usually appears in the Period column, and both are situated in the row identified as Countdown.) For a buy Countdown the requirement is a series of 13 closes less than or equal to the low two trading days earlier, and the requirement for a sell Countdown is a series of 13 closes greater than or equal to the high two trading days earlier. (This selection appears in the Sig-nal column and also in the row entitled Countdown.) Although I prefer in most instances to use less than or equal to and greater than or equal to for Countdown purposes, in inactive markets and when applying TD Sequential to short-term bar charts (1- to 10-minute intervals, for example), it is often prudent to remove "equal" and rely solely upon less than for buy Countdown and greater than for sell Countdown.

3. To establish whether Intersection should be active, the box in the Period column and Intersect row should be checked. You should check it despite the fact the Intersection requirement is applicable primarily to stocks and not necessarily to futures, commodities, or indices.

4. To identify in which trading bar to begin looking for Intersection, make certain that the Intersection box is checked, then initialize this process by inserting the start date for the Intersection test. A recommended choice is to use setup price bar number 8 to commence the search for Intersection (this selection appears in the Signal column in the row identified as Intersect) since the Countdown generally will commence the succeeding trading day. It is also important to realize that if an alternative Setup series or time period is selected, the Intersection selection should be changed as well to adjust to this change, since Countdown will automatically commence the following trading day.

5. To cancel an active buy or sell Setup, select one of the five options displayed in the Cancel column located in the first row of the category described in the Advanced column. You might choose CaHTH/CbLTL (Close above Highest True High for a buy Setup cancellation and Close below Lowest True Low for a sell Setup cancellation), since it requires a closing price to be recorded above the highest true high recorded during the entire buy Setup period for buy Setup cancellation and below the lowest true low recorded during the entire sell Setup period for sell Setup cancellation. This selection is checkmarked in the box in the row identified as CaHTH/CbLTL. The cancellation can occur anytime after the commencement of Setup until the day Countdown has been completed. However, remember that Countdown is perfected and a Recycle is avoided once a price flip has been recorded. The requirement of a price flip is eliminated if no Recycle possibility exists or if the Recycle options preclude it for any reason.

6. To cancel either a buy or a sell Setup prior to Countdown completion, a contradictory sell or buy Setup can appear—in other words, a buy Setup would be canceled if a sell Setup is formed prior to completion of the buy Countdown, and a sell Setup would be canceled if a buy Setup is formed prior to completion of the sell Countdown. To activate this cancellation process, check the box in the Cancel column and the Reverse. This is my preference.

7. To cancel a redundant Setup, thereby precluding a Recycle, whether buy or sell, which is contained by the extreme intraday high and low of the previous Setup—in other words, the second (or more recent) of two consecutive, redundant buy or sell Setups whose price extremes do not exceed the previously active Setup's extreme high and low price range levels—check the box at the bottom of the Cancel column and located on the Within row. If it is not checked, it assumes the same significance as a Recycle. I am currently experimenting with this option and was initially ambivalent regarding its value. However, if any Recycle option that "Ignores" the current smaller dis-

tance from high to low or highest close to lowest close, for example, is not selected, and the standard option Recycle "before, on, or after" is chosen, my current test results indicate that it be checked, thereby preventing the potential Recycle due to the Setup's inability to exceed the original Setup parameter extremes.

8. To determine whether Setup, Countdown, or "Both" Setup and Countdown are displayed on the chart, the Display column situated on the Setup row designates the option desired. You may prefer to display "Both" Setup and Countdown.

9. To identify graphically the specific price bar that qualifies Intersection, the box under the column Display and on the row Intersect must be checked. This selection is merely for identification, location, information, and overall formation purposes. You may prefer to leave it unchecked.

10. To specify whether the series of consecutive Setup days includes closes that are less than and greater than the close four trading days earlier depending on whether a buy or a sell Setup, as well as those days that are "equal," make the selection in the Parameter box in the Setup row. It is recommended that "not equal" be specified for Setup determination, although on occasion I have elected "equal."

11. To specify whether the series of Countdown closes includes closes that are "less than" the low two trading days earlier and "greater than" the high two trading days earlier depending upon whether a buy or a sell Countdown, as well as those closes that are "equal," make the selection in the Parameter box in the Countdown row. I recommend for daily charts that "equal" be used and for 1, 5, 10 minutes and other intraday time periods that "equal" be used for actively traded and volatile markets and that "not equal" be used for inactive markets and very short time intervals (minutes).

12. To apply Intersection to price activity that occurs only during the period encompassing the Setup phase—"only in Setup" should be selected, and if Intersection is allowed to occur before, during, or anytime after Setup occurs. This option is found in the Parameter box in the Intersect row. My preference is "in or after Setup."

13. To select the method of Recycle or the time to Recycle, refer to the Parameter column and the Recycle row. The possibilities include the following:

a. Option *a* is the standard, plain vanilla, conservative setting "Before, on, after," which indicates that a subsequent Setup—a minimum of nine or more consecutive closes less than or greater than the close four trading days earlier—either Before, on, or after the 13 Countdown days and prior to the first price flip day will produce a Recycle.

b. Option *b* is "Ignore smaller true high–true low" and is identical to option *c* except that true highs and true lows are used instead of chart highs and chart lows.

c. Option *c* is "Ignore smaller high–low" and specifies that a Recycle is canceled if the current Setup distance from maximum intraday high over the entire Setup period through the minimum intraday low over the same entire Setup period is less than the distance from the maximum intraday high over the entire immediately prior Setup period to the minimum intraday low over the same entire immediately prior Setup period— remember that a Setup is defined as a series of *at least* nine consecutive closes less than the close four trading days earlier or *at least* nine consecutive closes greater than the close four trading days earlier—both ending once a price flip occurs, and the Setup period can often continue further than the minimum Setup requirement of nine consecutive closes less than the close four trading days earlier for a buy Setup and greater than the close four trading days earlier for a sell Setup. Consequently, the highest high and the lowest low recorded over the entire Setup period is *not* just the minimum Setup period of nine.

d. Option *d* is "Ignore smaller close–close" and is identical to option *c* except maximum and minimum close are inserted instead of highest high and lowest low.

e. Option *e* is "Ignore current" and refers to disregarding the most recent Setup (a Setup in the same direction as the previous Setup and one that would constitute a Recycle condition for any of options *g* through *j*.

f. Option *f* is "Ignore all" and disregards all subsequent, redundant Setups that would constitute a Recycle in any of options *g* through *j* and proceeds through Countdown for each.

g. Option *g* is "Before or On" the thirteenth Countdown day, and Setup Recycle occurs if Setup takes place prior to or on Countdown day 13.

h. Option *h* is "on or after" the thirteenth Countdown day provides that Recycle can occur on or after Countdown day 13 prior to the day before the price flip.

i. Option *i* is "Only before" the thirteenth Countdown day.

j. Option *j* is "Only after" the thirteenth Countdown day and prior to the price flip.

My preferences are the default setting of "Before, on, after" and "Ignore smaller true high–true low." I also observe the Multiplier option when applying the latter proposition (see item 15).

14. To require a specified consecutive series of closes less than for a buy Setup or greater than for a sell Setup the close four trading days earlier other than the standard "9" required for a Recycled Setup, then a Recycle Count value can be selected to reflect any option from 5 to 15 consecutive closes less than the close four trading days earlier for a buy Recycle and greater than the close four trading days earlier for a sell Recycle. Your selec-

tion can be made in the Parameter box in the Recycle count row. My preference is the default setting of "9," which is identical to that required for Setup. At times, however, I will apply 10 or 11.

15. To disallow any Recycle option that begins with the expression "Ignore" even though the current Setup (from intraday high to intraday low) is greater than the previous Setup, the current Setup (from intraday high to intraday low) must exceed the previous Setup by a multiplier of $x$ times, and the Recycle Multiplier option selection determines the size of this factor. I prefer a multiplier from 1.618 to 3.0 times.

16. To liberalize the last of a series of Countdown bars, a selection entitled TD Termination Count is designed to allow the last element of the Countdown series to have a relationship in addition to that prescribed for the other Countdown days. It is defaulted to the closing price of day 13 of Countdown just like the other Countdown days; however, I occasionally select "open" to allow the opening price to operate simultaneously with the closing price, thereby increasing the probability of fulfilling the Countdown requirement. I also apply "low" for a buy Setup and "high" for a sell Setup.

17. To specify which Qualifiers to apply to Setup, select the Qualifiers contained in the Parameters box under the column entitled Parameter. The possibilities are numerous. The On box must be checked to activate the specific Qualifier and the Qual and With columns specify which days prior to, on, or subsequent to Setup completion are compared. The Qval and Wval columns specify which price levels are being compared. The Compare column specifies what type of relationship is selected—remember, if one comparison is made for a buy Setup, then the reciprocal should be selected for the sell Setup; for example, less than (<) for a buy Setup would complement greater than (>) for a sell Setup, and the combination would appear as b<s>. Even though you would like to see the low of day 9 of a buy Setup less than the low of day 6 and the high of day 9 of a sell Setup greater than the high of day 6, you may prefer not to activate these Setup Parameter settings when looking for a TD Sequential Setup indication; rather, you could activate it when you want to experiment or apply a qualifier(s) to just the Setup process for purposes of trading only Setups or to apply to TDST (TD Setup Trend) for purposes of defining the trend-reversal levels, but such an activity can best be manipulated within the qualifiers presented within the TDST study.

18. To specify whether the Setup and the Countdown continue to be displayed on a chart after the minimum period for Setup and Countdown has been met, "After signal" should be selected, and if only the minimum periods are to be displayed, then "Up to signal" should be selected. A good one is "Up to signal" unless you are either comparing Setup periods to determine a reversal of trend (see TDST), assessing the potential of the current Setup distance exceeding the distance of the previous Setup in the same direction and a Recycle option with "Ignore" has been selected, or evaluating the like-

lihood of the continuation of a move exceeding the most recent Setup in the other direction to determine whether the current price move is a reversal of trend (TDST) and will mature into full Countdown.

19. To specify the Qualifiers to be used for both Setup and Countdown, as well as their interaction, in order to perfect TD Sequential indications, select Qualifiers in the Advanced column. The comparison can be made between Setup days and between Countdown days, as well as between Setup and Countdown days. The On column must be checked to activate the specific Qualifier. The Qtype and Wtype determine whether the comparisons are within Setup, Countdown, or between Setup and Countdown. The Qval and Wval specify which levels within Setup or Countdown are compared. Qual and With columns specify which days prior to, on, or subsequent to either Setup or Countdown completion are compared. The Compare column relates to the specific comparison that is made. Note that if less than or equal to (<=) is used for a buy Setup or Countdown then the reciprocal greater than or equal to (>=) should be used for a sell Setup or Countdown, and this combination would be displayed as B<=s>=. You may prefer to have the close of day 13 of Countdown less than or equal to the close of day 8 of Countdown for a buy Countdown and the close of day 13 of Countdown greater than or equal to the close of day 8 of Countdown for a sell Countdown. At a minimum, you should specify the low of day 13 of Countdown be less than or equal to the close of day 8 of Countdown for buy Countdown and that you specify the high of day 13 of Countdown be greater than or equal to the close of day 8 of Countdown for sell Countdown. In those instances in which Countdown would have been fulfilled had the Qualifier(s) not been introduced, an Asterisk appears on the price chart to designate that fact.

20. To group-specific Qualifiers, six sets composed of elements from *a* to *d* have been provided. These groupings enable the user to create "and" as well as "or" conditions and statements within each group, as well as between groups for both Setup, Countdown, and combinations of Setup and Countdown.

You've seen my preferences for the preceding selection options. It would be a serious oversight not to devote additional time to describe further the various Setup Recycle options, since they are such a significant component of the TD Sequential process. Markets are like living organisms, inhaling (undergoing selling pressure) and exhaling (experiencing buying pressure). The flow of money into and out of the market dictates its price movement. Since the market has no obligation to conform to any trader's expectations, a trader must measure as best he or she can the market's price rhythm and pulse at any particular time. TD Sequential attempts to accomplish this goal by identifying prospective market top and bottom price exhaustion zones. However, events can change at any time to cause a resurgence in either selling or buying pressure. Just such inflows or price regenerations create Setup Recycles. An effective way to deal with these renewed price thrusts is to ignore those Setups that encompass less price distance than the prior price Setup distance. Setups begin with the first day that records a closing price less than (for a buy Setup) or greater than (for a sell Setup) the closing price four trading days earlier. The minimum buy Setup series is accomplished once nine consecutive closes are recorded; however, the Setup extends until a contradictory close greater than or equal to (buy Setup completion) or less than or equal to (sell Setup completion) the close four trading days earlier is recorded. Then the price comparison is made. If the current Setup distance from true high to true low is less than the original (previous) buy Setup distance from true high to true low, the current Setup is ignored if the selection "to ignore" is made. This Recycle condition is "ignore smaller true high/true low." If the current Setup is greater in price distance, a Recycle exists. There is one exception, and that occurs when the current Setup distance is greater than the original Setup distance by a factor of at least 1.618 to 3.0 times. This Multiplier feature is a precautionary device to alert the trader to a market's potential price exhaustion area. Figure 2.19 (the MidCap TD Sequential low in July 1996) presents such an event. The charts in Figures 2.38 through 2.43 illustrate other examples in which either "ignore smaller true high/true low" or the Recycle Multiplier was the proper method to use to deal with recycling.

## Implementation

The TD Sequential discussion is presented intentionally in the context of an indicator rather than as a system. All the variations and considerations presented for TD Sequential may seem intimidating, but mastering it should make your life as a trader more successful. Given its massive composition and its numerous variations, an entire book could be devoted to the TD Sequential indicator. Familiarizing yourself with its features and various important components will avail you of the opportunity to choose and experiment with selections of your own from this dynamic option matrix. In order to help you, I have designed a robust indicator capable of accommodating most elements of the numerous price pattern conditions and relationships that are apparent from time to time within the price structure of markets. This discussion will include the various aspects of TD Sequential, its salient elements, and its versatility and applicability to markets. Due to the comprehensive overview presented, the variables that may be introduced to arrive at TD Sequential price execution may vary from one trader to another. The various components and potential default selections I use

**Figure 2.38** By applying Recycle setting "ignore smaller true high/true low" and the Recycle Multiplier, the sell Setup that appeared just prior to the all-time high in the Japanese yen was not considered, and as a result, TD Sequential successfully identified the all-time high in that market. The only excuse to recognize the Setup would have been if the Setup were greater than the original Setup but less than two times the price difference (Multiplier Value).

**Figure 2.39** Note that TD Sequential with the Recycle option "ignore smaller true high/true low" and a Multiplier of more than two times the previous Setup identified precisely the three turning points in the Swiss franc in late 1994 through mid-1995. These zones are identified with an *X*. Also note that often when a market is inactive, as it was in October through December 1994, TD Sequential indications are more sensitive and precise.

**Figure 2.40(a)** At the August 1995 high a sell Setup was recorded but the price distance from true high to true low was less than the active sell Setup and consequently "ignored." As you can see, this was a proper decision, since TD Sequential identified the price peak.

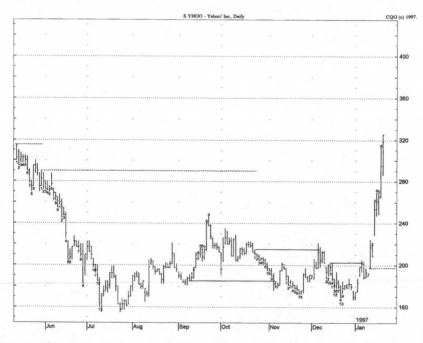

**Figure 2.40(b)** With the Recycle option setting "ignore smaller true high/true low," the precise December low was identified as a low-risk entry point. The conventional setting of "before, on, or after," correctly located the July low. TDST correctly identified trend reversals.

**Figure 2.41** The TD Sequential Countdown occurred close to the November 1996 low. As price rallied, there were two sell Setups, and the most recent Setup completed in late December was greater than the active Setup and less than the Multiplier value of 2. Consequently, the sell Setup was Recycled. The TDST breakout upside in November foretold of higher prices.

**Figure 2.42** By installing the Recycle option "ignore smaller true high/true low," the September 1996 price low was identified by TD Sequential.

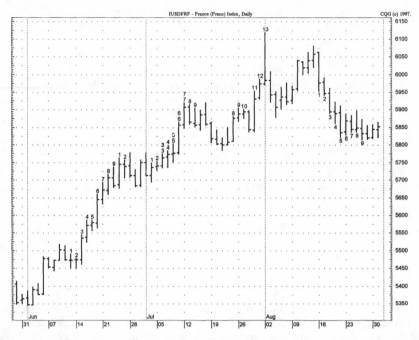

**Figure 2.43** The August 1996 high was identified by TD Sequential once the Recycle option "ignore smaller true high/true low" was introduced. Had it not, the Countdown would have been postponed due to the Recycle.

most often are presented. Although each item has been an important consideration in my construction of the TD Sequential indicator, many of these refinements are not crucial to the successful application and implementation of TD Sequential. Furthermore, there is no need for you to customize or optimize the variables to conform to the market being monitored. Although there probably exists an ideal set that measures the natural price rhythm and exhaustion tendencies of most markets, the suggested selections are generic in the sense that they are a good starting point from which to apply this indicator. Your evaluation and installation of the variables important to TD Sequential should be preceded by careful forethought and consideration of criteria such as, entry, exit, and stop-loss contingencies. For the sake of completeness, you should familiarize yourself with some of the following options as well.

*Entry:*  A major issue confronting a trader any time a "9-13" (completed Setup and Countdown) indication for basic TD Sequential is generated is the possibility of a Setup Recycle occurring prior to a price flip, thereby requiring the abort or cancellation of the Countdown and, consequently, the potential trade. The various entry techniques I propose include the following:

1. The most venturesome and risky approach is to take entry on the thirteenth day of Countdown.

2.  Another method intended to reduce the likelihood of a Recycle and ensure the chance of a successful trade is, subsequent to Countdown day 13, the first closing price recorded that is greater than the opening price is a good confirmation of a bottom, and the first closing price recorded that is less than the opening price is a good confirmation of a top.

3.  This option is added to option 2 and requires that (a) subsequent to Countdown day 13, not only is the closing price greater than the opening price the same day, but also the high that same day is greater than the previous trading day's close at a potential bottom and (b) not only is the closing price less than the opening price the same day, but also the low that same day is less than the previous day's close at a potential top. For more conservative traders who are willing to accept a less advantageous entry price, I suggest that instead of the requirement "the high the same day is greater than the previous day's close," the high is greater than the previous day's true high be applied and, likewise, instead of the requirement "the low the same day is less than the previous day's close," the low is less than the previous day's true low be applied. In either case, this search process commences the trading day following the thirteenth day of Countdown.

4.  Another more conservative method to avoid the risk of Recycle is to require a *price flip* (close greater than the close four trading days earlier at a low or a close less than the close four trading days earlier at a high) before entry is made and prior to a renewed price Setup. By definition, this approach guarantees no possibility of a Recycle, but unfortunately, this option often translates into a forfeiture of a more favorable entry price.

5.  Another technique to initiate or to add to an existing position is to place an additional order to buy just above the stop-loss level at a low and to sell just below a stop-loss level at a high (see stop-loss discussion that follows).

6.  Another approach applying a discipline similar to option 5 is to buy or sell an additional position when a 9-13-9 occurs—in other words, whenever a TD Sequential Reinforcement indication occurs (see following).

7.  Further, in order to prevent the possibility of Countdown proceeding to "12" and price reversing without recording a "13" Countdown, you might occasionally use the open price or low for buy and high for sell rather than the close—or a combination of the open, the low and the high, and the close—to arrive at the Countdown 13 indication (see Termination Count in previous Countdown discussion) to ensure entry. This last selection is called TD Termination Count in the software selection since a trader may elect to terminate Countdown with a value other than, or in addition to, the standard close for "13"—this option applies only to the final Countdown day.

8.  By synchronizing a shorter-term (time interval) TD Sequential low-risk indication (e.g., on a 1-, 5-, or 30-minute basis), the entry level and timing can be perfected further.

9. Another effective technique requires the construction of a TD Supply Line™ at a low and a TD Demand Line™ at a high to fine-tune the low-risk entry zones.

10. At least six other entry techniques used to define and refine low-risk entry include TD Combo, TD Diff, TD REBO, TD Open, TD Trap, and TDPOQ, as well as various other indicators presented in the book in combination with one another.

*Profit level:* Generally, you may look to take profits once an opposing Setup—in the other direction—is formed and the highest closing price of the current Setup period fails to exceed the intraday peak of the opposing Setup or the lowest closing price of the current Setup period fails to exceed the intraday low of the opposing Setup. This method conforms with the precepts for the TDST indicator. If, however, the closing price subsequent to a price bottom does exceed the intraday true high—or, subsequent to a price peak, the intraday true low—and is confirmed (see foregoing TDST), then generally expect price to continue through the Countdown process, and once Countdown is completed you can take profits and occasionally reverse at that time to participate in the primary trend. Obviously, other exit techniques can be used: dollar value profit-taking levels (once a prescribed profit is made, then exit); trailing dollar stop losses; a series of consecutive up closes (or down closes); a series of consecutive closes greater than the open (less than the open); the first profitable opening price; the first trading day with a price range at least double the range of the entry day or double the range of the previous trading day; the first day with a low greater than the entry day's high (high less than the entry day's low); and the introduction of other indicators presented in this book, such as TD Moving Average I (TDMA I), REBO, TD Open, TD Trap, and TD Lines.

*Stop loss:* Since this stop-loss technique was created over 20 years ago, it's been applied to a number of indicators. It still has an amazing ability to protect me from prematurely exiting a trade, as well as its ability to be sufficiently sensitive to changing market conditions. In fact, there have been individuals who have used TD Sequential, and once this stop loss has been triggered, they have exited the trade and have, at that same time, successfully reversed their positions, because when a TD Sequential trade does not work, as Paul Tudor Jones observed and described it, "it really doesn't work." So impressive was the stop-loss performance that I subsequently developed an indicator called TD Stop Reverse,™ which utilizes a similar approach, independent of any entry technique whatsoever, to initiate trades as well. Repeatedly, when a TD Sequential 9-13 low- or high-risk indication fails, price accelerates quickly in the breakdown direction. At the time it fails, the forces of supply and demand have shifted so dramatically that rapid adjustments to the price structure take place. The stop-loss method is as follows: At a price bottom, identify the lowest low, including all the days of Setup and Countdown. Then calculate the difference between the true high (the high recorded that same day or the previous day's close, whichever is greater) and that same day's price low. This true price range is then subtracted from the low that same day. Should price close below that value, the stop loss would be triggered. Conversely, a stop loss at a price peak is calculated as follows: Identify the highest high of the entire Setup and Countdown periods. Then calculate the difference between the high and the true low (the low recorded that same day or the previous day's close, whichever is less) and add that value to that same day's price high. If price closes above that peak, then the stop loss would be activated. A more liberal method would be to require two closes below and above the calculated stop-loss levels. A more conservative method (not recommended) would be to install stops at intraday—not closing—price-level violations. Another buy-stop loss identifies the lowest day of the entire Setup and Countdown period, calculates the difference between the intraday low and the close that same day, and subtracts that difference from that same day's intraday low—if there are recorded two consecutive closes below that level, then the stop loss is triggered. Conversely, a sell stop loss is calculated by subtracting the difference between the highest intraday high of Setup and Countdown and the close that same day. If price closes above that level for two consecutive days, then likewise the stop loss is triggered. Another stop-loss method applies a flat dollar amount to the entry price, and if price exceeds that value either intraday or on a closing basis, then the trade is exited.

To complement these stop-loss methods, it is suggested that as price approaches the stop-loss level an additional entry (entries) can be taken, since the risk associated with the trade diminishes. In other words, you may wish to lower your average price at a low or raise your average price at a high by adding to your position as price approaches your stop loss. Obviously, such a practice is gutsy, but if the stop loss is effective and if you are comfortable assuming the limited risk, it is an approach worthy of consideration.

An alert individual trader asked me what to do if an entry were to occur subsequent to the completion of Countdown and that entry price were outside the stop-loss zone. It was an astute observation on his part for the following reasons: For example, if a trader were to wait for a close greater than the open on a day subsequent to recording the thirteenth day of Countdown to execute a buy entry, and a close of a day subsequent to the thirteenth day of Countdown and prior to this entry is below the stop-loss level, then how should the trader deal with this event? Experience seems to indicate that whenever this situation occurs, price typically Recycles. (See Figure 2.44, the S&P December 1996 futures on November 9.) But such occasions arise only if a trader attempts to perfect his or her entries into a market, which, by the way, is the method I recommend for a trader to be successful.

Included in this chapter is a series of charts identifying TD Sequential low-risk 9-13 indications over a number of diverse markets using the conser-

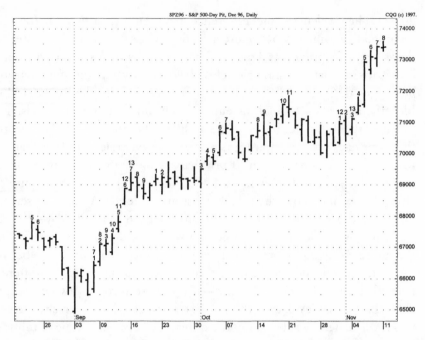

**Figure 2.44**   The thirteenth day of TD Sequential Countdown was recorded on November 4. If you do use entry techniques, such as a close less than the open and a low the same day less than the previous day's close, you would not have sold. In fact, the stop loss based upon the true price range of the highest trading day of the entire Setup-Countdown period is below the highest price appearing on the chart, and consequently the sell would not be taken because by the time it was effected, the stop loss was triggered.

vative Recycle qualifier "on, before, and after." In addition, there is a group of charts that have applied the more liberal Recycle qualifier "ignore smaller true high/true low," which compares the price distance traveled by the current Setup and then relates it to the previous Setup. If the difference is less, the current Setup is disregarded and Countdown is continued. Together with this latter option, "ignore smaller true high/true low," I have introduced the Recycle Multiplier, which ignores a Recycle if the price distance traveled for the current Setup is more than two (or three) times the previous Setup's price difference. Additionally, you'll find numerous observations that should benefit a trader who uses TD Sequential. First of all, inactive markets are generally more sensitive to TD Sequential indications and, consequently, if trading futures markets, you should often review the activity in distant contracts to confirm nearby, more active, contract TD Sequential Countdown indications (see Figures 2.45 and 2.46). You can also apply TD Sequential to intermarket and intramarket price spreads, low-priced stocks or even options, and statistical market data, such as upside and downside volume, and advancing and declining stocks, even economic statistics, with surprisingly good results. For example, Figures 2.47a through e illustrate such applications.

**Figure 2.45**   This is a chart of September 1996 U.S. Treasury bonds. In August of 1995 and January 1996, this contract was inactive. Nevertheless, TD Sequential generated Countdown 13 indications precisely at the low and the high. As the contract became more actively traded in May 1996, the 13 Countdown occurred as well at the low just as did the most actively traded bond futures contract at the same time.

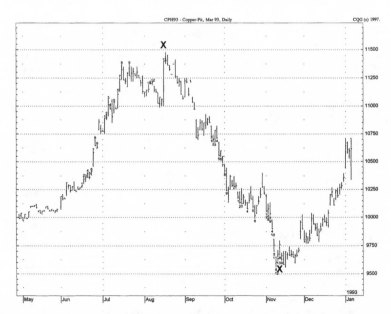

**Figure 2.46**   Although in both August and November 1992, the March 1993 copper contract was inactive, the TD Sequential low- and high-risk indications were precise—see *X*s on chart. Whereas Figure 2.45 used the standard Recycle default "before, on, or after," this example uses "ignore smaller true high/true low" difference with a Multiplier of 2.

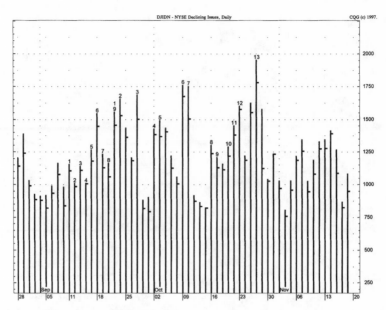

**Figure 2.47(a)**  This chart identifies the TD Sequential Setup and Countdown for the New York Stock Exchange declining issues daily. The same comparisons and time periods used for TD Sequential are applied, and amazing results are produced. See that the thirteenth day of Countdown occurred on October 25, 1996. Figure 2.47b shows the New York Stock Exchange Average and identifies October 25, 1996, to establish a perspective as to where the Countdown occurred for the market average.

**Figure 2.47(b)**  A comparable point in time to the October 25 thirteenth day of Countdown for the New York Stock Exchange declining issues which is identified in Figure 2.47a is marked on this chart for reference purposes. By comparing the two charts, it is easy to see that whereas the date on which the declining issues indicated a TD Sequential potential bottom, the NYSE Stock Index did as well (see Figure 2.47a). Consequently, it behooves a trader to integrate analyses for both indices to determine investment opportunities.

**Figure 2.47(c)**   Quite by accident, TD Sequential was applied to spreads and, amazingly, it worked well. One should await a reversal in the trend to indicate a low-risk entry zone. This chart displays the Euro Swiss franc–Euro lira spread, and the *X*s indicate the low-risk trend turns subsequent to the TD Sequential 13 Countdown days.

**Figure 2.47(d)**   Once again, the versatility of TD Sequential is demonstrated. Whereas Figure 2.47c was an intermarket spread, this example is an intramarket spread (as is Figure 2.47e). Also note TDST indications on chart.

109

**Figure 2.47(e)** The top of this intramarket soybean spread was correctly identified by TD Sequential Countdown 13.

Although it is necessary to establish guidelines and parameter settings for TD Sequential and not to deviate from them lest you enter the realm of optimization modeling, I have observed what appear to be anomalies in price behavior in various markets. These are noteworthy and should be addressed. For example, whereas I have always applied a Setup relationship of the current close versus the close four trading days earlier for a series of nine consecutive closing prices, in the cash currencies markets a Setup series of eight consecutive closes often appears to work as well, and you should evaluate similar adjustments and applications to the cash markets you may follow. However, you should remain consistent in your approach. Additionally, better results may accrue by using a combination of both the opening price and the closing price for the thirteenth day of Countdown for cash markets (see previous discussion of TD Sequential Termination Count), and as long as the opening and the closing prices occur at the same time each price period and a level of consistency is maintained, TD Sequential should continue to be effective and responsive.

## TD Sequential Reinforcement™

Throughout the years, I have observed a derivative TD Sequential pattern that has proven to be reliable and has produced credible results. This pattern is called TD Sequential Reinforcement because not only does it have a classic 9-13 low-risk buy or sell indication, but subsequent to the occurrence of a price flip, it also records another Setup, which serves in a sense to reinforce or confirm the original 9-13 indication. This reinforced Setup subsequent to the TD Sequential low-risk buy or sell Setup can occur above the lowest low of the previous buy Countdown and below the highest high of the previous sell Countdown, or it can occur below the low of the lowest buy Countdown day or above the high of the highest sell Countdown day (see Figures 2.48 through 2.50).

## TD Price Flip Trend™

Simple techniques such as variations of TD Price Flip are valuable starting points to construct methods for anticipating trend reversals. By definition, the first step for a market that is reversing trend upside is to record a close greater than the previous day's close. At the same time, the price action must be initialized by requiring that the close one trading day ago be less than the close two trading days ago. By extrapolating this concept further, potentially a new uptrend is defined whenever price closes greater than the previous trading day's close. Extending this reasoning to other price relationships, such as whenever price closes greater than the close four trading days earlier and the previous day's close is less than the close five trading days ago, other indications of a potential upside reversal confirmation can be defined and

**Figure 2.48**  TD Sequential Reinforcement is most effective when the lowest close of the Setup that is formed subsequent to day 13 of TD Sequential Countdown is contained by the intraday low or high, depending whether it is a potential buy or a sell indication.

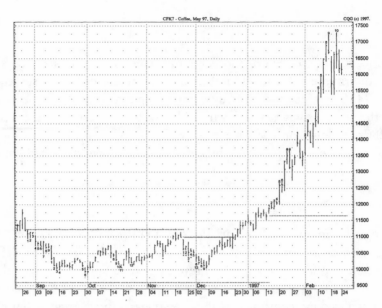

**Figure 2.49** TD Sequential Reinforcement patterns record the secondary or "reinforce-ment" Setup subsequent to the occurrence of a price flip. In the case of the recycle selection "ignore smaller true high/true low," the potential Recycle Setup may be ongoing at the time the low-risk 13 indication is given. A trader must wait to be certain that the current Setup does not exceed the distance of the previous Setup, and if it does, then it must be greater by the Multiplier amount. Because the Setup is ongoing at the time the "13" is recorded, this is not a true TD Sequential Reinforcement pattern or referred to as a "9-13-9." The price flip must occur prior to the last Setup. Note how well TDST identified the breakout in December.

**Figure 2.50** Gold identified a low-risk TD Sequential buy zone in January 1997. Subse-quently, a trader would likely have been stopped out. However a 9-13-9 TD Sequential Rein-forcement low-risk buy indication occurred one day before the low close. Coupled with the fact that TD Trend Factor indicated a bottom at that price level as well, a trader was pre-sented with a low-risk buy opportunity.

easily described. In other words, to commence an upside trend, the previous trading day's close must be less than the close two trading days ago or five trading days ago, whichever the trader might be inclined to select. Obviously, these suggestions are for upside breakouts. To accomplish the same conclusions for downside moves, the process should be reversed: The previous trading day's close must be greater than the close two trading days ago or five trading days ago, whichever the trader might be inclined to select. In any case, entry at the inception of a trend that is being established is ideal, since a trader is not only able to maintain an edge over the conventional trend followers, but also to confirm entry based upon other trend-anticipatory methods. However, the risk of price whipsaw in a nontrending, trading range market does exist when using this market timing approach. Consequently, it is prudent to set stop losses to prevent false starts. I am not espousing TD Price Flip Trend as a trading system by any means. Rather, with the introduction of a few minor adjustments and qualifiers, this technique can serve a trader well in confirming price trends and assuring entry at the inception of a trend reversal. In conclusion, other comparisons can be implemented as well. For example, if the close one trading day ago is less than the opening price that same day, and the current trading day's closing price is greater than the current day's opening price, then a similar indication exists. To apply this same methodology to the downside trend reversal, the close one trading day ago must be greater than the opening price one trading day ago, and the current day's closing price must be less than the current day's opening price.

Other price relationships and comparisons can be easily substituted and used for the TD Price Flip closes as well. For example, highs, lows, opens, midpoints, and averages can be compared with comparable prices $x$ number of days earlier, or different price comparisons can be made, such as close versus open or high versus low. A myriad of selections and time periods exist, and you should use those price levels and time series with which you are most comfortable. Just remember that the start of any market advance is always identified and clearly broadcast, as subtle as it may seem, by an initial price flip, whether it be a one-, two-, three-, or four-day (or some other) comparison. The trader's only dilemma is to distinguish between the legitimate and bogus price reversals. That is why I recommend using additional filters, such as the introduction and employment of a series of price comparisons, combinations, and qualifiers to confirm the possibility of the inception and the continuation of the trend reversal and to ensure the likelihood of further price follow-through by introducing other confirming indicators such as TD REBO into your analysis. Also, research indicates that once a basic price flip occurs similar to the first day of a buy Setup (close greater than close four trading days ago and the previous day's close less than the close five trading days ago), this positive closing price relationship typically extends for an additional three to five trading days. Conversely, you can reverse this relationship for suspected downside price reversals. Figure 2.51 illustrates the effectiveness of such a method in a trending market. However, to avoid false breakouts in trading range markets, qualifiers should be introduced and other indicators be followed to confirm these moves; you could use TD REBO, TD Trap, TD Open, short-term TD Sequential and TD Combo confirmations, and others. In conclusion, Figures 2.52 through 2.55 are presented for additional information.

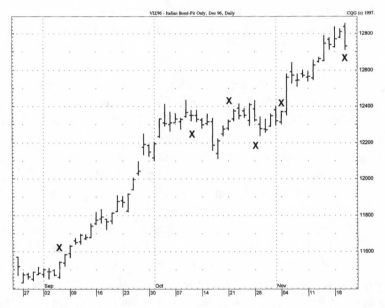

**Figure 2.51**  To identify the TD Price Flips, set the TD Sequential Setup to one consecutive close greater than or less than the close five trading days earlier instead of nine consecutive closes greater than the close four trading days earlier. Try experimenting with other TD Price Flip relationships. The letter *X* below the price bar on the chart identifies the TD Price Flips downside, which may be a precursor to the inception of a downside move, and conversely, the letter *X* above the price bar may be the precursor of the inception of a trend upside.

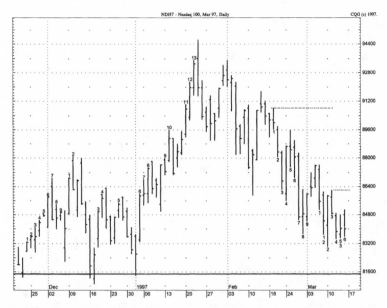

**Figure 2.52(a)** The TD Sequential low-risk sell indication for the NASDAQ 100 futures occurred on January 22, 1997—much earlier than the indication for the major indices (see Figure 2.53). The TDST level appears just below the 816 level.

**Figure 2.52(b)** For inactively traded markets or in sideways, nontrending markets—this pertains primarily to stocks—it is often preferable to require the TD Sequential Countdown process to exclude those closes that were equal to the high or low two trading days earlier. In other words, for a buy Countdown the close must be less than the low two trading days earlier or the close must be greater than the high two trading days earlier. Whereas this chart illustrates the TD Sequential buy indication "13" on December 26, this low-risk entry technique requires a close greater than the open on a subsequent trading day and whose high is greater than the previous trading day's close, a prerequisite fulfilled on January 2 (X). Note how the upside price movement in February is stopped cold at the TDST level (Y). Compare this chart with Figure 2.52c.

**115**

**Figure 2.52(c)** This chart applies the TD Sequential requirement, referred to in Figure 2.52b, that the close be *less than,* not "less than or equal" to the low or high two trading days earlier. Note again the TDST resistance apparent in February that repelled prices to the downside.

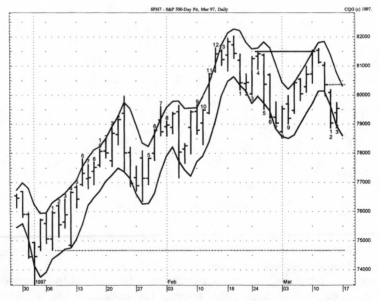

**Figure 2.53** Compared to Figure 2.52a, the S&P future low-risk sell indication came one month later. The first close less than the open and low less than the previous trading day's close is the high day. The TDST level was 815.00, and the March rally closing high was 815.00 precisely. Note how well TD Channel II (see Chapter 11) defines the various trading days' high and lows.

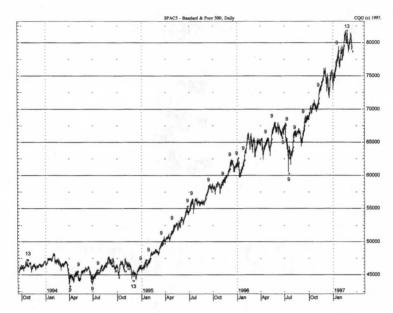

**Figure 2.54**  The TD Sequential high-risk 9-13 indication for the S&P cash in February was the first 9-13 since the 9-13 low-risk buy indication in late 1994. All subsequent "9"s recycled.

**Figure 2.55**  Note the buy Setup that was completed on March 24 was less in price distance from the intraday true high to intraday true low than the previous buy Setup completed in February. By electing to "ignore smaller true high/true low," the TD Sequential low-risk buy zone identified the intraday low prior to a significant rally. The TDST is also displayed, and indicated an advance through TD Sequential sell Countdown.

# Chapter

# 3

# TD Combo™

The late 1970s and early 1980s were marked by the tendency of many markets to operate within trading ranges. Not only were my range expansion breakout and volatility indicators beginning to experience a difficult time, but so were many of my confirming trend-following indicators. In addition, TD Sequential was not always identifying the low- and high-risk zones at their troughs and peaks as it had previously done so well. Sure, important reversal zones were being highlighted, but the accustomed accuracy and precision in identifying price extremes and exhaustion levels were lacking. Therefore I experimented and introduced a series of qualifiers that, by definition, stretched the Countdown process to price extremes and thereby ensured that the 13 Countdowns would have a tendency to seek the extreme price tops and bottoms. For example, my standard default selection required that the close of Countdown day 13 be less than or equal to the close of Countdown day 8 at a potential price low and that the close of Countdown day 13 be greater than or equal to the close of Countdown day 8 at a potential price high. Even this qualifier did not always ensure a price extreme, and by introducing an additional series of qualifiers I oftentimes precluded any indication whatsoever. Additionally, there was a risk of indicator optimization. At the same time, as a result of an increasing number of traders becoming familiar with the TD Sequential methodology, its effectiveness could conceivably diminish over time, and I wanted to maintain a trading edge. Consequently, TD Combo was born.

As with the other indicators presented throughout this book, the entire research project for TD Combo was conducted without any assistance and without the use of computers. Only as a result of long, tedious chart inspection and trial and error was this project accomplished. Although TD Combo has been applied to thousands of charts over various markets and time intervals for many years, I am discovering and developing new variations, applications, and interpretations for this methodology even to this day. Because this research effort is ongoing, after you have studied and applied TD Combo you should create and experiment with derivatives of your own. To perform effectively in the trading arena requires extensive research and analysis, and my suggested indicator settings may not necessarily be optimal and may, in fact, be inferior to those you may uncover and develop as a result of your own testing of these indicators. Should you be lacking in programming skills, at the conclusion of this book there's a list of authorized services to which you can subscribe that have already programmed TD Combo, as well as many of the other indicators in this book, into a master template you can use to introduce variations and qualifiers of your own in order to experiment and to customize these techniques. This announcement is not intended to advertise these vendors, but to alert you to the fact that if you are like I am and not computer literate, or if you do not have the time or the interest to be bothered with anything other than researching and developing indicator components and options, this is certainly a viable alternative to spending time creating and writing research programs that already exist.

There are two key elements to TD Sequential—Setup and Countdown—that are likewise critical to TD Combo. Whereas Intersection is a third component of TD Sequential, especially when this indicator is applied to individual stocks to protect against the double-edged threat of bankruptcy and buyout, TD Combo does not require Intersection to occur for either stocks, futures, indices, or any other market for that matter. Furthermore, although the requirements for Setup are the same for TD Sequential and TD Combo, they differ for Countdown in three important respects. Specifically, TD Sequential Countdown commences on day 9 of Setup, provided Intersection has occurred on either trading day 8 or trading day 9, and Countdown is postponed until the day Intersection occurs if Intersection takes place subsequent to day 9 of Setup. TD Combo, on the other hand, not only disregards Intersection totally, but it also begins Countdown on day 1 of Setup. This may appear contradictory and unorthodox: How is a trader able to begin Countdown on day 1 of a Setup if the minimum requirement for Setup—nine consecutive closes less than the close four trading days earlier for a buy Setup and nine consecutive closes greater than the close four trading days earlier for a sell Setup—has not even been accomplished at that time? The answer is simple: TD Combo backtracks in time once the minimum Setup requirement has been fulfilled. In other words, once the minimum price relationship required for Setup is complete, TD Combo refers back to day 1 of Setup and begins Countdown on that day. Hence the name Combo, since Countdown is not limited to the period subsequent to the perfection of Setup, as is the case with TD Sequential. The following discussion will describe the Countdown process for TD Combo in more detail and explain how this procedure differs from the traditional Countdown process employed in TD Sequential.

Generally, as buy Countdown for TD Sequential unfolds and successively qualified closing prices are recorded, ideally the ultimate low close approaches, and conversely, as price advances and sell Countdown progresses through completion, ideally the ultimate high close grows closer as well. This makes sense, since sooner or later the current Countdown close will be the last close of a series of lower closes, and the current Countdown close will be the last close of a series of higher closes. By working backward from major historical price lows and price highs, I experimented with many price combinations and relationships before arriving at a method to identify the termination points of price trends and to avoid Countdown occurring at a level other than a recent price bottom or top. The following conditions provided the major impetus for my research effort: (1) an increasing tendency of TD Sequential low-risk buy Countdown completions that occurred at elevated levels above the lows and low-risk sell Countdown completions that occurred at depressed levels beneath the highs and (2) the increasing frequency of markets to record Setup Recycles. TD Combo is specifically designed to circumvent the handicap of high-level 13 buy Countdowns at price bottoms and low-level 13 sell Countdowns at price tops. When first developed, it appeared to be an effective antidote to the plague of TD Sequential Recycles. Experience indicates, however, that Recycling is a bugaboo for TD Combo as well, but not necessarily to the same degree as TD Sequential, since TD Combo Countdown completions occur either quickly in both sharp market declines and steep market advances or slowly when a market is moving essentially sideways with a slight downside or upside bias. In either instance, the potential of TD Combo recycling is less likely than TD Sequential since in a fast market move the chance of Countdown completion is more likely because Countdown can commence the first day of Setup, and in a sideways market if a Recycle Setup occurs, it is usually before Countdown is complete. On the other hand, in the case of TD Sequential, Countdown can be completed in a trading range only to be Recycled once price breaks out. Just as with TD Sequential, I have attempted to eliminate the frequency and impact that Recycling can cause when applying TD Combo by introducing the same series of Recycling options presented in the discussion of TD Sequential. Similarly, these Recycle options address redundant Setups (Recycles) and serve to qualify overlooking their presence in certain circumstances. These filters enable a trader to perfect the TD Combo Countdown process by ignoring or eliminating Recycle occurrences. These options are discussed later in this chapter. Although Intersection is not a consideration with TD Combo, this does not preclude you from experimenting and creating Intersection applications of your own.

The process required to identify either a TD Combo buy or sell Setup is identical to the Setup procedure for TD Sequential in every respect. First of all, to establish a buy Setup, the first day of a buy Setup series must be initialized by requiring that the previous trading day's closing price be greater than or equal to the close four trading days before that trading day, and if you are looking for a sell Setup, the first day of a sell Setup series must be initialized as well by requiring that the previous trading day's closing price be less than or equal to the close four trading days before that trading day. Then proceed to compare the close of each succeeding trading day with the close four trading days earlier. Once a series of at least nine consecutive closes less than the close four trading days earlier for a buy Setup or a series of at least nine consecutive closes greater than the close four trading days earlier for a sell Setup has been recorded, then the minimum requirement for either a buy or a sell Setup has been met. Please note for purposes of applying Recycle qualifiers, as well as TDST, that Setup is not necessarily completed once a series of nine consecutive closes have been recorded. Rather, Setup continues for as long as the series of consecutive price relationships continue and is terminated only when the series is interrupted by registering a close greater than or equal to the close four trading days earlier for a buy Setup or a close less than or equal to the close four trading days earlier for a sell Setup.

Once the minimum requirement for either a buy or a sell Setup has been completed by recording a series of either nine consecutive closes less than or greater than the close four trading days earlier, Countdown for TD Combo commences. In order to identify a potential TD Combo buy Countdown day, I compare the close of day 1 of Setup and the low two trading days earlier. If it is less than or equal to the low two trading days earlier and the low that same day is less than the previous day's low and the close is less than the previous trading day's close, I have recorded day 1 of TD Combo Countdown. Subsequently, I compare the second day of Setup with the low two trading days earlier. If it is less than or equal to the low two trading days earlier and the low is less than the previous trading day's low and the close that day is less than Countdown day 1's close and also less than the previous trading day's close, then the second day of TD Combo Countdown is registered. Whereas for Countdown day 1, a trader is unable to compare the close that day with a prior Countdown day's close, since none existed previously, on Countdown day 2 this comparison can begin, since Countdown day 1 has been defined as a prior reference price. Next, I continue to evaluate each successive day and make the same comparisons. If any of the closes is less than or equal to the low two trading days earlier *and* the low is less than the low of the previous trading day *and* the close is less than the previous Countdown day's close *and* the close is less than the previous trading day's close, then another buy Countdown day is recorded. This is TD Combo version 1, and this process continues until 13 Countdown days are accumulated in this fashion. The key elements of TD Combo version 1 buy Countdown are threefold:

1. The close is less than or equal to the low two trading days earlier.
2. The Countdown day's low is less than the previous trading day's low.
3. Each successive Countdown day's close is less than the previous Countdown day's close—obviously, this requirement does not apply to day 1 of TD Combo Countdown since no Countdown day preceded it—and the previous trading day's close.

The key elements of TD Combo version 1 sell Countdown are as follows:

1. The close is greater than or equal to the high two trading days earlier.
2. The Countdown day's high is greater than the previous trading day's high.
3. Each successive Countdown day's close is greater than the previous Countdown day's close—obviously, to reiterate, this requirement does not apply to day 1 of Countdown since no Countdown day preceded it and, consequently, cannot be used as a closing comparison—and the previous trading day's close.

It should be clear that by definition the lowest close recorded over the entire series of TD Combo buy Countdown trading days once day 13 of TD Combo buy Countdown is completed is also the lowest close of the entire 13 Countdown days. Conversely, the situation is reversed for a sell Countdown, since the highest close of the entire TD Combo sell Countdown is the thirteenth Countdown trading day as well. By definition this is the case, and for that one trading day, at a minimum, the absolute low or high close of the most recent price trend is identified. Once the thirteenth day of Countdown has been recorded, only three trading considerations arise: (1) a subsequent closing price or series of closing prices that are below a TD Combo Countdown 13 bottom by a specified amount or above a TD Combo Countdown 13 top by a specified amount and that could thereby trigger a stop loss, (2) a renewed Setup that can cause a potential Recycling condition, and (3) the specific technique to be used as a filter to time market entry subsequent to recording a TD Combo 13. This is TD Combo version 1.

TD Combo version 2 differentiates itself from TD Combo version 1 in one respect only—the process by which the Countdown days subsequent to Countdown day 10 are calculated. Whereas TD Combo version 1 counts each day the same regardless of which Countdown day it is, TD Combo version 2 is less restrictive when identifying Countdown days 11, 12, and 13, since for a buy Countdown, days 11, 12, and 13 need neither close less than or equal to the low two trading days earlier nor record a lower intraday low versus the previous trading day's low, needing only to record three successively lower closes. That is, the close of Countdown day 11 must be less than the close of Countdown day 10, the close of Countdown day 12 must be less than the close of Countdown day 11, and the close of Countdown day 13 must be less than the close of Countdown day 12. Conversely, for a TD Combo version 2 sell Countdown, the identification process for Countdown days 1 through 10 is identical to version 1, but the counts for Countdown days 11, 12, and 13 merely require higher closes versus the previous TD Combo sell Countdown days. This is not as restrictive as the procedure for Countdown days 1 through 10, since it is neither required that these Countdown closes be greater than or equal to the high two trading days earlier nor that the high be greater than the high of the previous trading day. As you can readily see, TD Combo version 1 is more conservative than TD Combo version 2. I prefer to use TD Combo version 2, since I would rather have more candidates than fewer for buy or sell consideration and would prefer to weed out these buy and sell candidates with some of the other indicators presented throughout this book.

Just as with TD Sequential, there's a variable called TD Termination Count whose purpose is to serve as a substitute for, or in combination with, the standard selection of closing price for the final day (thirteenth day) of Countdown. Typically, I prefer to select the opening price, thereby increasing the opportunity that a TD Combo Countdown 13 will occur.

## Execution Settings

With the exception of Intersection and both the inception and the perfection of the Countdown process, TD Combo and TD Sequential are identical in most other respects, including their execution settings. Consequently, the following description of variable settings and entry and stop-loss options are identical to those described in the previous chapter on TD Sequential.

Once again, it is not my intention to provide you with fixed settings for any of the indicators. Hopefully, you will experiment and customize these selections to fit your specific trading style, expectations, and needs. Although I recommend the following selections, since these are the ones that have proven most effective and with which I am most comfortable at this time, they are not necessarily the optimal settings. The specific selection grid presented here is a version of the standard design that is implemented on most vendor networks:

1. To establish Setup, compare the close of the current price bar with the close four trading bars earlier. (This setting for the "close" appears in the Price column, which defines the price to be compared with a previous price level and "4" appears in the Period column since it defines the number of

price bars back to make the comparison and both are situated in the row identified as Setup.) Default for Setup completion is a series of nine consecutive closing price bars less than or greater than the close four trading bars earlier, depending on whether it is a buy or a sell Setup. (This selection appears in the Signal column and also in the row entitled Setup.)

2. To establish Countdown, compare the close of the current bar with the low or high two trading bars earlier, depending upon whether it is a buy or a sell Setup. (This setting for the "close" appears in the Price column, the "2" appears in the Period column, and both are situated in the row identified as Countdown.) A buy Countdown requires a series of 13 closes less than or equal to the low two trading days earlier, and a sell Countdown requires a series of 13 closes less than or equal to the low two trading days earlier, and a sell Countdown requires a series of 13 closes greater than or equal to the high two trading days earlier. (This selection appears in the Signal column and also in the row entitled Countdown.) Although I prefer in most instances to use less than or equal to and greater than or equal to for Countdown purposes, in inactive markets and when applying TD Combo to short-term bar charts (1 to 10-minute intervals, for example), it is often prudent to remove "equal" and rely solely upon less than for buy Countdown and greater than for sell Countdown. In addition, the low must be less than (or the high greater than) the previous day's low (high) and the close must be less than (greater than) the previous Countdown day's close. Version 1 continues this comparison throughout Countdown and Version 2 applies this method to Countdown days 1 through 10 and requires only three successive lower (higher) closes for Countdown days 11 through 13.

3. Since TD Combo does not consider Intersection, the Intersection selection should be left unchecked. However, generally I include the option of installing Intersection, just in case a trader may prefer to experiment with this variable.

4. Once again, since Intersection is not a factor in TD Combo, this particular setting is left vacant. Should a trader wish to research this indicator with Intersection, I typically include this option for his or her use. Usually, this option is programmed in such a manner that once the day of Intersection is selected, TD Combo will commence its search for Countdown the next trading day, just as in the case of TD Sequential. If you wish to include Intersection, then you must make certain that the Intersection box is checked and then initialize this process by inserting the Setup start date for the Intersection search.

5. To cancel an active buy or sell Setup, select one of the five options displayed in the Cancel column located in the first row of the category described in the Advanced column. A good choice is CaHTH/CbLTL (Close above Highest True High for a buy Setup cancellation and Close below Lowest True Low for a sell Setup cancellation), since it requires a closing price to be recorded above the highest true high recorded during the

entire buy Setup period for buy Setup cancellation and below the lowest true low recorded during the entire sell Setup period for sell Setup cancellation. This selection is checkmarked in the box in the row identified as CaHTH/ CbLTL. The cancellation can occur anytime after the commencement of Setup until the day Countdown has been completed. However, remember that countdown is perfected and a Recycle is avoided once a price flip has been recorded. The requirement of a price flip is eliminated if no Recycle possibility exists or if the Recycle options preclude it for any reason.

6. To cancel either a buy or a sell Setup prior to Countdown completion, a contradictory sell or buy Setup can appear—in other words, a buy Setup would be canceled if a sell Setup is formed prior to completion of the buy Countdown, and a sell Setup would be canceled if a buy Setup is formed prior to completion of the sell Countdown. To activate this cancellation process, check the box in the Cancel column and the Reverse. This is my preference.

7. To cancel a redundant Setup, thereby precluding a Recycle, whether buy or sell, which is contained by the extreme intraday high and low of the previous Setup—in other words, the second (or more recent) of two consecutive, redundant buy or sell Setups whose price extremes do not exceed the previously active Setup's extreme high and low price range levels—check the box at the bottom of the Cancel column and located on the Within row. If it is not checked, it assumes the same significance as a Recycle. I am currently experimenting with this option and was initially ambivalent regarding its value. However, if any Recycle option that "Ignores" the current smaller distance from high to low or highest close to lowest close, for example, is not selected, and the standard selection Recycle "before, on, or after" is selected, my current test results indicate that it be checked, thereby preventing the potential Recycle due to the Setup's inability to exceed the original Setup parameter extremes.

8. To determine whether Setup, Countdown, or "Both" Setup and Countdown are displayed on the chart, the Display column situated on the Setup row designates the option preferred. I prefer to display "Both" Setup and Countdown.

9. Once again, TD Combo does not require Intersection. However, should you wish to install it, this option enables the user to identify graphically the specific price bar that qualifies Intersection. To accomplish this, the box under the column Display and on the row Intersect must be checked. This selection is merely for identification, location, information, and overall formation purposes. You may want to leave it unchecked.

10. To specify whether the series of consecutive Setup days includes closes that are less than and greater than the close four trading days earlier depending on whether a buy or a sell Setup, as well as those days that are "equal," make the selection in the Parameter box in the Setup row. I recommend that "not equal" be specified for Setup determination.

11. To specify whether the series of Countdown closes include closes that are "less than" the low two trading days earlier and "greater than" the

high two trading days earlier depending upon whether a buy or a sell Countdown, as well as those closes that are "equal," make the selection in the Parameter box in the Countdown row. I recommend for daily charts that "equal" be used and for 1, 5, 10 minutes and other intraday time periods that "equal" be used for actively traded and volatile markets and that "not equal" be used for inactive markets and very short time intervals (minutes).

12. Once again, TD Combo does not apply Intersection. However, should you wish to include it, this option enables you to apply the Intersection requirement *only* if it occurs during the Setup phase *or* and if Intersection is to be applied before, during, or anytime after Setup. These options is found in the Parameter box in the Intersect row. This option should be left vacant since TD Combo does not include Intersection in its analysis.

13. To select the method of Recycle or the time to Recycle, refer to the Parameter column and the Recycle row. The possibilities are as follows:

a. Option *a* is the standard, plain-vanilla, conservative setting "Before, on, after," which indicates that a subsequent Setup—a minimum of nine or more consecutive closes less than or greater than the close four trading days earlier—either Before, On, or After the 13 Countdown days and prior to the first price flip day will produce a Recycle.

b. Option *b* is "Ignore smaller true high–true low" and is identical to option *c* except that true highs and true lows are used instead of chart highs and chart lows.

c. Option *c* is "Ignore smaller high–low" and specifies that a Recycle is canceled if the current Setup distance from maximum intraday high over the entire Setup period through the minimum intraday low over the same entire Setup period is less than the distance from the maximum intraday high over the entire immediately prior Setup period to the minimum intraday low over the same entire immediately prior Setup period— remember that a Setup is defined as a series of *at least* nine consecutive closes less than the close four trading days earlier or *at least* nine consecutive closes greater than the close four trading days earlier—both ending once a price flip occurs, and the Setup period can often continue further than the minimum Setup requirement of nine consecutive closes less than the close four trading days earlier for a buy Setup and greater than the close four trading days earlier for a sell Setup. Consequently, the highest high and the lowest low recorded over the entire Setup period is *not* just the minimum Setup period of nine.

d. Option *d* is "Ignore smaller close–close" and is identical to option *c* except maximum and minimum close is inserted instead of highest high and lowest low.

e. Option *e* is "Ignore current" and refers to disregarding the most recent Setup (a Setup in the same direction as the previous Setup and one that would constitute a Recycle condition for any of options *g* through *j*.

f. Option *f* is "Ignore all" and disregards all subsequent, redundant Setups that would constitute a Recycle in any of the options *g* through *j* and proceeds through Countdown for each.

g. Option *g* is "Before or on" the thirteenth Countdown day, and Setup Recycle occurs if Setup takes place prior to or on Countdown day 13.

h. Option *h* is "On or after" the thirteenth Countdown day provides that Recycle can occur on after Countdown day 13 prior to the day before the price flip.

i. Option *i* is "Only before" the thirteenth Countdown day.

j. Option *j* is "Only after" the thirteenth Countdown day and prior to the price flip.

My preferences are the default setting of "Before, on, after" and "Ignore smaller true high–true low." I also observe the Multiplier option when applying the latter proposition (see item 15).

14. To require any Recycle to consist of a specified consecutive series of closes less than or greater than the close four trading days earlier other than the minimum "9" required for a valid Setup, then the Recycle Count value must be selected to reflect any option from 5 to 15 consecutive closes less than the close four trading days earlier for a buy Recycle and greater than the close four trading days earlier for a sell Recycle. Make your selection in the Parameter box in the Recycle count row. My preference is the default setting of "9," which is identical to the standard Setup minimum. At times, however, I will apply 10 or 11.

15. To disallow any Recycle option that begins with the expression "Ignore" even though the current Setup (from intraday high to intraday low) is greater than the previous Setup, the current Setup (from intraday high to intraday low) must exceed the previous Setup by a multiplier of *x* times, and the Recycle Multiplier option selection determines the size of this factor. My preference for a multiplier is 2 (or 3) times.

16. To liberalize the last of a series of Countdown bars, there's a selection entitled TD Termination Count, which is designed to allow the last element of the Countdown series to have a relationship in addition to that prescribed for the other Countdown days. It is defaulted to the closing price of day 13 of Countdown just like the other Countdown days; however, you should occasionally select "open" to allow the opening price to operate simultaneously with the closing price, thereby increasing the probability of fulfilling the Countdown requirement.

17. To specify which Qualifiers to apply to Setup, select the Qualifiers contained in the Parameters box under the column entitled Parameter. The possibilities are numerous. The On box must be checked to activate the specific Qualifier and the Qual and With columns specify which days prior to, on, or subsequent to Setup completion are compared. The Qval and Wval

columns specify which price levels are being compared. The Compare column specifies what type of relationship is selected—remember, if one comparison is made for a buy Setup, then the reciprocal should be selected for the sell Setup; for example, less than (<) for a buy Setup would complement greater than (>) for a sell Setup, and the combination would appear as b<s>. Even though I would like to see the low of day 9 of a buy Setup less than the low of day 6 and the high of day 9 of a sell Setup greater than the high of day 6, my current preference is not to activate these Setup Parameter settings when looking for a TD Combo Setup indication; rather, I prefer to activate it when I want to experiment or apply a qualifier(s) to just the Setup process for purposes of trading only Setups or to apply TDST (TD Setup Trend) for purposes of defining the trend-reversal levels, but such an activity can best be manipulated within the qualifiers presented within the TDST study.

18. To specify whether the Setup and the Countdown continue to be displayed on a chart after the minimum period for Setup and Countdown has been met, "After signal" should be selected, and if only the minimum periods are to be displayed, then "Up to signal" should be selected. I prefer "Up to signal" unless I am either comparing Setup periods to determine a reversal of trend (see TDST), assessing the potential of the current Setup distance exceeding the distance of the previous Setup in the same direction and a Recycle option with "Ignore" has been selected, or evaluating the likelihood of the continuation of a move exceeding the most recent Setup in the other direction to determine whether the current price move is a reversal of trend (TDST) and will mature into full Countdown.

19. To specify the Qualifiers to be used for both Setup and Countdown, as well as their interaction, in order to perfect TD Combo indications, select Qualifiers in the Advanced column. The comparison can be made between Setup days and between Countdown days, as well as between Setup and Countdown days. The On column must be checked to activate the specific Qualifier. The Qtype and Wtype determine whether the comparisons are within Setup, Countdown, or between Setup and Countdown. The Qval and Wval specify which levels within Setup or Countdown are compared. Qual and With columns specify which specific days prior to, on, or subsequent to either Setup or Countdown completion are compared. The Compare column relates to the specific comparison that is made. Note that if less than or equal to (<=) is used for a buy Setup or Countdown then the reciprocal greater than or equal to (>=) should be used for a sell Setup or Countdown, and this combination would be displayed as b<=s>=. In those instances in which Countdown would have been fulfilled had the Qualifier(s) not been introduced, an Asterisk appears on the price chart to designate that fact.

20. To group specific Qualifiers, six sets composed of elements from *a* to *d* have been provided. These groupings enable the user to create "and" as well as "or" conditions and statements within each group, as well as between

groups for both Setup, Countdown, and combinations of Setup and Count-down.

The ensuing discussion is identical to the one presented with TD Sequential in Chapter 2 since it has application to both techniques. You've seen my preferences for the preceding selection options. It would be a serious oversight not to devote additional time to describe further the various Setup Recycle options, since it is such a significant factor in the TD Combo process. Markets are like living organisms, inhaling (undergoing selling pressure) and exhaling (experiencing buying pressure). The flow of money into and out of the market dictates its price movement. Since the market has no responsibility to conform to any trader's expectations, a trader must measure as best he or she can the market's price rhythm and pulse at any particular time. TD Combo accomplishes this goal by identifying prospective market top and bottom price exhaustion zones. However, events can change at any time to cause a resurgence in either selling or buying pressure. Just such inflows or price regenerations create Setup Recycles. An effective way to deal with these renewed price thrusts is to ignore those Setups that encompass less price distance than the prior price Setup distance. Setups begin with the first day that records a closing price less than (for a buy Setup) or greater than (for a sell Setup) the closing price four trading days earlier. The minimum buy Setup series is accomplished once nine consecutive closes are recorded; however, the Setup extends until a contradictory close greater than or equal to (for a buy Setup completion) or less than or equal to (for a sell Setup completion) the close four trading days earlier is recorded. Then the price comparison is made. If the current Setup distance from true high to true low is less than the original (previous) buy Setup distance from true high to true low, the current Setup is ignored if the selection "to ignore" is made. This Recycle condition is "ignore smaller true high/true low." If the current Setup is greater in price distance, a Recycle exists. One exception exists when the current Setup distance is greater than the original Setup distance by a factor of at least 2. This Multiplier will alert the trader to a market's potential price exhaustion area.

## Implementation

The TD Combo discussion is presented intentionally in the context of an indicator rather than as a system. All the variations and considerations presented for TD Combo may seem intimidating, but mastering it should enhance your trading success. Given its massive composition and its numerous variations, I could have devoted an entire book to the TD Combo indicator. Familiarizing yourself with its features and various important components will avail you of the opportunity to choose and experiment with selections of your own from this dynamic option setting. In order to help you, I have provided a robust indicator capable of accommodating most elements of the numerous price pattern conditions and relationships that are apparent from time to time within the price structure of markets. The discussion will include the various aspects of TD Combo, its salient elements, and its versatility and applicability to markets. Due to the comprehensive overview presented, the variables that may be introduced to arrive at TD Combo price execution may vary from one trader to another. The various components and potential default selections I use most often are presented. Although each item has been an important consideration in my construction of the TD Combo indicator, many of these refinements are not crucial to the successful application and implementation of TD Combo. Furthermore, there is no need for you to customize or optimize the variables to fit to the market being monitored. Although there probably exists an ideal matrix that conforms to the natural price rhythm and exhaustion tendencies of most markets, the suggested selections are generic in the sense that they are a good starting point from which to apply this indicator. Your evaluation and installation of the variables important to TD Combo should be preceded by careful forethought and consideration of criteria such as, entry, exit, and stop-loss contingencies. For the sake of completeness, you should consider some of the following options as well.

*Entry:* A major issue confronting a trader any time a "9-13" (completed Setup and Countdown) indication for basic TD Combo is generated is the possibility of a Setup Recycle occurring prior to a price flip, thereby requiring the abort or cancellation of the Countdown and, consequently, the potential trade. The various entry techniques I propose include the following:

1. The most venturesome and risky approach is to take entry on the thirteenth day of Countdown.
2. Another method intended to reduce the likelihood of a Recycle and ensure the chance of a successful trade is, subsequent to Countdown day 13, the first closing price recorded that is greater than the opening price is a good confirmation of a bottom, and the first closing price recorded that is less than the opening price is a good confirmation of a top.
3. This option is added to option 2 and requires that (a) subsequent to Countdown day 13, not only is the closing price greater than the opening price the same day, but also the high that same day is greater than the previous trading day's close at a potential bottom and (b) not only is the closing price less than the opening price the same day, but also the low that same day is less than the previous day's close at a potential top. For more conservative traders who are willing to accept a less advantageous entry price, I suggest that instead of the requirement "the high

the same day is greater than the previous day's close," the high is greater than the previous day's true high be applied and, likewise, instead of the requirement "the low the same day is less than the previous day's close," the low is less than the previous day's true low be applied. In either case, this search process commences the trading day following the thirteenth day of Countdown.

4. Another more conservative method to avoid the risk of Recycle is to require a *price flip* (close greater than the close four trading days earlier at a low or a close less than the close four trading days earlier at a high) before entry is made and prior to a renewed price Setup. By definition, this approach guarantees no possibility of a Recycle, but unfortunately, this option often translates into a forfeiture of a more favorable entry price.

5. Another technique to initiate or even add to an existing position is to place an additional order to buy or to sell just above the stop-loss level at a low and just below a stop loss level at a high (see stop loss that follows).

6. Another approach applying a discipline similar to option 5 is to buy or sell an additional position when a 9-13-9 occurs—in other words, whenever a TD Combo Reinforcement™ indication occurs (see following).

7. Further, in order to prevent the possibility of Countdown proceeding to "12" and price reversing without recording a "13" Countdown, you can occasionally use the open price or low for buy and high for sell rather than the close—or a combination of the open, the low and the high, and the close—to arrive at the Countdown 13 indication (see TD Termination Count in previous Countdown discussion) to ensure entry. This last selection is called TD Termination Count in the software selection since a trader may elect to terminate Countdown with a value other than, or in addition to, the standard close for "13"—this option applies only to the final day of Countdown.

8. By synchronizing a shorter-term (time interval) TD Combo low-risk indication (e.g., on a 1-, 20-, or 60-minute basis), the entry level and timing can be perfected further.

9. Another effective technique requires the construction of a TD Supply Line at a low and a TD Demand Line at a high to fine-tune the low-risk entry zones.

10. Six other entry techniques used to refine entry include TD Combo, TD Diff, TD REBO, TD Open, TD Trap, and TDPOQ, as well as various other indicators presented in the book in combination with one another.

*Profit level:* Generally, you should look to take profits once an opposing Setup—in the other direction—is formed and the highest closing price of the current Setup period fails to exceed the intraday peak of the opposing Setup or the lowest closing price of the current Setup period fails to exceed the intraday low of the opposing Setup. This method conforms with the precepts for the TDST indicator. If, however, the closing price subsequent to a price bottom does exceed the intraday true high—or, subsequent to a price peak, the intraday true low—and is confirmed (see foregoing TDST), then generally expect price to continue through the Countdown process, and once Countdown is completed you can take profits and occasionally reverse at that time to participate in the primary trend. Obviously, other exit techniques can be used: dollar value profit-taking levels (once a prescribed profit is made, then exit) trailing dollar stop losses; a series of consecutive up closes (or down closes); a series of consecutive closes greater than the open (less than the open); the first profitable opening price; the first trading day with a price range at least double the range of the entry day or double the range of the previous trading day; the first day with a low greater than the entry day's high (high less than the entry day's low); and the introduction of other indicators presented in this book, such as TDMA I, REBO, TD Open, TD Trap, and TD Lines.

*Stop loss:* Since the stop-loss technique was created over 20 years ago, it's been applied it to a number of indicators. It still has the amazing ability to protect me from prematurely exiting a trade, as well as its ability to be sufficiently sensitive to changing market conditions. In fact, there have been individuals who have used TD Combo, and once this stop-loss has been triggered, they have exited the trade and have, at that same time, successfully reversed their positions, because when a TD Combo trade does not work, as Paul Tudor Jones observed and described it, "it really doesn't work." The stop loss performed so impressively that subsequently I developed an indicator called TD Stop Reverse that utilizes a similar approach, independent of any entry technique whatsoever, to initiate trades. Repeatedly, whenever a TD Combo 9-13 low- or high-risk indication fails, it really fails, and price accelerates quickly in the breakdown direction. At the time it fails, the forces of supply and demand have shifted so dramatically that rapid adjustments to the price structure occur. The stop-loss method is as follows: At a price bottom, identify the lowest low, including all the days of Setup and Countdown. Then calculate the difference between the true high (the high recorded that same day or the previous day's close, whichever is greater) and that same day's price low. This true price range is then subtracted from the low that same day. Should price close below that value, then the stop loss would be triggered. Conversely, a stop loss at a price peak is calculated as follows: Identify the highest high of the entire Setup and Countdown periods. Then calculate the difference between the high and the true low (the low recorded that same day or the previous day's close, whichever is less) and add that value to that same day's price high. If price closes above that peak, then the stop loss would be activated. A more liberal method would be to require two closes below and above the calculated stop-loss levels. A more conservative method (not recommended) would be to install stops at intraday—not closing—price-level violations. Another buy-stop loss identifies the lowest day of the entire Setup and Countdown period, calculates the difference between the intraday low and the close that same day, and subtracts that difference from that same day's intraday low—if there are recorded two consecutive closes below that level, then the stop loss is triggered. Conversely, a sell stop loss is calculated by subtracting the difference between the highest intraday high of Setup and Countdown and the close that same day. If price closes above that level for two consecutive days, then likewise the stop loss is triggered. Another stop-loss method applies a flat dollar amount to the entry price, and if price exceeds that value either intraday or on a closing basis, then the trade is exited.

To complement these stop-loss methods, as price approaches the stop-loss level an additional entry (entries) can be taken, since the risk associated with the trade diminishes. In other words, you may wish to lower your average price at a low or raise your average price at a high by adding to your position as price approaches your stop loss. Obviously, such a practice is gutsy, but if the stop loss is effective and you are comfortable assuming the limited risk, it is an approach worthy of consideration.

An alert individual trader asked me what to do if an entry were to occur subsequent to the completion of Countdown and that entry price were to occur outside the stop-loss zone. It was an astute observation on his part for the following reasons: For example, if a trader were to wait for a close greater than the open on a day subsequent to recording the thirteenth day of Countdown to execute a buy entry, and a close of a day subsequent to the thirteenth day of Countdown and prior to this entry is below the stop-loss level, then how should a trader deal with this event? Experience indicates that whenever this situation occurs, price typically Recycles. But such occasions arise only if a trader attempts to perfect his or her entries into a market, which, by the way, is the method I recommend for a trader to operate successfully in the markets.

Although it is necessary to establish guidelines and parameter settings for TD Combo and not to deviate from them lest you enter the realm of optimization modeling, I have observed what appear to be anomalies in price behavior in various markets. These are noteworthy and should be addressed. For example, whereas I have always applied a Setup relationship of the current close versus the close four trading days earlier for a series of nine consecutive closing prices, in the cash currencies markets, it seems a Setup series of eight consecutive closes often appears to work as well, and you should evaluate similar adjustments and applications to the cash markets you may follow. However, you should remain consistent in your approach. Additionally, better results may accrue by using a combination of both the opening price and the closing price for the thirteenth day of Countdown for cash markets (see previous discussion of TD Combo Termination Count), and as long as the opening and the closing prices occur at the same time each price period and an established level of consistency is maintained, TD Combo should continue to be effective and responsive.

## TD Combo Reinforcement

Throughout the years, I have observed a derivative TD Combo pattern that has proven to be reliable and has produced credible results. This pattern is called TD Combo Reinforcement because not only does it have a classic 9-13 low-risk buy or sell indication, but subsequent to the occurrence of a price flip, it also records another Setup, which serves in a sense to reinforce or confirm the original 9-13 indication. This reinforced Setup subsequent to the TD Combo low-risk buy or sell Setup can occur above the lowest low of the previous buy Countdown and below the highest high of the previous sell Countdown, or it can occur below the low of the lowest buy Countdown day or above the high of the highest sell Countdown day. A more liberal method would be to require two closes below and above the calculated stop-loss levels. A more conservative method (not recommended) would be to install stops at intraday, not closing, price level violations.

To complement these various stop-loss methods, as price approaches the stop-loss level an additional entry (entries) can be taken, since the risk associated with the trade diminishes accordingly. In other words, you may wish to lower your average purchase price at a low or raise your average price at a high by adding to your position as price approaches your stop loss. Obviously, such a practice is gutsy, but if the stop loss is effective and you are comfortable assuming the limited risk, it is an approach worthy of consideration.

Numerous charts are included for your review to describe the TD Combo Setup and Countdown processes. As you can easily see, TD Combo has application to numerous unrelated markets with equal success. All charts displayed are TD Combo version 2, since that condition is more liberal than version 1. Figures 3.1 and 3.2 display the TD Combo high-risk indications that occurred the first week of September 1992, just before the collapse of the British pound on a daily, as well as a weekly, basis. The fact that both time periods confirmed one another by generating simultaneous warnings of impending market weakness undoubtedly foreshadowed the intensity of the impending decline. Additionally, see how well the other TD Combo weekly indications performed at the 1990 high and mid-1991 low. Just as Figures 3.1 and 3.2 demonstrated, using basic TD Combo without ignoring Recycling has been successful in identifying prospective tops and bottoms for the cash currencies. Figure 3.3 (cash yen) demonstrates TD Combo's versatility and

**Figure 3.1** Note how well TD Combo identified the high-risk area for the British pound in September 1992 before its historic decline. This is entirely consistent with the weekly TD Combo indication generated at the same time (see Figure 3.2 small *a′*). TDST identified a trend reversal.

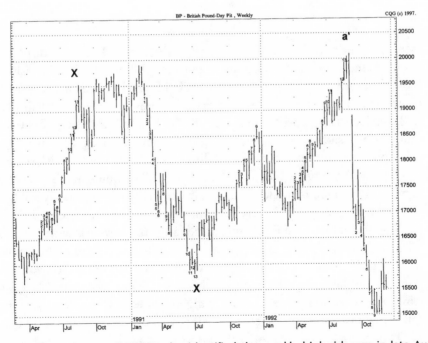

**Figure 3.2** See how well TD Combo identified the weekly high-risk area in late August 1992—as well as the high in the summer of 1991 and the low in July of 1992 (see *X*s). Letter *a′* identifies on a weekly chart the location of the TD Combo low-risk sell indication on the previous chart (Figure 3.1) of the daily British pound at the same time.

135

**Figure 3.3** The August 1992 yen low and subsequent January 1994 high were identified by TD Combo.

sensitivity in both bear and bull markets. Figures 3.4 and 3.5 display two more examples of TD Combo and its uncanny ability to locate low-risk entry zones. Figure 3.5 also identifies two TDST levels—one that was broken downside and the other that served as upside resistance. Figure 3.6 displays a daily cash currency spread (Japanese yen/Swiss franc) with both TD Combo and TDST showcased. Figure 3.7 illustrates the speed with which TD Combo is able to reverse itself from low-risk buy zone to low-risk sell zone. Figure 3.8 shows the ECU with the low-risk TD Combo and TDST. Once again, TD Combo is applied to a weekly chart (Figure 3.9, weekly gold), and TDST is also included. Figure 3.10 illustrates the importance of TDST, as well as the ability of TD Combo to identify the low-risk entry area. TD Combo has application to exotic markets as well, such as the Irish punt (Figure 3.11). Figures 3.12 and 3.13 have Countdown day 13 one to two months after Countdown days 10 and 11. This is not uncommon for TD Combo since the closes must be successively higher for each Countdown day into a projected price peak and successively lower into a projected trough. Unlike TD Sequential, they are more difficult to accomplish.

The charts focus primarily upon daily and weekly currency, both cash and futures, and world market metals. TD Combo has worked well in iden-tifying the exhaustion points for indices, spreads, and individual equities and

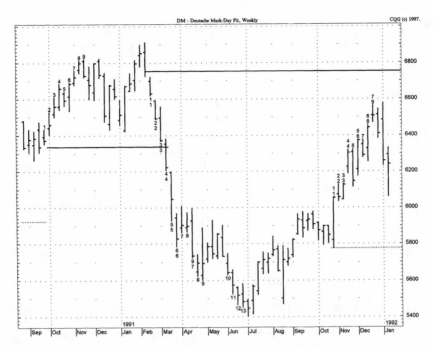

**Figure 3.4** This chart demonstrates TD Combo applied to another currency, but in this example it is a weekly futures chart of the German mark. TDST is also included.

**Figure 3.5** Once again this weekly chart demonstrates TD Combo's ability to identify prospective low-risk entry levels. Additionally, see how well the breakdown below the TDST level in the first quarter of 1991 was a prelude to a sharp decline and the market's inability to exceed on a closing basis the TDST level in 1992 at the 13 Countdown forecast the subsequent decline.

**Figure 3.6**  The previous TD Combo charts were applied to individual currencies, both cash and futures. This chart applies TD Combo to a currency spread and includes TDST as well.

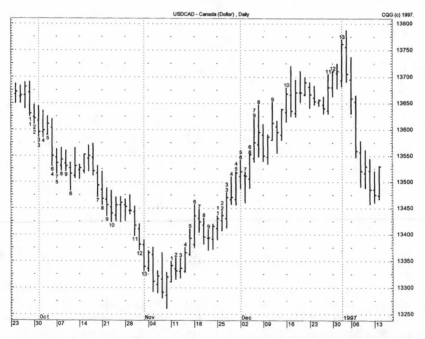

**Figure 3.7**  This chart of the cash Canadian dollar displays the TD Combo low-risk entry levels.

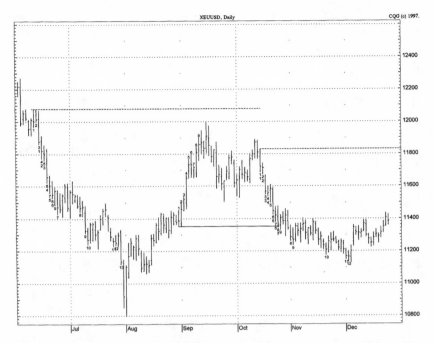

**Figure 3.8**   Once again TD Combo identified a low-risk entry for the ECU. The first close greater than the open and high greater than the previous day's close occurred the day of the low. TDST defined the critical upside breakout level.

**Figure 3.9**   Weekly gold responded to a TD Combo high-risk indication, but the downside was limited to a buy Setup, which failed to close below the previous sell Setup as identified by the TDST line on the chart.

**Figure 3.10**   Note how the rally off the low-risk TD Combo 13 stalled precisely at the TDST level and then broke sharply below the TDST level in May when the precise intraday high met resistance at the TDST level. However, the next day the market opened above the TDST level, which is an example of TD Critical Qualifier being activated.

**Figure 3.11**   The Irish punt recorded a TDST upside breakout in late October, and subsequently proceeded to generate a TD Combo 13 Countdown at the precise high. Note that it took close to a month for Countdown to advance from 12 to 13.

**Figure 3.12**   TD Combo correctly identified the world lead market high in May 1996.

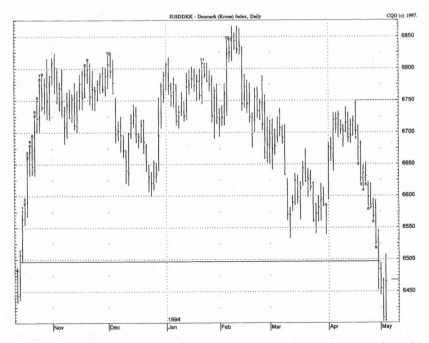

**Figure 3.13**   As in Figure 3.11, it is not uncommon to see TD Combo Countdown 11, 12, or 13 occur much later than the other Countdown days.

commodities, as well as financial futures. For example, Figures 3.14 and 3.15 display the Dow Jones Utilities and the Goldman Sachs Commodity Index. Figures 3.16 and 3.17 show the Biotechnology and Health Care stock indices, respectively. Figure 3.17 illustrates an "add-on" pattern reminiscent of TD Sequential, which I refer to as TD Combo Reinforcement since a TD Combo high-risk 13 was recorded in June and subsequently another rally attempt took place one month later and another Setup was recorded at that time, prior to the decline, which coincidentally exhausted itself at the TDST level defined by the sell Setup low in early May. Figure 3.18 of the Dow Jones Industrial Average has a similar TD Combo Reinforcement indication in October after the precise high was identified by the thirteenth day of Countdown in mid-September. The next three charts (Figures 3.19 to 3.21) illustrate how diverse markets such as 5-year government yields, the Dollar Index, and Live Cattle have a common denominator, that is, TD Combo low-risk entry levels and TDST breakouts. Not to be outdone, the following group of charts show TD Combo indications for stocks. Note that by waiting for a close above the open and a high greater than the previous day's close at a low and, conversely, a close less than the open and a low less than the previous day's close at a high, entries can be perfected. Figure 3.22 shows the

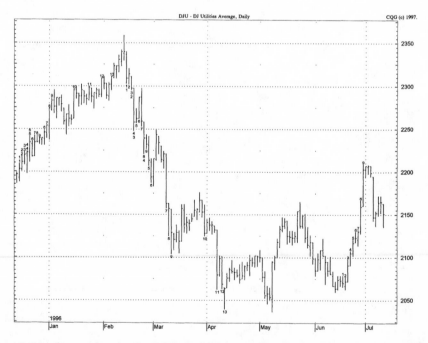

**Figure 3.14**  As you can see, the February high, as well as the April low, were identified by TD Combo. In order to perfect entry, various techniques can be applied, such as, at a low, close greater than open and high same trading day greater than previous trading day's close or, at a high, close less than open and low less than previous trading day's close.

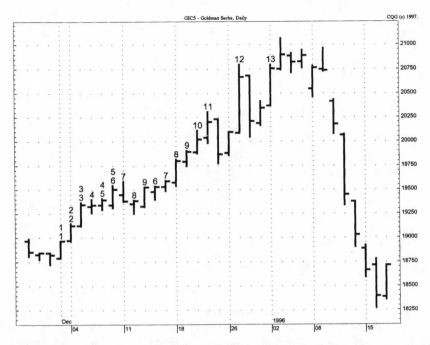

**Figure 3.15**   As you can see the Goldman Sachs Commodity Index topped out coincident with TD Combo Countdown 13.

**Figure 3.16**   TDST served as resistance to the upside in May. Price broke below the TDST level in June, forecasting a potential decline through TD Combo Countdown completion and a low-risk entry zone. Various entry techniques can be used to perfect the timing.

**Figure 3.17** The Health Care Index recorded a TD Combo 9-13-9. A TD Combo Reinforcement indication at the July high broke the TDST level on day 1 of a buy Setup. Subsequently, price declined on day 8 of Setup approaching the TDST level but never closed below it, thereby indicating an imminent price reversal and resumption of the uptrend. Then price exceeded the TDST level upside in August and September, indicating a price that should continue through Countdown completion.

**Figure 3.18** As in Figure 3.17, TD reinforcement indication is given. It appears in situations such as this one, where the last impulse to buy must be exhausted before price is able to decline. Also note how well TDST served as resistance in August and support in November for short periods of time.

144

**Figure 3.19** TD Combo correctly identified the increase in yields and confirmed the upside trend by recording a TDST breakout.

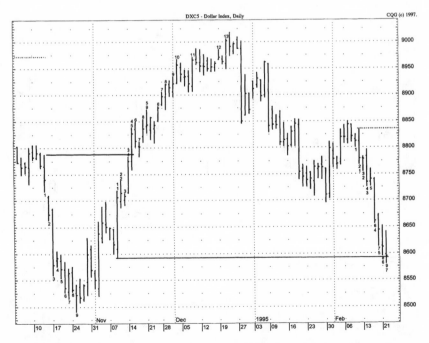

**Figure 3.20** The Dollar Index exceeded the TDST breakout level upside on its way to a Countdown 13 recorded at the market high. The TD Combo low-risk entry occurred co-incident with the high.

145

**Figure 3.21**   The live cattle peak in November was an upside exhaustion move predicted by TD Combo. The TDST breakout downside forecast lower prices.

**Figure 3.22**   TD Combo Countdown 13 occurred three days prior to the high, but the first subsequent day to record a close less than the open and low less than the previous day's close occurred on the high day.

TD Combo high for Oxford Health: By postponing entry until both a close less than the open and a low less than the previous day's close is recorded the same trading day, the high day was identified. Figure 3.23 shows a similar situation with IBM. Figure 3.24 provides an example of a TDST failure to break out downside in October, immediately followed by a TDST breakout upside within seven trading days, which suggested that TD Combo would likely continue through Countdown, which it did.

Figure 3.25, Mercantile Stores, demonstrates the length of time it took for the TD Combo peak to be formed and how quickly the subsequent TD Combo low occurred. In other words, the ability of TD Combo to operate in both environments once again demonstrates its flexibility. Furthermore, the stop loss at the high was not in jeopardy of being triggered and, as price approaches the stop loss in early June is a prudent time to add to your position, since the risk is diminished substantially from the level of the initial commitment. Figures 3.26 and 3.27 show that if the TDST breakout level is not broken subsequent to a TD Combo low-risk indication, the underlying trend is likely to resume, and it is a low-risk opportunity to enter the market once the TDST breakout failure is apparent, which usually occurs upon

**Figure 3.23**  As in Figure 3.22, by awaiting a close less than the open and a low less than the previous day's close, the TD Combo low-risk entry zone was the high day (*X*). Furthermore, TD Sequential generated a 9-13 low-risk sell two days before the high, which was perfected by the down close and low less than the previous trading day's low on the high day as well. Note the TDST breakout in January, forecasting the continuation of the rally through TD Combo Countdown.

**Figure 3.24** The TDST downside breakout failure in October was quickly followed by a TDST upside breakout, which continued through TD Combo Countdown.

**Figure 3.25** The TD Combo low-risk top area was somewhat premature, but the stop loss was never close to being activated. By awaiting a close greater than the open subsequent to the TD Combo low and a penetration of the previous day's close, an ideal entry zone was identified.

**Figure 3.26**   The TD Combo 13 Countdowns took a period of time to complete but both were precise. Subsequent to both, the Setups failed to exceed the TDST level, and price rallied to new highs.

Setup completion. This method is similar to the one applied as price approaches the stop-loss level. In a delayed and exaggerated context, Figure 3.27 shows a three-month lag between days 11 and 13 of TD Combo. The subsequent buy Setup failed to exceed the TDST level on a closing basis, and the price proceeded to new rally highs.

As with TD Sequential, by ignoring Setup Recycles if the current Setup from true high to true low is either less than the previous Setup or if the current Setup from true high to true low is more than two times the previous Setup in price distance, TD Combo Countdowns increase from those instances that have the conservative "before, on, or after" Recycle condition. The copper weekly (Figure 3.28) displays an example of the Recycle Multiplier feature. Note that Figure 3.29 confirms Figure 3.30, which is a good example of the Recycle exception "ignore smaller true high to true low" as well as of using a Recycle Multiplier of at least two times. By evaluating Figure 3.29 in the context of its weekly TD Combo indication, confirmation of the market peak is obtained. Figure 3.31 is an additional example of a continuing TD Combo Countdown through the Setup Recycle, and this technique is particularly applicable to actively traded markets, since it is a not an uncommon experience for a Setup Recycle to occur at market turning points, and it is prudent to apply the "ignore" Recycle options to participate in these moves.

**Figure 3.27**   TD Combo Countdown coincided with the price peak and the subsequent decline failed to close below the TDST level, implying a subsequent attempt to challenge the high.

**Figure 3.28**   By "ignoring" a Recycle Setup of less price distance from true high to true low than the previous Setup or "ignoring" a Setup that is more than two times the previous Setup's price distance, a TD Combo 13 appeared at the June 1996 copper weekly low confirming the TD Sequential daily low.

**Figure 3.29**  By applying the open as a "Termination Count" to week 13 of TD Combo, the all-time weekly price high was identified.

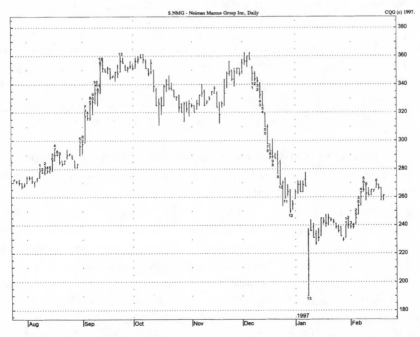

**Figure 3.30**  Figure 3.29 provides a weekly perspective for Nieman Marcus Group, and this chart identifies the TD Combo high and subsequent low by introducing the Recycle exceptions "ignore smaller true high low" and the Multiplier of at least two times the previous Setup.

**Figure 3.31**   "By ignoring the Recycle" because the current Setup covered less price distance than the previous Setup from true high to true low, a low-risk TD Combo indication appeared in March and a high-risk TD Combo in late May. Keep in mind that by perfecting the entry levels using various price comparisons, trading this volatile stock became much easier. Note how TDST stopped advance in April and supported decline in June.

As indicated throughout the discussion of TD Sequential, I like to follow distant futures contracts to obtain TD Combo indications, and the same preference applies to inactively traded markets. Figure 3.32 is an example of a distant market generating a TD Combo low-risk sell entry and Figures 3.33 and 3.34 display two relatively inactive foreign stocks that trade domestically.

To continue to display more markets and to discuss more opportunities presented by TD Combo and TDST would be redundant. The reason for so many examples is to present the indicator and its many ramifications, as well as its interaction with the trend-following and confirmation indicator, TDST. It would have been simple to present a few charts and rules and go on to other topics, but TD Combo is such a valuable tool and complement to TD Sequential that not to present numerous examples of its application to a wide spectrum of markets would be remiss. My failure to focus on short-term intraday examples of TD Combo has nothing to do with its lack of application or success within this time arena. Much to the contrary, I have witnessed many TD Combo one- and five-minute, as well as hourly, charts that were precise, and many individuals have profitably traded on this level. It's not that it doesn't work, but complications outside the indicator's control

**Figure 3.32** The late April TD Combo 13 Countdown was confirmed by the nearby contract expirations as well.

**Figure 3.33** This stock is relatively inactive, and consequently the TD Combo and TD Sequential indications generally are reliable, similar to those given by distant futures contacts. Note the TD Combo Reinforcement high-risk indication subsequent to the TD Combo 13 in late December. Also, the TDST levels are identified on the chart, and the last one forewarned of a continuation of TD Sequential Countdown through day 13. This example indicates the utility of combining TD Combo and TD Sequential since TD Combo correctly identified the high-risk zone in October and TD Sequential located the low-risk area in April.

**Figure 3.34** This chart displays an inactively traded stock. Once again note that the TD Combo 13 Countdown was accurate in identifying the high-risk area in October. See how well the TDST levels worked as support and resistance.

often dictate the difference between profits and losses: Order delays, slippage, order flow, late tape, and so on can all have an impact. I strongly recommend that if you are committed to trade at an intraday level you use TD Combo—and TD Sequential and TDST, for that matter—to ensure that the overriding trend is in your favor. In other words, if you are using a one-minute TD Combo, it would be prudent not only to have confirmation from TD Sequential but also to have the 5-minute, 30-minute, or hourly TD Combo confirming as well by generating a Setup or Countdown completion at close to the same time.

As you have observed, TD Combo is a valuable complement to TD Sequential, since it is intended to identify extreme market highs and lows. It has been designed to address the deficiencies inherent in TD Sequential by requiring that each Countdown day be successively exceeded at a prospective market low by a lower close and at a prospective market high by a higher close. There are two versions of TD Combo Countdown, and the distinction between the two relates to the methodology applied to the last three days of Countdown. Version 1 is more conservative in this regard since it maintains the same criteria applied to the prior 10 Countdown days. Numerous benefits accrue from both versions of TD Combo. On many occasions I have witnessed this indicator precisely identify both market tops and bottoms. As with TD Sequential, TD Combo's versatility and applicability to various markets over a wide spectrum of time periods is a valuable feature. I have seen TD Combo fail to identify some tops and bottoms, however, while at the same time and over the same period TD Sequential has correctly identified them. That is why I prefer to use both indicators in tandem in my analysis of markets. In fact, experience suggests whenever both speak at the same time, it pays to listen attentively.

For more examples, see Figures 3.35 through 3.41.

**Figure 3.35(a)**    The TD Combo low-risk sell indication occurred on the same day as the TD Sequential low-risk indication (see Figure 3.35b). TDST also appears.

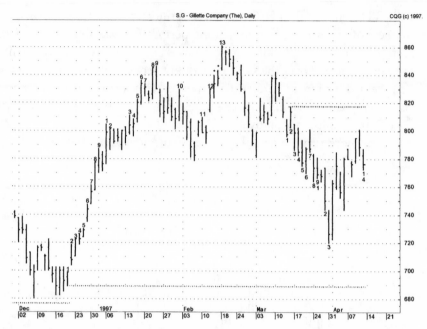

**Figure 3.35(b)** The TD Sequential low-risk sell indication at the high is identical to the previous chart (Figure 3.35a), which is example TD Combo. TDST also appears.

**Figure 3.36(a)** TD Combo low-risk sell indication appears at the precise high in this example as opposed to Figure 3.36b, which displays the TD Sequential low-risk sell at a different level. TDST is displayed as well.

**Figure 3.36(b)**  This figure is the TD Sequential counterpart to the chart in Figure 3.36a, which shows a TD Combo low-risk sell indication.

**Figure 3.37**  TD Combo identified the low-risk sell opportunity zone at the high. TDST identified the breakout in late December and the support in March–April.

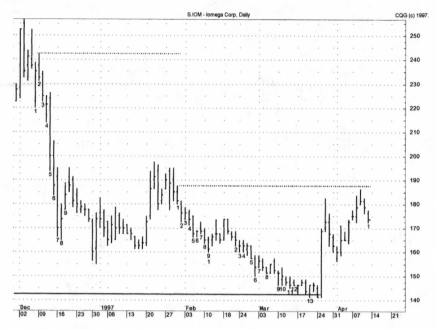

**Figure 3.38** Whereas TD Combo was silent in this example, TD Sequential and TDST spoke loud and clear.

**Figure 3.39** TD Combo low-risk sell appeared at high. TD Trend Factor levels also appear.

**Figure 3.40**  TD Combo high-risk indication did not appear, but TD Sequential did, right at the high. TDST also appears.

**Figure 3.41**  Once again, TD Combo did not identify high-risk zone, but TD Sequential did. The TD Trend Factor levels appear.

# Chapter

# 4

# TD Lines

*Observation:* When I initially studied market timing approaches, I applied and experimented with most of the commonly used conventional technical methods, including trendlines, moving averages, cycles, and so on. Trendline analysis was the first method researched. I applied trendlines to all sorts of markets, fundamental data, and economic statistics. Nothing escaped the scope of my research. My naïveté, enormous appetite for market timing information, and an obsession to create simplistic methodologies made me more pliable and willing to experiment. Once I had developed my own trendline model, no data source was considered sacrosanct. I was determined to apply TD Lines, as I refer to my specific form of trendline analysis, to everything conceivable. An incident occurred in a conference room of an investment counseling company where I worked in 1974, where a presentation by a visiting economist was taking place. Constructing a TD Line and applying it to a chart of interest rates that appeared in the *Wall Street Journal,* I volunteered my interest rate forecast, which contradicted the consensus opinion expressed by the other individuals in attendance. My prediction, unbeknownst to the others, was based solely upon this form of analysis. This forecast proved to be accurate. It made an obvious impression upon the visitor and the salesperson who accompanied him, since shortly after my interest rate projection was fulfilled, I was contacted by both of them. Thinking back on that episode, I'm gratified that the simple technique I'd created and applied was so well received, for that long-ago visitor is currently held in

high esteem, both politically as well as within the overall investment and economic communities: He is Alan Greenspan, chairman of the Federal Reserve
Board.

Whether an analyst is a fundamentalist or a technician, at one time or
another he or she has likely drawn a trendline to construct and extrapolate a
trend, as well as to identify a potential breakout point. Obviously, enough
instances in which trendline analysis benefited the user were observed to justify their application by these individuals. However, it seems the process most
individuals use to construct these lines is generally arbitrary and fraught with
subjectivity and inconsistency. This belief was recently confirmed. I gave a
speech to a gathering of floor traders and asked the attendees how many of
them used trendlines to arrive at trading decisions. It was almost unanimous:
Most did. Next, I presented the identical price chart to five individuals seated
in the front row and requested that they draw trendlines of the price action of
the same market. Every trendline was different. The same person will likely
construct completely different trendlines when presented the same chart at
different times. The fact that most traders use trendlines attests to their
acceptance and the simplicity of their application and interpretation, as well
as their perceived value. However, no prescribed checklist exists for their
proper construction, interpretation, and qualification.

I experimented with a series of trendline variations before uncovering
various common denominators present in most successful breakouts. Once
the two points required to draw a trendline were selected properly and then
connected, many benefits were derived. Since a trendline is merely a graphic
representation of supply and demand, it is important that it be redefined and
redrawn continually as the composition and the relationship between supply
and demand change, in keeping with the dynamics of the marketplace.

I developed a series of steps to construct trendlines properly, to qualify
intraday breakouts, and to calculate price projections. This process consists
of the following:

1. Identify key pivot, price exhaustion, or price-reversal levels (TD Supply
   and Demand Points).

2. Connect the two most recent TD Supply Points to create a TD Supply
   Line and the two most recent TD Demand points to create a TD
   Demand Line.

3. Continuously reassign the TD Points™ to connect only the two most
   recent ones (i.e., select the farthest-right TD Point and the second-
   farthest-right TD Point just prior to that one). In other words, instead of
   drawing a trendline by focusing upon the left side of the price chart projecting into the future, as is the most common method and the most natural one, the TD Line should be drawn from the rightmost TD Point to

the second rightmost TD Point then extended from the most recent TD Point on the chart into the future.

4. Determine whether the prerequisites exist to qualify intraday entry of a price breakout or, if none are present, whether the possibility exists to fade (do the reverse) the "disqualified" breakout.

5. Calculate an upside price objective based upon the extreme price movement below a descending TD Supply Line, and calculate a downside price objective based upon the extreme movement above an ascending TD Demand Line. These are derived as a result of the market's symmetrical tendencies to both replicate downside the extreme price movement that occurred above the TD Line prior to a downside breakout and upside the extreme price movement that occurred below the TD Line prior to an upside breakout.

6. Install additional qualifiers to perfect the breakout identification process.

7. Evaluate the succeeding day's price activity to determine whether cancellation of the original breakout is warranted.

8. Ideally, operate within the context of the overall market trend if possible. In other words, generally make certain that the TD Line breakout price objective is in the same direction and contained within the price objective established by the breakout of a higher-level TD Line. This serves to establish the underlying market trend. If this doesn't work, concentrate upon fading the "disqualified" breakouts.

A TD Point level 1 low is defined as an intraday price low that is both preceded and succeeded the day immediately before and the day immediately after by higher intraday price lows. Conversely, a TD Point level 1 high is defined as an intraday price high that is both preceded and succeeded the day immediately before and the day immediately after by lower intraday highs. True lows and true highs should be used instead of chart lows and chart highs. (A *true high* is the high that trading day or the previous trading day's close, whichever is greater, and a *true low* is the low that trading day or the previous trading day's close, whichever is less. A *chart high* and a *chart low* are the actual price levels depicted on the chart.) This is accomplished by disregarding both a TD Point low if the close on the trading day before the low is less than the TD Point low and a TD Point high if the close on the trading day before the TD Point high is greater than the TD Point high. If you were to use chart lows and chart highs rather than true lows and true highs, more TD Lines will appear; however, research indicates that true highs and true lows are more effective. If you wanted to construct a TD Line of a level higher than level 1, you would merely identify those TD Points of a magnitude greater than or equal to your selection, connect the two most recent TD points, and then extend the TD Line into the future. For example, a TD

Point Low level 3 requires three or more higher lows on the three trading days immediately before and after the low day, and a TD Point High level 3 requires three or more lower highs on the three trading days immediately before and after the high day. Figure 4.1 displays the various TD Points and their respective levels on the chart. The Level One TD Points are connected to draw level 1 TD Lines. I have identified the Disqualified TD Lines—those breakouts that fail to meet at least one of the TD Line Qualifiers (see following)—with dotted lines.

   TD Points are significant in the sense that they identify a pivot or reversal price at either a low or a high where the pressure from either supply or demand exhausts itself, depending upon whether the TD Point is a high or a low. By connecting the two most recent TD Point Lows or TD Point Highs, a mechanical method for identifying prospective price support and resistance levels is created. The critical factor in the construction of these TD Lines is the necessity to continually readjust them as new TD Points are formed and as breakouts fail to occur. The specific TD Point level may vary, subject to the degree of change in either supply or demand. Instead of relying upon the standard TD Point level 1 setting, a trader may elect to intro-

**Figure 4.1**    This chart displays both TD Point Highs (highs immediately surrounded by one or more lower highs) and TD Point Lows (lows immediately surrounded by one or more higher lows). These TD Points are connected to draw TD Lines. In this example, both Qualified (solid line) and Disqualified (dotted line) Lines appear. Note that all TD Points greater than level 1 are also level 1 TD Points, and that is why a level 6 can be connected to a level 1 whenever level 1 is selected. The solid horizontal lines identify the price objectives.

duce higher-level TD Points to arrive at long-term TD Line breakout levels and to calculate higher and lower price objectives depending upon whether the breakouts are upside or downside. In any case, if you desire to screen your TD Line selection, generally it is recommended, regardless which level is selected, that a higher-level TD Line be monitored in addition to ensure that the overall market environment is consistent with both the lower-level TD Line breakout in the respect that the higher-level TD Line downside price objective is below the lower-level TD Line price objective and that the higher-level TD Line upside price objective is above the lower-level TD Line price objective. Furthermore, by definition, TD Point levels 2, 3, 4, and so on are a TD Point level 1 as well, since the prerequisite for a TD Point level 2 requires two higher lows on each side of a bottom and two lower highs on each side of a top. Another important consideration is the possibility of a disqualified higher-level TD Line occurring subsequent to the qualified breakout of a lower-level TD Line but prior to the fulfillment of the lower-level TD Line price objective, since a position may have to be closed at that time rather than awaiting the movement of price into the price objective zone. Furthermore, if an opposing (reversal) qualified TD Line breakout occurs prior to the price objective zone, it is prudent to exit and possibly reverse direction on the breakout. Since it is instructive to retain the TD Line price objectives on a chart regardless of the fact that a contradictory breakout indication may have been generated, its trading purpose no longer exists, and consequently the objective should be ignored.

Extensive research with TD Points and TD Lines has uncovered a confirmation technique that helps perfect TD Line selection. After reviewing many charts of relatively flat TD Lines and TD Line breakouts that did not work, a common denominator emerged. Specifically, if you construct a TD Supply Line that connects successively lower TD Point highs, and this TD Line is somewhat flat, then to confirm the TD Point selection of highs, you should make certain that either the closing price of the most recent TD Point High day is below the closing price of the first (farther-left TD Point) TD Point high day or that the low of the most recent TD Point High day is below the low of the first (farther to the left) TD Point high day. Conversely, whenever you construct a TD Demand Line that connects successively higher TD Point lows, and this TD Line is relatively flat, then you should make certain that either the close of the most recent TD Point low is above the closing price of the first (farther-left TD Point) TD Point low day or that the high of the most recent TD Point low is above the high of the first (farther to the left) TD Point low day. An alternative confirmation method for a TD Supply Line could apply either successive lower lows or successive lower closes, and for a TD Demand Line, either successive higher highs or successive higher closes. Generally, TD lines are relatively steep, and the necessity for this confirmation process or condition does not exist. However, the concern arises in those instances in which the lines are relatively flat. The reason many flat trendlines fail to produce good price breakouts is because this critical confirmation process is lacking. Superficially, upsloping or downsloping lines can be drawn, but since the closes and highs or closes and lows are not confirming this interpretation, it is usually wise to disregard this questionable trendline or, more important, search for those instances in which these "unconfirmed patterns" occur simultaneously with a "disqualified" trendline breakout. It is precisely for these reasons that many of the approved indicator software packages include a selection option that requires that the closing and/or high or low prices associated with the price bars selected to construct TD Demand and TD Supply Lines be upsloping and downsloping and also to confirm the TD Lines. Figures 4.2a, b, and c illustrate this confirmation process. Figure 4.2a displays only "disqualified" TD Lines. These disqualified TD Lines do not meet even one of the qualifiers to justify intraday entry at the breakout level, and consequently trading in the direction of the breakout should be avoided. However, a trader can do the opposite and fade the breakout. In fact, I have experimented with combining disqualified

**Figure 4.2(a)**   This chart displays *only* TD Line level 1 *Disqualified* breakouts (see discussion presented in this chapter). Most TD Lines are steep, and the closes and highs/lows confirm this relationship. The two instances in which they fail to confirm are identified on the chart with *X*s. This lends credence to the possibility of a false breakout, and if by chance a Disqualified breakout is indicated at the same time, the chance is greater the breakout will fail. "Disqualified" TD Lines eventually become qualified at some point in time. Consequently, you must be careful to monitor the situation daily and follow with a tight stop loss.

**Figure 4.2(b)** The solid lines are qualified TD Lines. The horizontal lines are price objective zones identified once breakouts occurred. Often the breakout levels will be fulfilled, but in late January a price objective was generated that superseded a prior objective. In fact, the first objective was derived as a result of a breakout that was "not confirmed" since the more recent close was above the prior close (*X*). Also, many breakouts are succeeded by breakouts that occur in the other direction, thereby canceling the prior breakout and accompanying price objective.

**Figure 4.2(c)** All TD Lines presented are qualified and consequently solid. Once again, price objective zones are presented by horizontal lines. These price objectives are retained regardless of the fact that they are often reversed by a contradictory breakout, identified on the chart with an *x*.

166

breakouts and unconfirmed TD Lines, and these are identified with an $X$ on the chart. Keep in mind that disqualified TD Lines eventually become qualified, and as a result, a disqualified trade must be liquidated on the close the day of entry or be monitored closely.

Figure 4.2b and c describe qualified TD Lines, but as you can readily see, with one exception in each case, the TD Lines were confirmed. The solid lines are differentiated from the TD Lines that appear in Figure 4.2a, which are dotted since they are disqualified trades. Also presented are horizontal lines that serve as price objective areas. In many cases, these objectives are superseded by a TD Line breakout that reverses the previous TD Line breakout in the other direction.

## TD Breakout Qualifiers™

One of the features of my first book, *The New Science of Technical Analysis*, was the release of three special conditions that serve to qualify or to disqualify not only TD Line breakouts, but also TD Retracements and TD Trend Factors™, as well as other trend-following methods. This presentation was important since it attempted to filter those trading opportunities that presented themselves intraday to traders but that traders were often unwilling to take advantage of for fear that the closing price might fail to confirm the suspected intraday breakout. In order to eliminate these numerous trading forfeitures, I shared these previously undisclosed qualifiers. Since that time, these filters have been improved. In fact trading disqualified TD Lines is consistent with my particular trading style of selling into market strength and buying into market weakness. The qualifiers for an intraday upside breakout above a TD Supply Line are as follows:

1.  The close on the trading day before an upside breakout must be a down close. This implies that most traders in that market are expecting the market to move lower and will initially be skeptical of any upside breakout and, consequently, when it occurs intraday will be reluctant to enter the trade until the close approaches. At that time they likely will concede the breakout is legitimate and reverse their positions. In fact, these traders may initially sell the suspected breakout anticipating a failure, and their mistake and eventual capitulation becomes apparent into the market's close when price moves generally accelerate in the direction of the breakout.

2.  The close on the day before the upside breakout is an up close, and consequently Qualifier 1 is not active. Despite that fact, if the opening price is above the TD Line, then the dynamics of the marketplace have more than likely shifted so dramatically in favor of buyers and the upside since the previous day's close that the breakout is legitimized. *However,* two

additional conditions, not included in my previous book, must also be present to confirm Qualifier 2. First of all, the opening price must not only be above the TD Supply Line but also above the previous day's close since it is possible, if the TD Supply Line is very steep, that price can open above the line but below the previous day's close. Second, price must follow through upside by at least one or two price ticks above the opening price level since the opening could be a last gasp of demand in a price vacuum caused by the specialists or market makers, and this exhaustion would not present a buying opportunity; rather, it would coincide with a price peak.

3. Even if the close the previous trading day is up and the current day's opening price is below the TD Supply Line or fails to follow through after the open, if the current day's high is able to surpass a measure of the previous day's demand and then exceed the TD Supply Line, this demand should be sufficient to justify an intraday upside breakout, which will be confirmed for a conventional chartist by a closing price above the TD Supply Line. Calculate the previous day's expression of demand or buying by subtracting the difference between the previous day's closing price and that same day's true low (that same day's low or the previous trading day's close, whichever is less). Then add that value to the previous day's close to identify the level at which the buying pressure expressed that trading day will be replicated the current trading day. If this value is beneath the TD Supply Line and subsequent to price exceeding this measurement of demand and then exceeding the TD Supply Line, there is sufficient buying to justify intraday entry on the upside breakout. However, if the TD Supply Line breakout upside occurs prior to the measure of demand exceeding the previous day's level, Qualifier 3 is not fulfilled.

4. A potential new Qualifier that I am currently researching for inclusion to the Qualifier set relates the true price range the day before a breakout to the breakout level. Specifically, if that price range is doubled and the breakout level added to the previous trading day's close for an upside breakout (subtracted from the previous trading day's close for a downside breakout) exceeds these price levels, then the breakouts are disqualified. Otherwise they are qualified. Note that this is preliminary work, however.

To qualify intraday entry at downside breakout levels of TD Demand Lines, reverse these conditions. Specifically, Qualifier 1 specifies that the close on the trading day before the downside breakout be an up close, and consequently, the subsequent downside breakout through the TD Demand Line on the following trading day will likely be viewed suspiciously by traders. Qualifier 2 requires that the open of the current trading day be less than the TD Supply Line, less than the previous day's closing price, and price must trade at least one or two ticks below the opening price level. Qualifier 3 provides that the current day's selling pressure surpass the previous day's measure of selling, which is calculated as the difference between the previous day's true high (that same day's high or the previous trading day's close, whichever is greater) minus the close that same day subtracted from that same day's close, and subsequently, the current day's low must decline below the TD Demand Line. This breakout below the TD Demand Line must occur after the level established by the previous trading day's selling pressure is first exceeded. Just as in the case of an intraday upside breakout of a TD Supply Line, a breakout downside below a TD Demand Line can be qualified by any one of these conditions, and not all three are required.

When introducing an individual or a group to my methodology to construct a trendline, I describe and discuss the various breakout qualifiers and ask them if certain TD Line breakouts could be taken intraday. If a particular pending breakout does not meet the requirements of either Qualifiers 1, 2, or 3, generally I ask them what trade exists. The unanimous response is usually that it is prudent not to take any trade whatsoever since no qualifier has been met, which is incorrect. Then I demonstrate to them that there is a great trading opportunity and that is to trade in the opposite direction of the breakout—in other words, if none of the qualifiers are met, then instead of buying an upside breakout, do the reverse and sell at the suspected false breakout price. If a downside breakout occurs and no qualifiers are fulfilled, then buy the suspected false breakout. It may be difficult to fight the flow of activity and sentiment by trading against the prevailing trend and buying into suspected price exhaustion, but great opportunities and price reversals exist. The only requirement is that the entry be exited on the close that same day or that the TD Line be extended into the future to protect against recording a subsequent breakout that is qualified. For this reason, a trader should install a tight stop-loss or profit level in case price reverses and exceeds either what will become a qualified TD Line or the price range of the entry day. Therefore you should change the computer setting if the TD Line selection is programmed from "end at first" to "end at qualified" to protect from just such unplanned events if you elect to remain in a disqualified TD Line breakout trade, since eventually it will meet the requirements for qualification. These disqualified trading opportunities should be either exited on the close or followed with a tight stop loss.

Figures 4.3 and 4.4 present a series of Disqualified level 1 TD Line breakouts. Other examples of TD Lines with Qualified breakouts and accompanying price objectives appear on Figure 4.5. Figure 4.6 displays TD Line level 1 Qualified (solid) and Disqualified (dotted) lines.

Market price movements above and below a TD Line are symmetrical, and oftentimes when price penetrates and exceeds a qualified TD Supply Line upside, the extreme price movement beneath the TD Line to the value of the TD Line immediately above it on that same day is reproduced above the line when added to the TD Line breakout level. When price penetrates and exceeds a qualified TD Demand Line downside, the extreme price

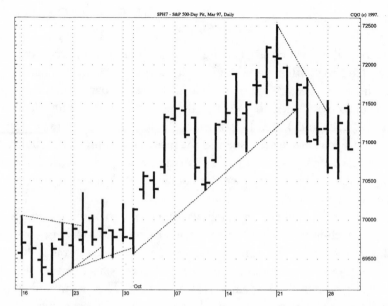

**Figure 4.3** Only the disqualified TD Lines are displayed on this chart. Note that in each instance, none of three Qualifiers were met, and consequently price reversed at least on that day. Certainly the outlook for most traders was for a continuation of the short-term move, and since they were already positioned for this opportunity, figuratively speaking, the last short-term buyer or seller was already in the market and the trend was exhausted. Furthermore, it is recommended exiting on the close or a tight stop loss or an awareness of the breakout level of a subsequent qualified TD Line.

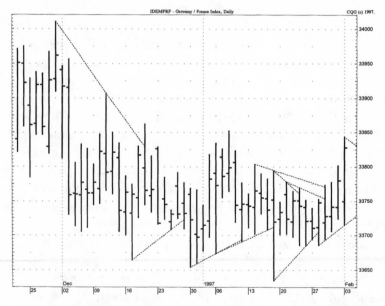

**Figure 4.4** This chart demonstrates the application of disqualified TD Lines level 1 to the German mark–French franc cross rates. It is a testimony to the effectiveness of this technique to see that all price penetrations, whether upside or downside breakouts, repelled price progress and were great opportunities to do the reverse. Keep in mind that eventually the disqualified breakouts will become qualified, and consequently either a trader should exit on the close or follow with a tight stop loss.

**Figure 4.5** The various TD Line level 1 Qualified breakouts are identified on this chart. The price objective zones are presented as well. Note that the objective level in late December was hit precisely.

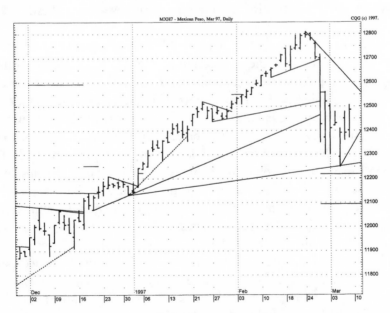

**Figure 4.6** This chart displays both Qualified and Disqualified level 1 TD Lines. A penetration filter of three price ticks was applied since this market trades relatively thin. As you can easily see, on both December 13 and January 17, dotted or Disqualified TD Lines identified the precise reaction lows. The solid or Qualified lines identified breakouts within the ongoing trend.

movement above the TD Line to the value of the TD Line immediately below it on that same day is reproduced beneath the line when subtracted from the TD Line breakout level. This price objective is valid or active until either fulfilled or reversed by a Qualified TD Line breakout in the other direction or until a Disqualified breakout occurs, which will reverse the trade. The description of the three types of price projections is presented in the discussion of execution settings that follow, and the previous charts displaying Qualified TD Line breakouts display the price objectives. Obviously, Disqualified breakouts do not include an accompanying price objective, since the breakout is not qualified and consequently does not produce one.

## Execution Settings

It is not the object of this book to provide you with fixed settings for TD Lines or any of the other indicators presented here for that matter. Hopefully, you will experiment with and customize the possible selections to fit your specific trading style, needs, and expectations. The following settings have proven to be effective, but they are not necessarily the best.

1. To construct a TD Line, level 1 TD Points should be selected first. This process includes the connection of the two most recent level 1 TD Points. Although this is not a requirement, nor is it essential since at times it limits the number of TD Line opportunities, in order to define the overall market environment as either uptrending, downtrending, or neutral, some higher-level TD Line should also be constructed (e.g., level 5, 8, 13). Provided that the upside breakout objective of the higher-level TD Line is greater than the price objective of an upside TD Line level 1 upside objective, you should be trading in the direction of the prevailing trend, which in this instance is up. Conversely, to be certain you are trading in the context of the prevailing down trend, the downside breakout objective of the higher-level TD Line must be below the TD Line level 1 downside breakout objective (the setting for the level appears beneath the column entitled Level). A good choice is to use TD Point level 1, and on occasion also use a higher level of 5 or 8 to make certain that the higher-level TD Line price objective exceeds the TD Line level 1 price objective.

2. To ensure that TD Points are defined properly, use only true lows and true highs rather than chart lows and chart highs—all price gaps caused by a current day's high or low failing to intersect the previous day's closing price are consequently filled (two options are available in the TD Point (TDP) column. They are True and Chart). Using True is preferred.

3. To gain an overall perspective of all trends within the market, a display of both TD Demand Lines (upsloping TD Line) and TD Supply Lines (downsloping TD Line) can be displayed. Either one separately can also be

shown (the selection options appear in the column Display row), but displaying both is preferred.

4. To specify which TD Points to connect for both TD Supply and Demand Lines, various price selections can made. A good choice is highs for TD Supply lines and lows for TD Demand lines (both appear in columns entitled Supply and Demand).

5. To indicate how many times a specific TD Point can be used to construct a TD Line, a selection must be made. You may prefer a limit of 8 to 10, although the likelihood of using the same TD Point this many times is remote (the number of possible times a TD Point can be used is indicated in the box in the Connect column).

6. To construct TD Lines from TD Points extending more than 200 trading days is not as effective as those drawn from shorter time intervals due to the market's tendency to experience memory lapse as time passes (the number of days surveyed to draw TD Lines is entered in the Lookback column in the TD Line Trend row). Consequently, generally concentrate upon shorter time intervals of 25 to 50 days maximum for TD Lines of level 1; however, for higher levels the Lookback will increase accordingly.

7. To perfect intraday breakouts, qualifiers are introduced. If *any* and *not* necessarily all of the qualifiers exist, intraday entry is justified, but if none exist then *no* entry in the direction of the trend is justified and, if Disqualified, it may in this instance be prudent to take the trading position opposite to what may appear to be correct—in other words, fade (do the reverse) the intraday breakout trade that would have occurred had any of the TD Line qualifiers been present. Qualifiers *a*, *b*, and *c* appear in the Qualifier column.

a. Qualifier *a* requires a close one trading day prior to the TD Line breakout less than the close two trading days ago to justify entry intraday on an upside breakout above a declining TD Line (supply line) and requires a close one trading day prior to the TD Line breakout greater than the close two trading days ago to justify entry intraday on a downside breakout below an advancing TD Line (demand line). The logic associated with Qualifier 1 correctly predicting whether the intraday breakout will be valid relates to the fact that false breakouts are more likely to occur if the close the trading day before an upside breakout is up versus the prior day's close or if the close the trading day before a downside breakout is down versus the prior day's close, since most traders have already positioned themselves in anticipation of this event occurring. Consequently, if traders have already taken their positions expecting a breakout, their activity is complete. However, if the close the trading day before an upside intraday breakout above a TD Supply line is a down close versus the prior day's close or if the close the day before a downside breakout below a TD Demand line is an up close versus the prior day's close, then not only is the general expectation for the continuation of the decline or advance in line with the previous trading day's closing price change, but also if price does breakout intraday then there is a degree of skepticism initially associated with the breakout, which in turn helps to propel prices further.

b. Qualifier *b* requires not only an opening price above a TD Supply Line or below a TD Demand Line, but also requires an open above the previous day's close in the case of a TD Supply Line or below the previous day's close in the case of a TD Demand Line, as well as that price follow through in the direction of the opening breakout by a couple of price ticks above the open for a TD Supply Line upside breakout and below the open for a TD Demand Line downside breakout.

c. Qualifier *c* requires that the TD Supply Line be greater than the difference between the previous trading day's close and that same trading day's true low (that day's low or the previous day's close, whichever is less) and that the TD Demand Line be less than the difference between the previous trading day's close and that same trading day's true high (that day's high or the previous day's close, whichever is greater). If the TD Supply Line or TD Demand Line, whichever the case may be, is subsequently penetrated intraday, then that implies the demand or supply not only exceeds the previous day's expression of demand and supply but that the market is sufficiently strong enough that, once it exceeds the TD Line, it should continue to trend in that direction as well.

To summarize, experience indicates that only one of the three qualifiers be active at any one time. Generally, markets do the unexpected, and that is either (1) break out in one direction after a close was recorded the previous trading day in the other direction, (2) gap above a declining TD Line and the previous day's close or gap below an advancing TD Line and the previous day's close, as well as demonstrate some minor price follow-through in the direction of the breakout after the open, or (3) exceed the previous day's expression of demand for a TD Demand Line breakout or exceed the previous day's expression of supply for a TD Supply Line breakout, *then* subsequently record a breakout above the TD Supply Line or below the TD Demand Line.

8. To enhance the potential of a valid intraday breakout, you can add additional price tick requirements to Qualifiers *b* and *c* above—the box appears in the Qpen (Qualified price penetration) column. One suggestion is to increase or decrease, depending upon whether the move is upside or downside, each Qualifier by two ticks to reduce the likelihood of rounding off decimals or introducing Qualifier error in the direction of conservatism.

9. To invalidate or Cancel a TD Line Qualified breakout entry, one of the three following conditions must occur the following day:

a. The open on the trading day following an upside breakout exceeds downside the TD Line that was penetrated upside the previous trading day, or the open on the trading day following a downside breakout exceeds upside the TD Line that was penetrated downside the previous trading day—box 1 in Qcan (Cancellation) column.

b. The open on the trading day following an upside breakout is less than the previous trading day's close and price closes below the declining TD Line that was broken the previous trading day, or the open on the day following a downside breakout is greater than the previous day's close and price closes above the advancing TD Line that was broken the previous trading day—box 2 in Qcan (Cancellation) column.

c. The high on the trading day after an upside breakout fails to exceed the breakout day's high, or the low on the trading day after a downside breakout fails to exceed the breakout day's low—box 3 in Qcan (Cancellation) column.

A good choice may be to select and activate all three cancellations, but there may be instances where you want to turn off option *c*.

10. To invalidate a TD Line Disqualified breakout entry, the three conditions in item 9 must be reversed, since you are performing the same function, but in reverse. That is, if all three conditions are not met, then the cancellation of the Disqualified TD Line breakout does not exist—boxes 1, 2, and 3 in Dcan (Cancellation) column. You may prefer not to check any of these boxes, since Disqualified breakouts are usually active only for the trading day on which the TD Line is penetrated; if you elect to hold a position any longer, you must closely follow the trade with a stop loss since Disqualified breakouts eventually become qualified and active on a subsequent trading day by fulfilling at least one Qualifier.

11. To suspend the TD Line after the "First breakout" attempt, whether Qualified or Disqualified, this box must indicate the selection of either "End at first" or "End at qualified." A good choice would be to always use "End at first" for Disqualified TD Lines and most of the time for Qualified TD Lines. The reason to use "End at first" is because Disqualified TD Lines eventually become Qualified on a subsequent day provided at least one of the Qualifiers is met and no subsequent TD Point has been formed—this selection appears in the Parameter column.

12. To specify which of three methods to use to approximate breakout price objectives, the Level column is filled with either Type 1, 2, or 3. *Type 1* is the standard and most common setting. It calculates the difference between the extreme intraday low price and the TD Supply Line value immediately above it and adds that difference to the upside breakout, or it calculates the difference between the extreme intraday high price and the TD Demand Line value immediately below it and subtracts that difference from the downside breakout. *Type 2* calculates the difference between the intraday low of the lowest close day beneath the TD Supply Line and the

value of the TD Supply Line immediately above it and then adds this difference to the upside TD Supply Line breakout price and calculates the difference between the extreme intraday high of the highest close above the TD
Demand Line and the TD Demand Line immediately beneath it and subtracts this difference from the TD Demand Line breakout price. *Type 3*
reverses the selections of Type 2 by calculating the differences between the
closes of the intraday low and high below and above the TD Line and then
adds or subtracts this value to and from the breakout price. The preferred
choice is Type 1 and I rarely use Types 2 and 3 which are more conservative;

13. To display both Qualified (solid line) and Disqualified (dotted line)
TD Lines at the same time is preferable (Display column). Occasionally you
may elect to show one or the other because not all computer printers differentiate between dotted and solid lines.

14. To increase the price objective calculated based upon the breakout
of the TD Line by various percentages of the Type 1 value, a percentage can
be introduced in the Parameter column—a good choice is 100 percent, but
on occasion you may want to increase it by multiples of 100 percent, since
the market has a tendency to advance and decline in incremental bursts.

15. To raise the TD Supply Line or to lower the TD Demand Line by
a prescribed number of ticks to be more conservative regarding breakouts,
the Breakout selection is adjusted accordingly—normally you would enter
"1" (or "2") tick(s).

16. To require the breakout to exceed the TD Line by $x$ number of
ticks, the Breakout selection is indicated with a number other than "0"—a
good choice might be "1" (or "2") tick(s).

17. To include custom Qualifiers, you can create them by developing
them. No additional qualifiers are necessary at this time.

Some readers of my first book have conducted their own research on
the indicators presented there. Several individuals experimented with variations of TD Points, TD Lines, and TD Gaps. Surprisingly, they indepen-
dently developed a technique I had researched many years earlier. Although
their research did not include breakout qualifiers and price projection techniques, nevertheless it was refreshing to witness their creativity. These individuals exhibited the contagious enthusiasm, interest in experimenting, and
propensity to perfect their ideas that I hope may be the legacy of my books.
Specifically, by connecting a TD Point with the first subsequent price gap
(price high failing to intersect the previous day's low upside or price low failing to intersect the previous day's high downside) or price lap (price high failing to intersect the previous day's close or price low failing to intersect the
previous day's close) by means of a line, a variation of a TD Line can be constructed, called a TD Line Gap™. Research indicates the construction and
the interpretation assigned to these TD Line Gaps (trendline gap lines) are
identical to those applicable to conventional TD Lines. Figure 4.7 describes

the construction of a TD Line Gap for the March 1997 German Bund. The methodology used for drawing the TD Line Gap originates with a TD Point, which is in turn connected to the nearest subsequent price gap or lap. The breakout calculation and qualifier prerequisites are the same as the standard TD Lines. In one case, one additional price objective greater than the first projection is included on the chart as well. To accomplish this, the calculated objective was multiplied by two times rather than the standard one time. My recommendation is to connect the TD Point low with the subsequent low recorded the day of the upside gap or, conversely, the TD Point high with the subsequent high recorded the day of the downside gap.

As this discussion illustrates, an analytical technique as mundane as trendlines can be massaged and molded into an objective, mechanical method of identifying trend reversals, establishing and distinguishing between qualified and disqualified price breakout levels, and calculating price objectives. Obviously, most conventional trendline approaches are reactive, imprecise, discretionary, and deficient on a number of other counts. On the other hand, TD Lines are defined and sufficiently clear so as to provide not only the traditional market trend follower with a practical methodology for identifying price breakouts, but they are also capable of assisting the contrarian trader who is inclined to sell strength and to buy weakness to identify successfully Disqualified breakout levels, which are opportunities to

**Figure 4.7**  The TD Line Gap breakouts with price objectives are marked on this chart. The technique used to construct the TD Lines Gaps requires a TD point that is subsequently connected to the closest price gap or lap. The method for projection, as well as the Qualifiers, is the same as for conventional TD Lines. Price projections have also been presented.

**Figure 4.8** The TD Supply Line level 12 broke out with a price gap upside on September 12. The upper price projection displayed is two times the standard price objective and was fulfilled on February 18. All intermediate TD Line level 1 Supply Lines with a price objective below the 100% or standard price objective shown by the lower horizontal line on the chart should be hit, since they are contained by higher-level (level 12) price objective.

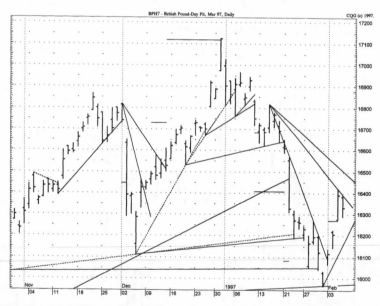

**Figure 4.9** The dotted TD Lines are disqualified, and price movement should be repelled from these levels for at least one trading day or until they become qualified. The solid TD Lines are qualified. Although the breakout that occurred in early December was qualified, it was reversed by a qualified upside breakout the following trading day. The price objectives are retained, however, on the chart, despite the fact they are no longer active when reversed. The upside price objective zone in late December was fulfilled precisely.

act against the emotionally charged and psychologically driven trend-following crowd. In conjunction with TD Sequential and TD Combo Setup and Countdown completions, many traders use both Qualified and Disqualified TD Lines to fine-tune low-risk entries. For example, once either TD Sequential or TD Combo Setup or Countdown are completed, a penetration of a qualified TD Line will confirm suspected low-risk entry zones. Furthermore, a breakout of a disqualified TD Line prior to completion of Setup or Countdown will identify levels from which to operate against the trend. Finally, as you can see, by combining TD Lines with the various other indicators, the chance of increasing the odds of trading success is enhanced considerably.

# Chapter

# 5

# TD Retracements

*Observation:* A number of years ago I developed a mechanical method to calculate retracement projections. Unlike many market letter and tout sheet writers who are notorious for identifying a series of retracement levels off a price bottom or a top, thereby not only increasing their odds of accuracy, but also concealing their apparent confusion as to which of these various price levels to use to calculate the price targets, this technique objectively selected the key price levels. Because this process was totally mechanical, the results could be reproduced regardless of when or by whom it was conducted. My comfort and satisfaction with this process increased markedly when this same retracement technique was applied to calculate retracement levels for non-market-related statistical information. Specifically, I applied retracement analysis on obscure statistical data, such as the migration trends of geese to Horicon Marsh in Wisconsin, the population growth of a large metropolitan city, economic statistics, and the support level for a fund manager's assets under management. Not surprisingly, this methodology worked well, producing accurate results for all of the unrelated, nonmarket samples.

## TD Relative Retracement™

Many traders rely upon retracements to project potential entry or support and resistance levels. It is amazing to me how convenient it is for market letter writers to arbitrarily calculate a series of retracement levels and, once one prediction proves accurate, to extol its accuracy and then conveniently ignore the numerous other projections that failed miserably in the process. This epitome of disregard for consistent methodology was found in one market letter writer's forecast and his accompanying presentation of a number of retracement levels to support his predictions. In a subsequent letter, only the correct retracement projection was presented—the additional incorrect ones vanished entirely from the accompanying chart. This practice seems to be widespread. If a purely mechanical technique were to be implemented to calculate these projections, however, artistic license would not become a factor or an issue. No excuse would exist for the writer to avoid the admission of a mistake, since there would be a consistent, reproducible methodology to replace the confusing, unscientific approaches most traders use to calculate retracement levels. They could not select one retracement level one week and a totally different level the following week for the same price chart over the same time period. Retracement levels should be calculated *objectively*. Due to various considerations such as price patterns and relationships between price levels, retracements are calculated differently depending upon how each is qualified. The first and most common retracement technique is TD Relative Retracement.

My various retracement approaches date back to 1971. At that time, I was introduced to Elliott wave analysis and Fibonacci numbers. Other than possibly artists and mathematicians, few individuals were aware of either the wave concept, the "golden mean" (61.8 percent ratio dominant throughout nature), or the Fibonacci number series. From the archives of the public library I retrieved Elliott's seminal piece *Nature's Law* in order to familiarize myself with his concepts. From the little information gleaned there, I made adaptations and then researched and experimented further. Since the application of these principles to the markets and price behavior appeared totally subjective, it was impossible to identify a definitive process for the selection of which precise retracement ratios to apply, as well as the correct calculation procedures required to arrive at the retracement objectives. Consequently, it was possible to develop various mechanical approaches to select retracement price levels and retracement ratios. One such technique is an objective process of identifying a recent price low, referring to the left of the chart to the last time price traded below that level, and then selecting the highest high in between those two points in order to establish a reference price level, called the TD Critical Price™. To project upside retracement or resistance levels, merely calculate the difference between these two prices—the "TD Critical Price" and the recent price low—and then multiply this value by the various ratios. The procedure is simple, mechanical, consistent, and universally applicable to all markets. Conversely, to project downside support levels, conduct the same process only in reverse: Identify a recent price high, refer to the left of the chart to the last time price traded above that level, and then select the lowest low in between those two points to establish a reference price level called the "Critical Price." Next, calculate the difference between the recent high and the low, then multiply that difference by the various ratio factors to arrive at support levels. The Fibonacci retracement ratios or factors of 0.382, 0.618, 1.382, 1.618, 2.236, 2.618, 3.618, and so on were selected, and an original retracement level, called the "TD Magnet Price™," was introduced. Most recently published technical analysis research books devote a section to the significance of the "golden mean" and the Fibonacci number series, as well as their prominence and dominance in nature. Examples include the angle of the outer walls of the Egyptian pyramids and the conversion factor from miles to kilometers. These ratios are applied within the context of a unique, mechanical methodology of calculating retracement levels. This retracement process is called TD Relative Retracement because it relates the current price low to the last time price traded at a lower low, using the intervening highest price high (TD Critical Price) to calculate upside retracement levels, and because it relates the current price high to the last time price traded at a higher high, using the intervening lowest price low (TD Critical Price) to calculate downside retracement levels.

A major conflict exists between a universally accepted belief regarding price retracements and what in actuality occurs in market price activity. Research revealed that the calculation of both upside and downside price projection levels is accomplished by using the Fibonacci ratios and the retracement methodology just described—with one major exception. Contrary to the widely held belief that price movement would eventually find resistance upside and support downside at the extreme intraday low and high TD Critical Price levels once the 50 or 61.8 percent retracement levels were exceeded, in actuality price movement behaved quite differently. Specifically, there existed a more valid retracement level than the conventional, widely followed expectation of a full 100 percent upside and downside retracement objective, and its implementation produced a much better record of success. By close inspection, you are able to see that there exists an obvious tendency for price to gravitate to the intraday high day's close *not* high for upside retracement moves and intraday low day's close *not* low for downside retracement moves. Consequently, this key retracement level—the TD Critical Price high or low day's closing price level—is called the TD Magnet Price. This statement will obviously contradict the expectations of most traders who apply retracement techniques to their work, since most traders operate under the mistaken notion that price will trade and find support or resistance at the extreme intraday high or low. The ratio series presented here is comprehensive. It is as follows: 0.382, 0.618, Magnet Price—the intraday high day's close or intraday low day's close or the Critical Price day's close—1.382, 1.618, 2.236, 3.618, 4.618, and so on. These factors are multiplied by the difference between the high and low and added to the low or subtracted from the high, depending upon whether an upside or downside retracement is calculated. To perfect intraday entry for suspected price breakouts, you may find success by applying the same Qualifiers used with TD Lines to TD Relative Retracements. Familiarize yourself with these Qualifiers, which appear in Chapter 4, as well as in the following discussion and in the parameter setting discussion.

## Qualifiers

One of the features of my first book, *The New Science of Technical Analysis*, was the release of three special breakout qualifiers that can be applied not only to TD Line breakouts, but also to TD Retracements and TD Trend Factors, as well as other trend-following methods. This information was important since it attempted to filter those trading opportunities that presented themselves intraday but which traders were often unwilling to take advantage of for fear that the closing price might fail to confirm the suspected intraday breakout. In order to eliminate these numerous trading forfeitures, I shared these previously undisclosed qualifiers. Since that time, I have improved upon these filters and recommended other methods to benefit by their installation. For example, you may prefer to trade disqualified TD retracement breakouts, since it is consistent with the recommended practice of selling into market strength and buying into market weakness. The qualifiers for an intraday upside breakout above a TD Relative Retracement level include the following:

1.  The close on the day before the breakout must be a down close. This suggests that most traders in that market are expecting a move downside and, as a result, will initially be skeptical of any upside breakout and when it occurs intraday will be reluctant to enter the trade until the close approaches and they are confident that the breakout is legitimate. In fact, these traders are more likely to sell the suspected breakout anticipating a failure.

2.  The close the day before the breakout is an up close, and consequently, Qualifier 1 is not applicable. Despite that fact, if the opening price is above the TD Relative retracement level, then the dynamics of the marketplace have more than likely shifted so dramatically in favor of buyers and the upside since the previous day's close that the breakout is legitimized. *However,* one additional condition must also occur to confirm Qualifier 2. Price must trade higher than the opening price level by at least one or two ticks. Otherwise the opening gap could merely be a last gasp of demand caused by the specialists or market makers, and would not represent a buying opportunity, but would coincide with a price peak.

3.  Even if the close the previous trading day is an up close and the current day's opening price is below the TD Relative Retracement level, if the

current day's price activity is able first to surpass a measure of the previous day's buying pressure or demand and then subsequently exceed the TD Relative Retracement level, the buying should be sufficient to justify an intraday breakout. Measure the previous trading day's demand or buying by subtracting the difference between the previous day's closing price and that same day's true low (that day's low or previous trading day's close, whichever is less) and then adding that value to the previous trading day's close to identify the level at which that buying pressure will be replicated. If this value is beneath the TD Relative Retracement level and price is able to exceed both levels, there is sufficient buying to justify intraday entry on the upside breakout. However if the retracement level breakout upside occurs prior to the measure of demand exceeding the previous day's level, Qualifier 3 is not fulfilled.

4.  A potential new Qualifier that I am currently researching for inclusion to the Qualifier set relates the true price range the day before a breakout to the breakout level. Specifically, if that price range is doubled and the breakout level added to the previous trading day's close for an upside breakout (subtracted from the previous trading day's close for a downside breakout) exceeds these price levels, then the breakouts are disqualified. Otherwise they are qualified. Note that this is preliminary work, however.

To qualify intraday entry at downside TD Relative Retracement breakout levels, these same conditions are reversed. Specifically, Qualifier 1 provides that the previous day record an up close, and consequently, the subsequent downside breakout through the TD Relative Retracement level on the following day will likely be viewed suspect. Qualifier 2 requires that the open be less than the TD Relative Retracement level and trade at least one or two ticks below the opening price level. Qualifier 3 specifies that the current day's selling pressure surpass the previous day's measure of selling, which is calculated as the difference between the previous day's true high (that day's high or the previous trading day's close, whichever is greater) minus the close that same trading day subtracted from that trading day's close, and subsequently, the current day's low must decline below the TD Relative Retracement level. Just as in the case of an intraday upside breakout of a TD Relative Retracement level, a breakout downside below a TD Relative Retracement level can be qualified by any one of these conditions, and not all three are required.

Due to their significance, it is important to reiterate these trading filters or TD Retracement Qualifiers. The first condition relates to those instances in which intraday price movement either exceeds an upside or a downside retracement level, but fails do so on a closing price basis. Generally, a trader is able to anticipate the occurrence of this event if none of the three breakout qualifiers are fulfilled. However, if *any one* of the three qualifiers are met, then intraday entry is qualified:

1. A down close the day before an upside breakout above the TD Relative Retracement level
2. An open above the retracement level with at least a one- or two-tick price follow-through above the opening
3. Buying pressure or demand exceeding the previous day's level and subsequently the current day's intraday high price exceeding the TD Relative Retracement level.

Calculate the previous day's expression of demand or buying pressure by subtracting the difference between the previous day's closing price and that same day's true low; then add that value to the previous day's close to identify when the current day's buying pressure will replicate that demand. If this buying pressure value is beneath the retracement level and both are exceeded, sufficient demand exists to justify intraday low-risk entry. Conversely, to determine whether price is likely to close below downside retracement or support levels, any one of the following three qualifiers must be met:

1. An up close recorded the day before a downside breakout below the TD Relative Retracement level
2. An open below the retracement level with at least a one- or two-tick price follow-through downside below the opening
3. Selling pressure or supply exceeding the previous day's level and subsequently the current day's intraday low price exceeding the retracement level.

Calculate the previous day's expression of supply or selling pressure by subtracting from the previous day's close the difference between the previous day's true high and that same day's close to identify when the current day's selling pressure will replicate that supply. If this selling pressure value is above the retracement level and both are exceeded, sufficient supply exists to justify intraday low-risk entry.

Figures 5.1 through 5.14 illustrate TD Relative Retracement with numerous examples.

*Observations:* There are other retracement relationships that serve to complement those just presented. Provided a high exceeds an upside retracement level and closes greater than the previous trading day's close or a low exceeds a downside retracement level and closes less than the previous trading day's close, but in either case the close fails to close above the upside or below the downside retracement level, then price can be expected generally to rally or price can be expected to decline (whichever the case might be) one-half the distance between the failed retracement level and the next retracement level. For example, one-half the distance between the 0.382 and

**Figure 5.1** This chart of the S&P March futures contract displays three TD Relative Retracement calculations—one upside in mid-December and two downside, one in late December and one in early February. Two trading days after the December low, the market opened above the 38.2% retracement level and made its intraday low precisely at that level. It closed on the 61.8% level, and one and four trading days later price reversed precisely at the Magnet price level where the disqualified breakout indication appeared. The subsequent decline bottomed exactly at the Magnet price, and this low was coincident with a disqualified breakout indication, which implied a downside breakout failure. Also, two retracements in one day occurred at that time. The later decline also bottomed precisely at the Magnet price, and more than one retracement in one day was recorded at that time as well indicating price exhaustion and a trend reversal. Note that the price levels used to calculate retracements were defined by referring to the left of the chart to the last time price traded at an equivalent level and then using the TD Critical price between these levels.

**Figure 5.1(a)** This 60-minute snapshot of the S&P March contract demonstrates the applicability of TD Relative Retracements to intraday price activity, as well as long-term periods. See how well the TD Magnet Price resisted the upside movement in both January and February and how precise both the TD Magnet Price low identification and the double retracement projection in one price bar in late February were.

**Figure 5.1(b)** See how well the disqualified breakout in mid-December at the Magnet Price identified the top in late December. Likewise the January 2 low was coincident with both the Magnet Price and a double retracement in one trading day, and the February high met resistance at the disqualified 2.618 level. Furthermore, this occurred at the same time as a TD Sequential low-risk sell indication.

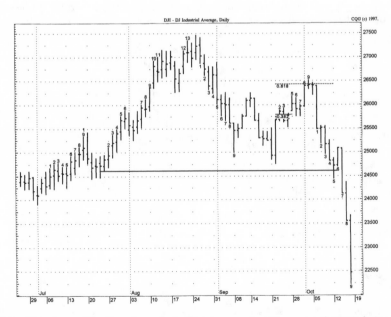

**Figure 5.2** This chart of the Dow Jones Industrial Average includes not only TD Relative Retracement levels, but also TD Sequential and TDST. Note the dotted TD Relative Retracement 0.618 level indicates that the successive breakout was not qualified, and as a result, price should fail at that level. Also, a sell Setup coincided with this failure and supported the possibility of failure. Subsequently, the TDST level was broken on day 5 of the buy Setup, and this breakdown was a prelude to the 1987 stock market crash, which was initially identified by the TD Sequential 9-13 indication of high risk in August.

**Figure 5.3** This chart is instructive on a number of different indicator levels. Specifically, last October this futures expiration was thinly traded and a 9-13 TD Sequential high-risk Countdown occurred at the peak price. Subsequently, a buy Setup occurred, which failed to break the TDST level that was considerably lower, suggesting that the price decline was merely a reaction in an uptrend. Then a sell Setup was recorded at the high day. Coincidentally, the other contracts of other energy components generated TD Sequential Countdowns at that same time, thereby confirming a potential price top. TD Relative Retracements identified potential support levels at the 0.382 and 0.618 retracement areas. Note the 0.618 was violated two times on a closing basis, but both times the following trading day's opening price gapped above that level consistent with the TD Critical Qualifier. Finally, TD Trend Factor identified the first support level at 0.9444 on the chart, and price gapped downside and ultimately found support at the third TD Trend Factor level, never trading below it, thereby confirming an advance of the TD Relative Retracement level.

**Figure 5.4** Note the TD Combo 9-13 at the high close in December. The 38.2% TD Relative Retracement level was exceeded, and Qualifier 2 was fulfilled, indicating a further decline to the 61.8% retracement level that was hit in late December. A rally ensued and two retracement levels were exceeded for the first time the first week of January, which identified the exhaustion of the upside move. See that a 100% retracement objective was not met as most timers generally expect. Subsequently, price declined both below the 61.8% level the first day of February and once again four trading days later. Finally, the TDST level was broken downside in mid-February, indicating that TD Combo should continue through Countdown completion.

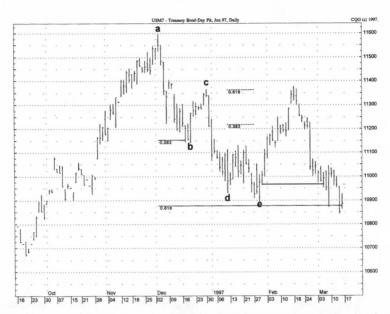

**Figure 5.5** The TD Relative Retracement from point *a* found 0.382 initial support two trading days prior to point *b*, since the break to that level was disqualified. Subsequently, an equal leg downside (*c* to *d*) comparable in price distance from leg *a* to *b* was recorded. Usually, 61.8% rallies occur off the low of the most recent second leg, and that's exactly what happened. Additionally, drawing a diagonal line from *a* to *b* and an identical price/time line from *c* to *e* identifies point *e* as the terminus of the most recent decline. The first March decline to the 61.8% level was disqualified, and price rallied. The second penetration was qualified, however. Furthermore, the TDST level was the precise February highest close, and the March decline broke the TDST downside.

**Figure 5.6** The TD Relative Retracement level of 38.2% proved to be resistance in February, and the 61.8% retracement level identified the price exhaustion in July. Note the two lows in January and November were TD Sequential 9-13 bottoms, and the intervening TD Sequential high in June included the option "ignore smaller true high/low."

**189**

**Figure 5.7** The TD Relative Retracements in late June, August, October, and January were upside resistance and price exhaustion levels. The downside retracement levels in December and January were levels of support. Also, the 9-13 TD Sequential low-risk bottom occurred the first week of January precisely at the Magnet level. In order to make the identification of the retracement levels more obvious, the TD Sequential Setups have been removed from the chart and only the Countdown is displayed.

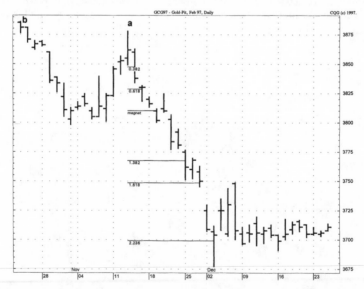

**Figure 5.8** TD Relative Retracement requires that to establish a high as a valid reference, it should be related to the last time price traded at a higher price level—in other words, relate one to the other (point *a* to *b*). This example is instructive since it identifies a series of TD Relative Retracement levels. The first downside breakout (0.382) was preceded by an up close. Consequently, the break was qualified. The 0.618 break was not qualified the first day it occurred, and price rallied into the close. The next day it was qualified, and the following trading day, which recorded an open below the Magnet price as well (Qualifier 2). The 1.382 fulfilled Qualifier 3, and the 1.618 was qualified. However, the 2.236 level did not meet any qualifier, and price held at that level. When it did close lower four trading days later and it was not qualified, price quickly adjusted the next trading day by gapping back above the retracement level—TD Critical Qualifier.

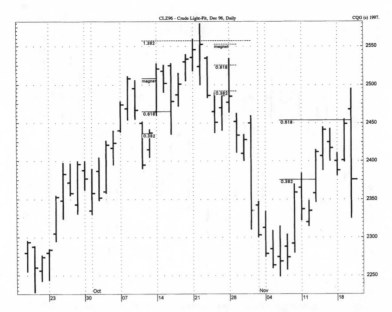

**Figure 5.9** This chart illustrates a number of TD Relative Retracement levels. The upside move on October 14 traversed two retracement levels—0.618 and the Magnet—for the first time since the low on October 10, suggesting price exhaustion. Both five and six trading days later the breakouts above the 1.382 level were disqualified and predicted price failure. On October 28, two retracements in one trading day occurred again. Off of the November 6 bottom, price failed at the 0.382 level. The breakout was not qualified, and it ran precisely into the 0.618 retracement level six trading days later.

**Figure 5.10** The October 10 TD Relative Retracement upside indicated a failure on October 21 due to the fact the breakout was disqualified. On October 28 Qualifier 2 was fulfilled; however, the TD Critical Qualifier canceled the breakout on the opening the next trading day. On November 6 the breakout was disqualified and two retracements were exceeded the previous trading day. Ultimately, the 2.618 retracement level provided resistance to the rally. The advance off the December 5 low failed on a disqualified move to the Magnet Price level, and the December 9 low was exactly the 0.382 level. The TD Trend Factor projection off of the high was hit precisely on December 5.

**Figure 5.11** The price distance from the December 3 high to the December 6 low was equal to the price decline from December 10 high to the December 16 low. Generally, after a two-equal-leg decline, a 0.618 retracement occurs. Also, the diagonal price/time comparison is equal. Included are TD Retracement Arcs, which identified the December 26 price failure and the January 5 breakout.

**Figure 5.12** The TD Relative Retracement downside in September found support precisely at the Magnet Price, and the October decline initially held at exactly the 0.382 retracement level, as well as the 0.618 level. The December high hit resistance at the 1.618 level. Also, the TDST level was not violated during the downside buy Setup phase in late October coincident with the 0.618 retracement support.

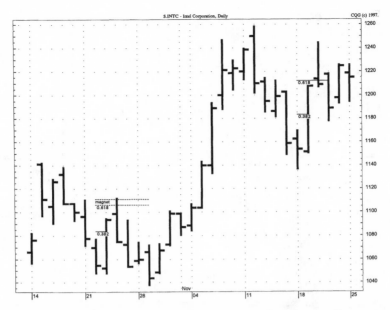

**Figure 5.13(a)** Two TD Relative Retracements in one trading day usually translates into a price reversal or consolidation. Two examples appear on this chart.

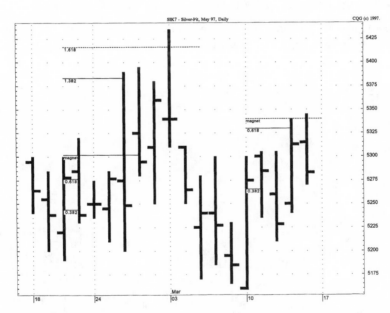

**Figure 5.13(b)** Two relative Retracements in one trading day generally identifies a price reversal or consolidation. February 20 and March 13 are two examples.

193

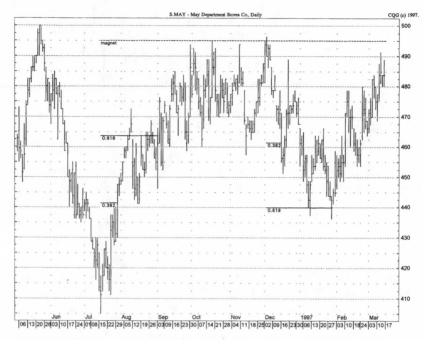

**Figure 5.14**   The Magnet Price served as resistance on the upside, and the 0.618 retracement level provided support on the downside.

**Figure 5.14(a)**   The TD Relative Retracements for Ford Motor are displayed on this chart. Once again, dotted lines indicate disqualified breakout levels—instead of trading with the anticipated breakout, traders should fade the trade (do the reverse).

0.618 retracement levels is 0.50, and one-half the distance between the 0.618 and Magnet Price will vary depending upon the specific level of the Magnet Price, which is in turn dependent upon the TD Critical Price day's high and low close.

Another important observation from my retracement research fore-warns of peculiar and unexpected price activity at retracement levels. This price activity is called TD Double Retracement™ since it applies to those instances in which two or possibly three retracement levels are exceeded in one price day on either an intraday or on a closing basis. Such extreme range movement and volatility over a one-day period is usually associated with the termination of a short-term trend, and price exhaustion and is not, as most traders might expect, a prelude to a price breakout. To perfect this condition, price should exceed both or all these retracement levels for the very first time and no prior price movement since the retracement level low or high should have exceeded any of these retracement levels, thereby enhancing the possibility that the move can be characterized as extreme and increasing the likelihood that price exhaustion will occur. Therefore, if price trades above or below two or more retracement levels for the first time in one day, it is not uncommon for price to reverse this trend or move sideways the next few days. Additionally, if price should close above or below two or more retracement levels for the first time in one price day, then it is not uncommon to record a price gap contrary to the previous day's trend, which retraces to at least the nearest retracement level just exceeded. Figures 5.13a and b and 5.14a (in September) display two examples of this phenomenon.

Most traders believe it is merely important for price to exceed a retracement level intraday in order to qualify further price movement to the next retracement level. Such an assumption is naive and an open invitation to trading losses. There are a number of factors that may cause price movement to fail at a retracement level and reverse its trend, to accelerate its movement to its next retracement projection, or to continue to trend but at a decelerated pace. Furthermore, there is an important qualifier, called the TD Critical Qualifier, that may negate a retracement breakout altogether and that can be successfully applied to most, if not all, indicators presented in this book as well. As a filter, the TD Critical Qualifier is an invaluable component in the validation of price breakouts and one that is improperly ignored by all market timers. So important is this final filter or screen for legitimizing price breakouts that it has application to most widely used market timing indicators and likely to most systems you may be trading at this time. Not only is the closing price level important in defining a price breakout, but what is even more important to the breakout confirmation process is the opening price of the following trading day. Here's why. If a specific TD Relative Retracement price level or TD Line breakout level (Trend Factor, for example) is exceeded on a closing basis, most market timers would likely perceive this event as a price breakout and a prelude to an acceleration of the trend. In most instances, this may be true, but a subsequent event could conceivably undermine and reverse this development, and that is the opening price on the day following the breakout. A closing price can be influenced artificially, and consequently there is a chance of distortion and misrepresentation of the true supply and demand condition of the market. For example, price activity can be exaggerated short term, especially when volume is light and the market price movement is news-driven, thereby misrepresenting the true market equilibrium level. Therefore, if the closing price were unduly influenced, the next session's opening price generally reestablishes price equilibrium by gapping either below or above the retracement level. Often the closing price of the S&P futures is influenced, since futures trading extends for an additional 15 minutes after the official close of the cash markets, and light futures trading volume can move prices significantly. This is especially pronounced on the last trading day of the week, the last trading day of the month, and during sessions in which program trading is active, and it is often accentuated by option, stock, and stock futures expirations. The opening price the following trading day is "king," and this price level serves effectively as a Critical Qualifier of price breakouts. Sure, the closing price is important, and you may want to relate the closing price to that same trading day's opening price to measure daily accumulation or distribution, but to reestablish price equilibrium after an apparent breakout, you should refer to the next trading day's opening price for confirmation. This price serves to correct any distortions caused by extraordinary events and activities that may have produced atypical price behavior. Most of the time the TD Critical Qualifier will serve to confirm legitimate breakouts, but at the same time, it will on occasion save a trader money by invalidating presumed price breakouts.

It's beneficial to identify and measure wave movements within the context of a market advance or decline and then apply retracement analysis to arrive at price projections. Often the individual price moves, or *legs* as they are referred to by technicians, will replicate one another in distance. To arrive at measurements, you can relate and calculate the distance from the closing price of the lowest intraday low to a subsequent intraday high or from the closing price of the highest intraday high to a subsequent intraday low. Next, add this value to a more recent closing price that is preceded by a price decline in the case of an upside move and that is preceded by an advance in the case of a downside move, encompassing at least 25 percent of the distance from the closing price of the preceding price leg's low and the subsequent intraday high in the same direction or from the closing price of the preceding price leg's high and the subsequent intraday low in the same direction. Price will generally experience support downside or resistance upside at this 25 percent level. Once penetrated, the next level of downside support is derived by subtracting 50 percent from the intraday high rather than the close that day. To arrive at upside resistance, add 50 percent to the intraday low rather than the close that same day. Furthermore, after two approximately equal legs down or up are recorded, a market will usually record a 61.8 percent TD Relative Retracement price recovery.

In a general sense, you can regard a market that has experienced two successive moves upside or downside that are comparable in distance as opportunities to apply TD Relative Retracement calculations. Specifically, a situation often occurs in which the market records two approximately equal legs down or up. Once the market begins its rally, you can generally calculate a 61.8 percent retracement level upside and expect price to meet that objective. Conversely, once a market begins to decline after recording two approximately equal up legs, you can calculate a downside price objective based upon a 61.8 percent decline. In each instance, you can apply the retracement theory described within the discussion of TD Relative Retracement.

Finally, for short term trading purposes, you can calculate and apply the TD Fibonacci Intraday Indicator. This indicator relates the current trading day's opening price relative to retracement levels calculated based upon the previous trading day's true price range (the difference between the previous trading day's high or the close two days ago, whichever is greater, and the previous trading day's low or the close two days ago, whichever is less). If the current trading day's open is less than 38.2 percent of the previous trading day's true range plus the previous trading day's true low, and the current trading day's high is greater than 38.2 percent of this value plus the previous day's low, expect price to rally to 61.8 percent of the true range plus the low. Conversely, if the current open is greater than 38.2 percent of the previous trading day's true range subtracted from the previous trading day's true high, and the current trading day's low is less than 38.2 percent of this value subtracted from the previous day's true high, expect price to decline to 61.8 percent of the true range subtracted from that day's intraday high. This exercise and series of calculations and price objectives is referred to as the TD Fibonacci Intraday Indicator™.

The various selections for TD Relative Retracement along with the preferred settings are as follows:

1. The Price column displays whether the retracement originates from a low, a high, or whatever reference point you desire.

2. The Date column identifies the date from which the retracement originates.

3. The Time column identifies the time at which the retracement reference is recorded.

4. The Direction identifies the direction of the retracement calculations.

5. The Breakout penetration column refers to the number of ticks to add to the retracement level to ensure a breakout is legitimate.

6. The Breakout end column determines whether the breakout qualifiers are active for the first time price exceeds the breakout level or whether
it continues active after it has been invalidated or disqualified. This selection
is similar to the "end at first" or "end at qualified" selection, which is presented in the discussion of TD Lines.

7. The Qualifier column determines which qualifier(s) are applied to
each suspected breakout in order to justify intraday entry—identical to qualifiers used with TD Lines. To perfect intraday breakouts, these qualifiers are
introduced. If *any one* and *not* necessarily all of the qualifiers exist, intraday
entry is justified, but if none exist then *no* entry justification in the direction
of the trend exists, and it may in this instance be prudent to take the trading
position opposite to what may appear to be correct for that day only and exit
on the close or follow with a stop loss—in other words, fade (do the reverse)
the intraday breakout trade that would have occurred had any of the qualifiers been present. Qualifiers *a*, *b*, and *c* appear in the Qualifier column.

a. Qualifier *a* requires a close one trading day ago less than the close two
   trading days ago to justify entry intraday on an upside breakout above an
   upside retracement level and requires a close one trading day ago greater
   than the close two trading days ago to justify entry intraday on a downside breakout below a downside retracement level. The logic associated
   with this event occurring is that false breakouts are more likely to occur
   if the closing price on the trading day before the upside breakout is above
   the previous trading day's close and the closing price the day before the
   downside breakout is below the previous trading day's close, since this
   suggests that most traders have already positioned themselves in anticipation of this event occurring. Consequently, if traders have already
   taken their positions expecting a breakout, their activity is complete.
   However, if the close the trading day before an upside intraday breakout
   above a TD Relative Retracement level is less than the close of the previous trading day, or the close the day before a downside breakout below a
   TD Relative Retracement level is greater than the close of the previous
   trading day, then not only is the general expectation for the continuation
   of the decline or the advance, but also if price does breakout intraday then
   there is a degree of skepticism initially associated with the breakout,
   which in turn helps to propel prices further.

b. Qualifier *b* requires not only an opening price above the TD Relative
   Retracement level upside or below the TD Retracement level downside,
   but also requires that price follow through in the direction of the breakout by a couple of price ticks above the opening for an upside breakout
   and below the opening for a downside breakout.

c. Qualifier $c$ requires that the TD Relative Retracement level be greater than the difference between the previous day's close and that same day's true low (that day's low or the previous day's close, whichever is less) for an upside price move or less than the difference between the previous day's close and that same day's true high (that day's high or the previous day's close, whichever is greater) for a downside move. If the TD Relative Retracement level is penetrated intraday, then that implies the demand for an upside move and supply for a downside move not only exceeds the previous day's expression of demand and supply but that the market is sufficiently strong enough that, once it exceeds the TD Relative Retracement level, it should continue that trend. To summarize, experience indicates that all three qualifiers should be active at all times. Generally, markets do the unexpected, and that is either (1) break out in one direction after a close was recorded the previous trading day in the other direction, (2) gap above or below a TD Relative Retracement level, as well as show some minor price follow-through in the direction of the breakout after the open, or (3) exceed the previous day's expression of demand for a TD Relative Retracement breakout upside or exceed the previous day's expression of supply for a TD Relative Retracement breakout downside, *then* subsequently record a breakout above the TD Relative Retracement level upside or record a breakout below the TD Relative Retracement level downside.

8. The Qpen column refers to the additional price ticks attached to Qualifiers 2 and 3 to insure a valid intraday breakout;

9. To invalidate or cancel a TD Relative Retracement breakout entry, one of the three following conditions must occur the following day:

a. The open on the trading day following an upside breakout exceeds downside the TD Relative Retracement level that was penetrated upside the previous trading day, or the open on the trading day following a downside breakout exceeds upside the TD Relative Retracement level that was penetrated downside the previous trading day—box 1 in Cancel column.

b. The open on the trading day following an upside breakout is less than the previous trading day's close and price closes below a downside TD Relative Retracement level that was broken the previous trading day, or the open on the day following a downside breakout is greater than the previous day's close and price closes above the upside TD Relative Retracement level that was broken the previous trading day—box 2 in Cancel column.

c. The high on the trading day after an upside breakout fails to exceed upside the breakout day's high, or the low on the trading day after a downside breakout fails to exceed downside the breakout day's low—box 3 in Cancel column.

A good choice may be to select all three cancellations, but there may be instances where you want to turn off option *c*.

10. The Limit column refers to the number of trading days surveyed to arrive at TD Relative Retracement calculations.

11. The Display refers to the TD Relative Retracement levels that appear on the chart.

The preferred default settings are either low or high, depending on whether the retracement is upside or downside; the date, time, and direction that appear are subject to the low or high selected; the breakout penetration is set at 2; the breakout end is set at valid; all the qualifiers are on; the Qpen is set at 2 for qualifiers 2 and 3; the cancellations are sometimes on and sometimes off; the limit is set at 200 days, and all the retracements are checked.

In conclusion, the observations regarding retracements are significant for screening trading opportunities:

1. The same Qualifiers developed for TD Lines are also applicable to screening and qualifying price entries for intraday retracement price breakouts.

2. Surpassing two or more key retracement levels (38.2 and 61.8 percent, or 61.8 percent and Magnet Price) for the first time in one day (price period), since the price low or high generally coincides with price exhaustion, translates into, at a minimum, a price consolidation or, more likely, a price trend reversal.

3. Despite the fact that price may close above or below a specific retracement level, the opening of the ensuing day (price period) is referred to as a TD Critical Qualifier in confirming whether the suspected breakout is valid.

4. If price exceeds intraday and closes in the direction of the breakout but fails to record a price reversal by closing above an upside retracement level or below a downside retracement level, it often indicates price will continue its trend to one-half the distance from the retracement level just exceeded intraday and the next retracement level.

5. The TD Fibonacci Intraday Indicator can be applied to arrive at intraday levels of price thrust and support and resistance.

## TD Absolute Retracement™

*Observation:* Years ago, I made market forecasts, based on simple price calculations, that proved to be amazingly accurate in predicting three historic price declines. Two occurred just prior to the 1987 stock market crashes in the United States and England, and one preceded the extended stock market decline in Japan after its all-time price high was recorded in January 1989. The following demonstration of the process applied will allow you to formulate your own conclusions regarding this technique. In the case of the Dow Jones Industrial Average, the record high of August 25, 1987, was multiplied by the Fibonnaci ratio of 0.618 to arrive at the subsequent October 20, 1987, low. In the case of the Nikkei Dow Jones Average, the historic high of December 1989 to January 1990 was multiplied by the Fibonacci ratio 0.382 to arrive at its August 1992 low—approximately 25,000 points lower. Additionally, the projection of a low in the London Financial Times Index from its all-time record high in July 1987 to its November 1987 low also represented a TD Absolute Retracement–level forecast applying the Fibonacci ratio of 0.618. The surprising fact regarding these forecasts is not necessarily their accuracy, but the relative ease with which these price projections were calculated. Most of the individuals with whom I shared these forecasts rejected them at the time, and even more perplexing was their unwillingness to accept the simple mechanical process used to derive them. The same methodology applies to all markets recording all-time highs as well as all-time lows. One market area that has conformed particularly well to this type of analysis is the new public stock issue market. Subsequent to the release and initial trading of many hot new issues, volatility has ensued. In many instances, the downside price support levels for these stocks were defined way in advance by TD Absolute Retracement–level calculations.

In those instances in which price is at a historic high or low—or, at the very least, at a high or low not equaled or exceeded in quite some time—and no reference high or low exists in recent history to which to compare a recent TD Relative Retracement high or low, a retracement technique called TD Absolute Retracement may be used. Prior to release of this retracement method many years ago, no one who used Fibonacci ratios to derive price objectives employed any kind of similar process. Specifically, in those instances where TD Relative Retracement is not applicable, you should either locate the highest high and multiply this figure by both 0.618 and 0.382 to arrive at downside price projection levels, or locate the lowest low and multiply this figure by 1.382, 1.618, 2.618, 3.618, 4.618, and so on. In exceptional cases where a price gap occurs the day after the highest high or lowest low, by using the close that day to calculate the TD Absolute retracement levels instead of the intraday high or low, you can achieve better results. You can successfully apply the same intraday retracement qualifiers used for TD Lines and TD Relative Retracements to TD Absolute Retracements to perfect intraday entry.

Experience indicates that it is not uncommon for price declines from the highs of recent public stock offerings to find price support at the TD Absolute

Retracement levels when these stocks experience price declines. Noteworthy examples that have demonstrated this tendency include Netscape, Yahoo!, Pixar, and Cox Radio. Additionally, volatile stocks that have limited shares outstanding and have wide public appeal and participation behave similarly. Such examples include Pairgain, Presstek, Zitel, and Iomega, among many others.

Figures 5.15 through 5.26 provide numerous TD Absolute Retracement examples.

The selection options available for TD Absolute Retracements include the following:

1. To select any of a number of price levels, refer to the Price column.
2. The column Date refers to the date on which the selected price appears.
3. The Time column refers to the time of day in which the selected price appears.
4. The Display column defines the series of retracement ratios and is accompanied by a checklist.

The preferred TD Absolute Retracement settings are either a high or a low depending upon whether you are projecting a retracement level down-

**Figure 5.15**   To arrive at a downside price objective if there is no reference price level and TD Relative Retracement cannot be applied, TD Absolute Retracement can be substituted. By multiplying the 1987 Financial Times Index by 0.618, the downside price objective is defined and displayed on the chart.

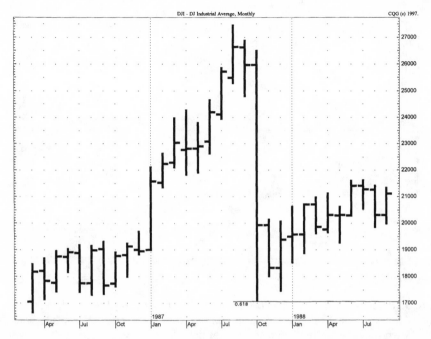

**Figure 5.16**  This chart is the complement to Figure 5.15. It displays the downside TD Absolute Retracement price objective for the Dow Jones Industrial Average in 1987.

**Figure 5.17**  Similar to Figures 5.15 and 5.16, this chart identifies the TD Absolute Retracement downside price objective. However, due to the price gap the month after the price high, use the close of that price bar to arrive at a price objective.

**Figure 5.18** To arrive at downside price objectives, simply apply the TD Absolute Retracement. Multiply the peak price by 0.618 and 0.382. Notice how price attempts to hold these levels. When they are broken, price accelerates downside.

**Figure 5.19** Stock price movements subsequent to many public stock offerings have had a tendency to decline to a TD Absolute Retracement level, possibly exceed it intraday, but close that same day above it. Once a closing price is recorded below the 0.618 level, price generally declines to the 0.382 level. By combining TD Absolute Retracement with TD Sequential, the July low was identified, as well as the December low if "ignore smaller true high/true low" is elected.

**Figure 5.20**    The previously penetrated 0.618 TD Absolute Retracement level proved to be formidable upside resistance in February subsequent to a break below the level on a closing basis in December. Note how the 0.382 level provided good support in March.

**Figure 5.21**    The July break below the TD Absolute Retracement level was disqualified because Qualifier 2 requires that price not only open below the retracement level, but it also must follow through downside by at least one price tick. In this instance, the open was the low. That was a warning that the breakdown would likely fail.

**Figure 5.22**   Price declined below the 0.618 TD Absolute Retracement level and found price support on a closing basis precisely at the 0.382 retracement level. The stock rallied 50% off of the July low.

**Figure 5.23**   Once price closed below the 0.618 level, the stock declined over 60 points in two trading days. When it closed below the 0.382 level, it declined another 35 points. Note in late June price bumped up against the 0.382 retracement level that it had previously broken. Despite the fact that good news was announced, causing a 12-plus-point upside gap opening, price failed to hold above that level on a closing basis.

**Figure 5.24**   The TD Absolute Retracement price objectives off of the April peak are displayed on the chart. The first was hit precisely at the July low and coincident with the TD Sequential low-risk entry. The 0.382 objective was hit in April 1995, approximately the same time as the TD Sequential low-risk entry.

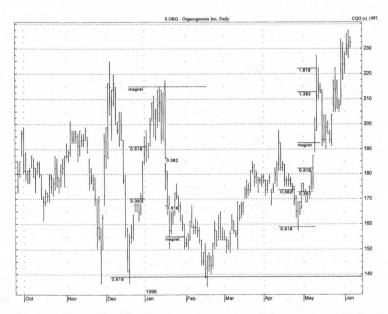

**Figure 5.25**   The December low that was equaled in February coincided with the TD Absolute Retracement level 0.618. The rally off of the December low failed precisely at the January peak. As you can see, it is possible to combine two forms of retracements.

**Figure 5.26**    Once again, the success of the combination of both TD Absolute and TD Relative Retracements is demonstrated on this weekly chart. Price gapped below the 0.618 level in January and in July found support at the 0.382 level. On the upside, the TD Relative Retracement levels defined price objectives.

side or upside. In rare instances in which a gap downside occurs the day following a high or a gap upside the day following a low, the close that trading day is substituted.

## TD Arc™

Most retracements occur within a specified period of time. However, both TD Relative Retracements and TD Absolute Retracements, as well as most other commonly used retracement techniques, concentrate upon only one dimension to arrive at price objectives, and that is *price*. Research suggests, however, that whenever price fails to retrace to the TD Relative Retracement price objective within a specified period of time, the market's momentum and ability to fulfill the price objective diminish. Consequently, price objectives should be adjusted to compensate for price erosion due to the market's inability to fulfill a price objective within a specified time window. In order to address this important element of time, which is ignored by most market timers, a meter is installed into the retracement analysis equation. This timing device is designed such that if a price objective is not realized within a defined period of time, the retracement level will adjust to compensate for the passage of time. Therefore, both considerations presented on a chart—price and time—are incorporated into TD Retracement Arcs. TD Arcs are a companion technique to TD Relative Retracements. They enable a trader to account for price erosion when calculating retracement levels. In a theoretical sense, the market's memory lapses over time and a price-time continuum ensures that either the retracement level is accomplished within a specified period of time or the price objective is adjusted to account for the passage of time.

As you can readily see, TD Relative Retracements and TD Absolute Retracements address only one dimension: price. When the element of time is introduced, you'll appreciate why markets tend to exhibit unexpected behavioral characteristics. In a sense, the price activity of a market is defined at particular points in time and price. If certain projected price levels are not fulfilled within a prescribed period of time, the price objective must be revised to reflect this erosion of time. That is the purpose of TD Arcs. First, diagonal lines were constructed from an initial closing price on an extreme range day, and that point was extended and connected to a subsequent extreme intraday high or low. Then a similar diagonal price/time line was positioned on a subsequent closing price to estimate the price/time range expectation for the market to complete its next leg. The price movement of the second leg may at times be less than the first leg in absolute terms. This occurrence may be attributed to the fact that the market's ability to replicate leg measurements diminishes with the passage of time. In many cases, however, the diagonals—depending upon the price and time scales—were approximately equal in distance despite the fact that their angle of ascent or decline may have been different when incorporating the two variables (price and time), provided an equivalent importance or value was assigned to both by allocating a square box to the time and the price increment.

To construct TD Arcs you should employ the same decision rules that apply to TD Relative Retracements. However, with regard to TD Arcs a different methodology is used to calculate the specific retracement levels. In this instance, extend a diagonal line from a recent price low or high back in time to a previous qualified high or low critical price. The price levels are selected in the same manner that the TD Relative Retracement levels are—in other words, refer back in time from a low to the last time a comparable or lower low was recorded, and conversely, refer back in time from a high to the last time a comparable or higher high was recorded. On that diagonal line, identify the specific ratio retracement levels and, by using the recent low or high as a fulcrum depending whether you are projecting upside or downside, construct an arc into the future. In order to ensure that the arc is capable of being reproduced regardless of price scale, anchor the points systematically on the chart by counting the same number of trading days from the low to the reference day high or from the high to the reference day low, depending on whether an upside or downside retracement is made, and then count an equal number of trading days back in time from that reference day high or low. The TD Arc is anchored in order to prevent one pattern for the arc at one price scale and a different one when it is changed to another price scale. Once drawn properly, the TD Arc takes on the shape of an ellipse and serves as a barrier of resistance or support for price retracements, and the market's attempts to advance or decline to specific retracement levels becomes an exercise in "beat the clock," whereby either price fulfills the prescribed TD Relative Retracement price objective within a specified period of time or it follows the time-price continuum path defined by the TD Arc. In addition, there are many times in which a price penetration of the TD Arc is a precursor to a similar, subsequent retracement of the TD Relative Retracement price levels as well. Consequently, it is good to apply the TD Relative Retracement and the TD Arc to a chart simultaneously and then relate one to the other. Figures 5.11 and 5.27 through 5.29 provide examples of TD Arc.

The selection options available for TD Arc Retracements include the following:

1. To select any of a number of price levels, refer to the Price column.
2. The column Date refers to the date on which the selected price appears.

**Figure 5.27** This chart includes a series of TD Relative Retracement projections plus TD Arcs off of the October 1994 low, which identified the December 1995 bond market peak.

**Figure 5.28** A combination of TD Relative Retracements and TD Arcs have proven effective in the identification of support and resistance. When one does not apply, the other does.

**Figure 5.29(a)** The TD Relative Retracements, TD Sequential low and high-risk 9-13 levels, the TD Arcs, and the TDST levels.

**Figure 5.29(b)**   This chart of the monthly Dow Jones Industrial Average illustrates a combination of TD Arcs and TD Relative Retracements. Note how well they complement one another and how the various retracement levels serve as price resistance and support.

3. The Time column refers to the time of day in which the selected price appears.

4. The Direction column is determined by whether the retracements are upside or downside.

5. The Mode column refers to the method of calculating the retracement arc, which is a diagonal line.

6. The Time scale determines the geometric construction of the TD Arc.

7. The Display column refers to which series of ratios or scales are applied to the chart. A checklist accompanies this display.

Preferred TD Arc settings are either a price high or low, depending upon whether you are projecting a retracement level downside or upside. The date, time, and direction are a function of this selection, and the various retracement ratios are all selected.

# Chapter

# 6

# Price Breakouts

*Observation:* One of the earliest video arcade games, called "Pong," involved two players who volleyed a rectangular pellet with knobs that served as paddles. Whenever a player failed to return the pellet to the opponent, the pellet's speed accelerated in that direction. I applied a similar technique to the price activity of various markets by devising a series of trading rules that can alert you to pending or potential price breakouts, at which time price would likely establish a trend and accelerate its movement. Since the late 1980s, this type of analysis has no doubt become quite commonplace, particularly among Commodity Trading Advisors (CTAs). The only characteristics that differentiate one trader who practices this methodology from another are the reference points they use, the ratios they apply, the price levels they select, and the markets they follow. The fact that most trading participants are using similar techniques affords a real advantage to those alert traders who are able to distinguish their trading style from this group by introducing additional trading filters and qualifiers, as well as techniques that are designed to perform contrary to the trading crowd. The structure used to execute this type of trend detection process is comprehensive and adaptable to most traders' needs.

## TD REBO™

TD REBO is an acronym for the indicator shell developed many years ago called Range Expansion BreakOut. It is a master template designed to accommodate and present various possible methods for expressing and calculating price breakout levels. The traditional or conventional applications of similar volatility breakout techniques are trend-following approaches that are widely used by traders even to this day. When I first experimented with breakout techniques, the markets enjoyed long periods of uninterrupted trends. The inflationary environment of the mid- to late 1970s played a major role in this regard. The evolution to a noninflationary economy, however, has produced a trading range environment for most markets and, consequently, played havoc with this methodology. Albeit there may be trending moves in world cartel markets (e.g., coffee, sugar, cocoa, energy, copper, tin, and even lumber), these are the exception rather than the rule. Over recent years, research suggests that markets as a whole operate within a trading range 78 to 82 percent of the time, and of the 18 to 22 percent of the time in which they are trending, typically a market is in an uptrend 12 to 14 percent of the time and in a downtrend 6 to 8 percent of the time. Research indicates that the amount of time markets trend up is approximately twice as long as the amount of time they trend down. This tendency can be attributed to two factors: (1) Buying is often a repetitive, cumulative decision, and increasing profitability, margin account increases, news events, positive research reports, and market psychology are key reinforcement factors that beget and perpetuate additional buying. (2) Selling, on the other hand, is typically a one-time decision—if any factor whatsoever concerns a trader, this excuse or reason may serve as a catalyst to force a trader to liquidate his or her entire position at that time without regard for any other considerations.

Much consideration and planning have gone into the design and construction of the TD REBO Indicator. It is sufficiently dynamic and capable of adapting to changing market conditions and environments, whether they be of a trading range or a trend-following variety. What distinguishes TD REBO from most volatility-based breakout approaches is the fact that it is so comprehensive. Whereas most conventional approaches merely calculate breakout levels by multiplying the previous day's price range by a fixed ratio and then adding that value to a base price (e.g., the previous day's close), TD REBO offers a plethora of design options, as well as a series of possible qualifiers. The versatility TD REBO provides to a trader is not necessarily to be perceived as an attempt to provide optimization capability to this analytical tool, whereby the trader is able to fit the price activity of various markets to conform with historical test results. Rather, the goal is to enable traders to differentiate themselves from other volatility-based traders by providing the building blocks essential to the creation of both complete trend-following techniques and price exhaustion approaches that are designed to sell strength and buy weakness within trading range markets and, consequently, operate against the trend-following tendency exhibited by the majority of breakout traders. By avoiding the competition created by other traders attempting to fill their orders in a trending market at comparable price levels, the potential risk of price slippage and skidding, price gaps, and unfilled limit orders is diminished considerably. TD REBO will provide a new dimension of volatility and range breakout analysis and opportunities to those traders inclined to operate in the markets with this type of trading methodology. It will also instill a psychological comfort level by demonstrating to traders that they are able to select from this vast indicator structure and reservoir of trading possibilities virtually any series of price relationships, options, and qualifiers needed to translate, document, experiment, and perfect their breakout methodologies.

Rather than present a long discourse on the derivation of TD REBO and its applications to markets, a better approach is to present its composition and the various selections built into its detailed architecture. You will no doubt agree that its options and structure make it a robust platform for the creation and introduction of volatility breakout and range expansion techniques. In retrospect, its construction and design are comparable to the development of a high-powered shotgun intended to kill a fly. Its designed capacity far exceeds any imaginable trading needs or requirements. Nevertheless, presenting an exhaustive, comprehensive trading template to enable you to construct your own trend-following methods and exhaustion techniques is preferable to leaving it deficient or handicapped in any respect whatsoever.

The various selection options are as follows:

1. The History checkbox refers to the option of presenting all the previous REBO indications or just the current day's REBO levels.

2. The Display column allows the trader to select either (a) "hits" or all the times in which REBO levels were fulfilled in the past as well as on the current bar, (b) "all" the REBO levels whether they were hit or not in the past as well as for the current bar, or (c) the "first" time in a successive series in which the REBO level was hit (note that an up level and down level can appear on the same day, since it is not possible to determine which occurred first on that particular day).

3. The Display column also allows the user to select either "chart" or "daily," thereby enabling the user to produce the daily REBO level only on the daily chart or to retain the daily REBO on any intraday chart of the same market as well.

4. The Base column displays the reference price used.

5. The Ago column lists the specific day from which to select the Base price.

6. The #Bars column indicates how many bars are included and surveyed, once the next column (Range type) has been defined, for the purpose of selecting a Base.

7. The Range type refers to the specific type bar(s) selected for the purpose of defining the Base.

8. The Range hi column and Range lo column display the values that are subtracted to arrive at a value for the purpose of adding/subtracting from the Base.

9. The Ago columns following both Range hi and Range lo specify which price bars are considered to arrive at a value to be added to the Base.

10. The #Bars refers to the number of price bars considered when calculating the value to be added/subtracted from the Base.

11. The Factor column specifies the ratio that is multiplied by the value prior to adding/subtracting from the Base.

12. The Qualifiers refer the numerous conditions that can be included in the REBO analysis to eliminate specific trades.

13. The On column determines whether that specific row's condition is active.

14. The Type column specifies whether the condition refers to one price bar to another price bar *or* whether one price bar refers to a group of price bars *or* whether a group of price bars refers to specific price bar *or* whether a group of price bars refers to another group of price bars.

15. The Multiplier column displays the ratio that is multiplied by the Price 1 column when a version of price range is selected in that column.

16. The Price 1 column refers to the specific price to be compared with Price 2.

17. The Ago 1 and Ago 2 columns specify which specific bar or series of bars are to be compared.

18. The Rel column defines the comparison relationship to be conducted.

19. The Price 2 column defines the specific price to be compared with Price 1.

20. The Ago 3 and Ago 4 columns specify which specific bar or series of bars are to be compared.

Another feature of TD REBO is its ability to apply any number of possibilities (e.g., close, open, midpoint, high, low, average, high for up and low for down, low for up and high for down, highest high and lowest low, lowest high and highest low, highest price, lowest price) for *x* days ago or over a specified day or series of days as the Base Price. Furthermore, to the Base Price can be added a percentage of a previous trading day's price range, a series of price day's ranges, a maximum or minimum day's range over *x* number of trading days, an average price range over a number of trading days, the range difference between the highest high and the lowest low price over a series of trading days, as well as price relationships other than range highs and lows. TD REBO is then capable of introducing various ratios that can be multiplied by these price ranges and added to or subtracted from the Base Price to arrive at threshold breakout-value levels. Additionally, to perfect this process further, a series of price relationships between individual trading days' price components, as well as a series or groups of trading days, can be compared to one another or other groups and series to qualify TD REBO trading opportunities.

For example, a series of possible settings or selections for TD REBO might consist of the following options: Calculate the difference between the previous trading day's true high and true low to arrive at a value described as $X$. Next, multiply this value by 0.382 (or 38.2 percent) and both add and subtract that value to the current trading day's opening price level. Once price has exceeded this price objective, the trend for the current trading day has likely been identified as up, and by subtracting that same value $X$ from the opening price, and if the low the current trading day exceeds that level downside, then the trend for that trading day has been defined as down. Instead of using the current trading day's opening price, by installing yesterday's closing price as the reference level, the entry areas will be redefined. In this instance, however, it is important that if you are reviewing the performance results produced by the application of this setting, you include the requirement that the current trading day's price activity intersect the entry area. Otherwise, if price gaps above or below this level occur, it would be impossible to enter the market at that price. By changing the ratio for TD REBO, the entries will adjust accordingly, and by introducing Qualifiers, the results can be improved further. One Qualifier you might want to apply to prevent both buying and selling the same trading day is as follows: The close one trading day ago must be less than the close two trading days ago for a buy indication, and the close one trading day ago must be greater than the close two trading days ago for a sell indication. Other Qualifiers can be introduced as well. Also, instead of calculating the price range one trading day ago, other trading days or combinations of trading days can be introduced as well, and the highest high and lowest low of this series can be applied. Numerous price relationships can be compared, such as a comparison of opening and closing price levels, price ranges, or highs and lows. As you can readily see, a multiplicity of variables can be considered and implemented. The choices are limited only by your level of interest and the time you may wish to devote to research and experimentation.

An observation made quite some time ago confirmed the utility of applying the current trading day's opening price as a key component of any TD REBO calculation you may consider. It has to do with my research conclusions regarding the opening price relationship and that same trading day's high and low price levels. Specifically, it is not uncommon to witness the opening price occur within 10 to 20 percent of any trading day's high or low. In fact, the open many times occurs precisely at a trading day's high or low. If the high and low for that trading day were known in advance, and once price deviates 20 percent of that price range from the opening, low-risk entry zones could be identified. Unfortunately, no one is able to predict the future consistently and accurately. Consequently, you should apply proxies for the current trading day's price range to calculate a 20 percent price entry level once the market opens. Reasonable alternatives to having the current trading day's price range is the previous trading day's price range or an average or a combination of a number of previous trading days' ranges. Additionally, instead of applying the price range, other options can be introduced, such as movement from open to high for an upside level and open to close for a downside level or a combination of these price comparisons. Among many other ideas, one currently being tested relates to calculating a 10 to 20 percent price movement of the TD Range Projection™ (see Chapter 12) for the following trading day added or subtracted to current trading day's opening price. One other variation being studied includes taking an average of a series of price levels for the previous trading day (such as open, high, low, and close) and then multiplying this value by a percentage and then adding and subtracting that value to and from the current trading day's opening price. Another derivative of TD REBO is TD Spring, which is explained below. As you can readily see, a myriad of relationships exists and can be applied to TD REBO. This indicator alone can be a trader's best friend and only trading tool. It just depends upon your trading preference and degree of interest.

TD REBO examples are presented in Figures 6.1 through 6.5.

It is readily apparent that TD REBO is a dynamic indicator with much power and market timing capacity. Encoded within this analytical outline is a comprehensive tool that can be used to experiment with and develop various forms of range expansion and breakout techniques. Just as with the other indicators presented throughout this book (TD Lines, TDST, etc.), this indicator is versatile. Not only can it be used as a trend-following device, it can be successfully used to identify zones of price or trend exhaustion. For example, if your experimentation and search for the identification of breakout levels is producing more losing trades than winning trades, then the parameters of TD REBO can be altered to take advantage of reversing your perspective from trend following to price exhaustion. In other words, if your trading suppositions are applied from an anti- or a contratrend perspective, you will be the beneficiary of even more trading opportunities, since TD REBO allows a user to partake of contratrend trading methodologies as well. With TD REBO, traders are limited in their research of breakout and range expansion techniques only by the degree of imagination they possess. By

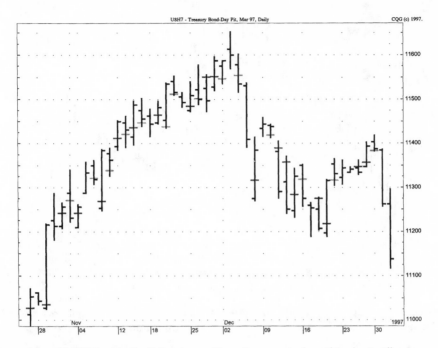

**Figure 6.1**   TD REBO with the following settings is presented on this chart. All price penetrations are displayed and a factor of 0.28 (28%) is used. This factor is multiplied by the true
price range of the previous trading day since only one price bar is selected rather than a
series of trading days. Only one low-risk entry Qualifier is introduced to ensure that only an
upside or a downside indication can be presented on a specific trading day, not both. The
Qualifier requires that for an upside move the close one trading day ago must be less than
the close two trading days ago. For a downside move, the close one trading day ago must
be greater than the close two trading days ago. The hash marks appearing on the chart
identify the low-risk entry level. To determine whether it relates to an upside or downside
breakout, compare the previous trading day's close versus the close two trading days ago.
The value calculated by multiplying the factor by the previous trading day's price range is
then added to or subtracted from the current trading day's opening price. Figure 6.2
applies the same procedure with the exception that its base is not the current trading day's
opening price, but the previous trading day's close.

adapting your perspective from trend-following to antitrend or exhaustion
techniques, the possibilities are increased even more.

## TD Spring™

Although TD Spring can be easily applied within the parameter selections
of TD REBO, this indicator is a unique, separate study because of its value
in forecasting breakouts from periods of lackluster, sideways price movement. When this indicator was developed in the late 1970s, numerous markets had undergone extended periods of price consolidation. For example, if

**Figure 6.2** As is apparent upon close review, the low-risk entries for Figure 6.1 are different from this chart only because the "Base" is the previous trading day's close.

**Figure 6.3** This chart is distinguished from Figures 6.1 and 6.2 in only one respect. Instead of calculating the true range difference of the preceding trading day, the minimum true price difference for each of the previous four trading days is evaluated and the minimum true range trading day is selected and multiplied by the 0.28 factor and added to or subtracted from the current trading day's opening price. Figure 6.4 applies this same calculation to the previous trading day's closing price.

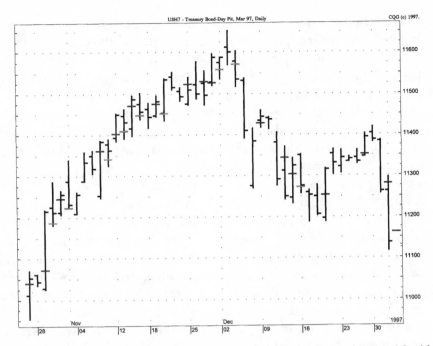

**Figure 6.4** The TD REBO settings for this chart are identical to those of Figure 6.3 with the exception that the previous trading day's close is used as a reference or "Base" instead of the current trading day's opening price.

**Figure 6.5** This version of TD REBO uses the current trading day's opening price as a "Base," uses the same multiplier of 0.28, but calculates the highest true high and lowest true low of the previous three trading days.

over a period of $x$ trading days prior to the current trading day (or series of trading days), the true price range (highest high over the time period or the close on the trading day prior to the first day of the series if that day's close is higher then all the highs of the series *minus* the lowest low over the time period or the close on the trading day prior to the first day of the series if that day's close is less then all the lows of the series) for the previous trading day, or series of trading days, is less than a defined percent of the true price range for the previous $y$ number of prior trading days, the market is trading in a relatively narrow price coil and about to "spring." To calculate the upside breakout zone, the current trading day's high must exceed a price level that is derived by multiplying the previous trading day's (or days') true range by a specified percent and then adding that value to the previous day's price close or current day's open. To calculate the downside breakout zone the current trading day's low must exceed a price level that is derived by multiplying the distance of the previous trading day's (or days') true range by a defined percent and then subtracting that value from the previous day's price close or current day's open to calculate. The critical factors are: (1) the selection of the price range—either the previous trading day or series of trading days, (2) the price range comparison period, and (3) the percentage to be applied to this value. The feature of the TD Spring indicator is the variability and versatility of its components. Once again, refinements, filters, and qualifiers, as well as additional indicators in this book can be introduced to perfect low-risk entry zones. Figures 6.6 and 6.7 provide examples of TD Spring.

## TD LV™

Typically, indicators are observed, tested, evaluated, then qualified before being introduced into my trading arsenal. One resource for potential market indicators: my "Waldo Patterns." Waldo Patterns were inspired by the children's cartoon character whose caricature is camouflaged within a background of numerous other cartoon figures. The game is to locate him. Once he has been identified, the task the next time becomes simple. However, the challenge is to accomplish this feat initially. Likewise with market observations and price patterns—the identification process is easy once successfully performed. That is why they are called Waldo Patterns. This set of market observations and experiences is significant and can impact your trading, but Waldo Patterns have not been researched and codified sufficiently to justify their inclusion within the indicator set. Oftentimes, all that is required to upgrade these trading observations and patterns to full-fledged indicators are just a few minor adjustments or additional indicator rules. One such trading opportunity that has been on deck for quite some time is TD LV.

**Figure 6.6** TD Spring is a version of TD REBO that is more specific. In this example, it relates the price range of the previous trading day with the price range of the prior three trading days. If the previous trading day's range is less than each of the prior three trading days, the market is generally coiled and ready to "spring" either upside or downside.

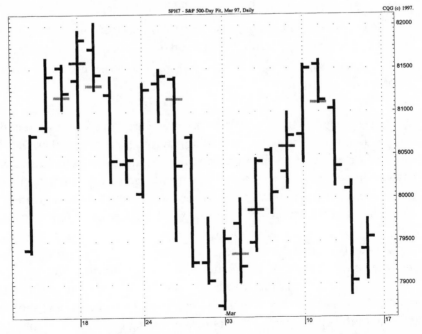

**Figure 6.7** This example of TD Spring uses a 0.382 multiplier instead of 0.28 and requires that the price range of the previous three trading days be less than the price ranges of four through eight trading days earlier.

TD LV is a pseudonym for a series of price comparisons generally associated with an impending price breakout. Since the key comparisons relate to the current trading day's closing price versus the series of 7 previous consecutive trading days' high or lows, as well as the series of 11 previous consecutive trading days' highs or lows, it was tempting to call this indicator 7-11. Lest it be confused with the gambling game craps, which is 7 and 11, its chosen name became the innocuous TD LV. There are five elements to TD LV for both upside and downside breakouts. The conditions that qualify the market environment for a potential breakout are as follows:

1. For a potential upside breakout, the previous day's closing price must be less than the closing price five trading days ago. Conversely, for a downside breakout, the previous trading day's closing price must be greater than the close five trading days ago. In other words, the price comparison between the previous trading day's close and the closing price four trading days prior to that day's closing price dictates whether you are to prepare for a possible upside or downside breakout.

2. The current day's closing price versus the series of seven previous trading days' highs for a potential upside breakout and versus the series of seven previous days' trading lows for a potential downside breakout.

3. The current day's closing price versus the series of 11 previous trading days' highs for a potential upside breakout and versus the series of 11 previous trading days' lows for a potential downside breakout.

4. The previous day's closing price relative to the close one trading day earlier to improve the potential for a breakout.

5. The market's potential to follow through the succeeding day(s) after the breakout indication.

*TD LV buy Setup:* To qualify for an upside breakout for the current day's trading, first of all, the close one trading day ago must be less than the close four trading days earlier—in other words, five trading days before the current day's trading. Next, if the close of the current trading day is greater than *all* the previous seven trading days' highs and, at the same time, not greater than *all* the highs of the trading days 8 through 11 (inclusive) trading days ago as well, then the price advance should fail. However, if the close of the current trading day is greater than *all* the previous seven trading days' highs and, at the same time, greater than *all* the highs of the previous trading days 8 through 11 as well—in other words, greater than *all* the previous 11 trading days' highs—then the advance should continue. Once again, you should be mindful of the opening price the following trading day relative to the breakout level, since the TD Critical Qualifier requires that the following trading day's opening price trade above the breakout level to confirm TD LV.

*TD LV sell Setup:* To qualify for a downside breakout for the current day's trading, first of all, the close one trading ago must be greater than the close four trading days earlier—in other words, five trading days before the current day's trading. Next, if the close of the current trading day is less than *all* the previous seven trading days' lows and, at the same time, not less than *all* the lows of trading days 8 through 11 (inclusive) as well, then the price decline should fail. However, if the close of the current trading day is less than *all* the previous seven trading days' lows and, at the same time, less than *all* the lows of the previous trading days 8 through 11 as well—in other words, less than *all* previous 11 trading days' lows—then the decline should continue. Once again, you should be careful to observe the following trading day's opening price relative to the breakout level, since the TD Critical Qualifier requires the open of that day be below the breakout level to confirm TD LV.

With respect to both TD LV buy and sell Setups and low-risk indications, if the prerequisites are not fulfilled as just described, most traders will probably decide that no trading opportunity exists, but in fact an alert individual could operate in reverse to the process followed when TD LV requirements for a valid price breakout are fulfilled and a low-risk entry indication exists. This type of trading tactic is similar to the Disqualified TD Line and TD Retracement approaches described in Chapters 4 and 5. You should note that despite the fact that the requirements for a trading indicator may be missing or disqualified, this does not cancel the possibility of operating in contradiction to your original intention of participating in a low-risk trend-following proposition, which implies fading a suspected breakout and operating against the prevailing market trend.

Figures 6.8 through 6.13 display examples of TD LV.

# TD Point Reversal™

Over the years, I have followed market price behavior subsequent to and coincident with potential TD Point level 1 lows and highs. Provided a subsequent TD Point low has not been formed or is not in the process of being formed by recording a low below the previous trading day's low or provided a subsequent TD Point high has not been formed or is not in the process of being formed by recording a high greater than the previous trading day's high, there are guidelines to establish the significance of these lows and highs. Specifically, after a TD Point low or a TD Point high is formed, you can apply a meter to market price action to evaluate the prospects for a price follow-through. In other words, to confirm a meaningful short-term low, either on the suspected TD Point low day or within the first four trading days after that low, the market must close above the closes of all four trading

**Figure 6.8** TD LV is often associated with breakout moves. The letter *X* identifies a closing price that exceeded all previous 7 trading days' highs, as well as all previous 11 trading days' highs *or* exceeded all previous 7 trading days' lows, as well as all previous 11 trading days' lows. The letter *Y* identifies an instance in which not all 7 trading days' highs were exceeded.

**Figure 6.9** TD LV low-risk opportunities are defined by the letter *X*. Often they occur coincident with a major price breakout. The letter *Y* identifies an instance where the close was less than all previous 7 trading days' lows but not all 11 trading days' lows. The reverse pattern occurred upside in January.

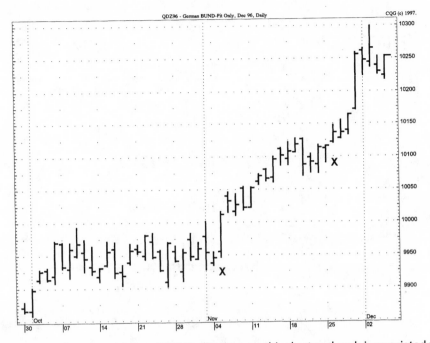

**Figure 6.10** There are only two TD LV indications on this chart and each is associated with breakouts. *X* identifies the days in which they occurred.

**Figure 6.11** Once again a breakout occurred coincident with a TD LV indication. A failure to close above all previous 7 trading highs but not all previous 11 took place in October (*Y*).

227

**Figure 6.12** TD LV indications appear on the chart accompanied by the letter X and the failures (7 NOT 11) are identified with a Y.

**Figure 6.13** TD LV indications are marked on the chart with the letter X. There were only three instances in which this pattern occurred.

days immediately preceding the TD Point low. Conversely, to confirm a meaningful short-term high, either on the suspected TD Point high day or within the first four trading days after that high, the market must close below the closes of all four trading days immediately preceding the TD Point high. Once again, you should apply the TD Critical Qualifier, which requires the opening price the following trading day maintain the breakout level of the previous trading day. See Figures 6.14 and 6.15 for examples of TD Point Reversal.

If a series of two or more upside price gaps occur since the most recent TD Point low, and the higher of the two is still below the highest close of the set of four closes prior to the TD Point low, the chance of price closing above the breakout level, which is the highest close of the four-day set, is unlikely and, if by chance it does, the following day's opening should reverse the breakout. Conversely, if a series of two or more downside gaps occur since the most recent TD Point high, and the lower of the two is above the lowest close of the set of four closes prior to the TD Point high, the chance of price closing below the breakout level, which is the lowest close of the four-day set, is unlikely and, if by chance it does, the following day's opening should reverse the breakout.

**Figure 6.14**  TD Point Reversal requires a close greater than all four trading days' closes prior to a TD Point low or a close less than all four trading days' closes prior to a TD Point high within four trading days after the TD Point low or high, whatever the situation may be. The letter *X* identifies the times it occurred.

**Figure 6.15**  TD Point Reversal indications are shown with the letter *X* on the chart. A TD Point can be formed the day in which an indication is generated, but it will not be confirmed as a TD Point until the following trading day is complete unless the potential TD Point be subsequently exceeded. This occurred at the January low.

## TD Double TD Point™

If a level 1 TD Point low is defined, and subsequently a second level 1 TD Point low is formed at a higher price level, then this secondary test of the original low generally confirms that the price trend should be up. On the other hand, if a level 1 TD Point high is defined, and subsequently a second level 1 TD Point high is formed at a lower price level, then this secondary test of the original high usually confirms that the trend should be down. Note that all TD Points that are higher than level 1 are by definition level 1 as well, since if two or more higher lows surround a TD Point low or two or more lower highs surround a TD Point high, then by definition the requirement for a level 1 TD Point is fulfilled. Research indicates that subsequent to the formation of the second TD Point low, once the high of the second TD Point low day is exceeded upside, then the trend should be up. Conversely, subsequent to the formation of the second TD Point high, once the low of the second TD Point high day is exceeded downside, then the trend should be down.

At the time TD Lines were developed by connecting TD Points, I observed this relationship between ascending TD Point lows and descending TD Point highs. In the past, this relationship was used to confirm trades in which I was already involved. Should you prefer to apply TD Double TD Point to your own trading, rather than merely using this technique to confirm your other market timing approaches, then the most recent day of the current TD Point set formation should constitute your low-risk entry zone to ensure that you are not entering the market at an exhaustion area. In the late 1970s most markets behaved similarly, and once the TD Double TD Point formation was formed the market responded and the low-risk entry zone selection was not a serious consideration since price typically trended from that point. In recent years, it has become more important to refine the low-risk entry level. My recommendation is to use the close of the most recent TD Point's last day of the set since there is no certainty as to whether this is a qualified TD Point until the last day of the three-day TD Point set is completed. Figures 6.16 and 6.17 include TD Double TD Point examples.

## TD Trap™

Although your first impression might easily and expectedly be that the various indicators in this book are complex due solely to their unorthodox nature

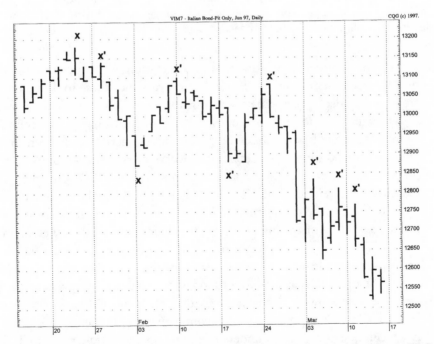

**Figure 6.16** TD Double TD Point requires a TD Point high succeeded by a lower TD Point high or a TD Point low succeeded by a higher TD Point low. Generally, these TD Points are level 1; however, you may substitute a higher-level TD Point. The letter *X* identifies the first of a series of TD Points and the letter *X'* identifies a succeeding lower or higher TD Point.

**Figure 6.17** From the November low when TD Combo generated a low-risk 9-13 indication, only three TD Double TD Points downside were formed (*Y*). Most TD Double TD Points occurred upside (*X*). Note that TDST failed to be exceeded downside in December and broke out upside in January. TD Double TD Point can be used with TDST to perfect entries and to confirm possible TDST breakout failures.

and unconventional application and interpretation, every attempt has been made to keep them simple and straightforward. Once these tools are understood and applied, most traders will probably agree. One such indicator that is easy to understand, simple to construct, and easy to apply is TD Trap. TD Trap is a trend-following method for entering the markets or for confirming your current position in the market. It works better when applied in conjunction with other indicators presented in this book—TD Sequential, TD Combo, REI, DeMarker, and TD ROC I and II. Within the context of these indicators, TD Trap can serve as an effective trigger mechanism for generating the execution of trading positions, provided the overall market environment as defined by the various price indicators indicates that the market is predisposed to advance or decline. Additionally, TD Trap can be used for pyramiding positions, as well as for money management purposes, by identifying successive low-risk entry points within a trending market environment. TD Trap, just like its market timing complement TD Open (see following), is a technique as simple to understand and apply as a trader can find. The complexity, if in fact any exists, arises once a set of qualifiers or filters are installed to perfect this basic timing approach.

Very simply, TD Trap low-risk entries are defined once the opening price for the day has taken place. If the current trading day's open is contained by the previous trading day's price range (i.e., is less than or equal to the previous day's high and greater than or equal to the previous day's low, and either the current day's high is greater than the previous day's high or the current day's low is less than the previous day's low) a TD Trap breakout is identified, either one tick above the previous trading day's high or one tick below the previous trading day's low. The critical variables are as follows: (1) The opening price must be contained or "trapped" within the previous trading day's price range and (2) either an upside or downside breakout beyond the confines of that price range must take place. Now in order to perfect these TD Trap indications, any series of qualifiers can be added. A number of recommended qualifiers to add from time to time to TD Trap include the following: For an upside move, the high one trading day ago must be less than the high two trading days ago, and conversely, for a downside move, the low one trading day ago must be greater than the low two trading days ago; for an upside move, the close one trading day ago must be less than the close two trading days ago, and conversely, for a downside move, the close one day ago must be greater than the close two trading days ago; and, as you can readily see, many other combinations and variations of similar comparisons can be introduced as well to qualify entries. These critical variables or qualifiers serve to distinguish TD Trap from most other short-term trend-following approaches. In addition to its simplicity, the other features of TD Trap include its versatility and variability, as well as its capacity to accommodate and introduce qualifiers and filters to its basic indicator formula. Figures 6.18 through 6.20 illustrate TD Trap.

The TD Trap options include the following:

1. The Display column includes "hits," "all," and "first" as variables and refers to the selection that can be displayed on the chart—a good choice is "hits" since it displays all instances in which TD Trap was activated, as opposed to "all," which displays each potential TD Trap possibility regardless of whether hit or not, and "first," which refers to the first TD Trap hit and disregards redundant hits in a series.

2. The Specific column provides a set of variables that price must exceed to activate TD Trap. Examples are highest/lowest, lowest/highest, narrowest, widest price range days, or other periods that are unconventional and consequently do not appear in the Price column and supersede any selections appearing in the Price column.

3. The Price column determines the reference price level used for TD Trap for both the open requirement as well as the penetration requirement.

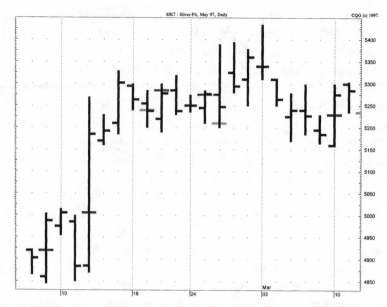

**Figure 6.18**   TD Trap requires a move greater than the previous trading day's high or less than the previous trading day's low after an opening price that is contained by the previous trading day's price range. As with TD Open, it is often better to exit a low-risk entry on the close or to use TD Trap to confirm another indicator. The opportunities arise to participate in big price moves—February 7 and 12—both up and down and to chip away at trades in the meantime. The series of qualifiers described on page 233, such as high/low one day ago less than/greater than high/low two days ago for an upside/downside move and close one ago less than/greater than close two ago, are included.

4. The Ago column establishes which day is used in conjunction with the Price column or which group of days is included in the Type column selection.

5. The Compare column determines whether the current day's open can be "equal to" as well as "greater than" and "less than."

6. The Other column refers to both the Qualifiers and Range that can be added to TD Trap. The Qualifiers are the standard options of comparisons, and Range includes the ability to attach an additional qualifier, such as a percentage penetration of the price range of a previous trading day or series of trading days to perfect the TD Trap entry level—this percentage component is similar to REBO.

Recommended settings for TD Trap are hits, up–true high/down–true low for the reference price as well as the penetration level, one trading day ago, with equal and with occasional qualifiers and occasional range penetration requirements. Figures 6.21 through 6.24 display TD Open examples.

TD Trap should be researched and used in conjunction with other indicators in this book. TD Trap is a suitable counterpart and complement

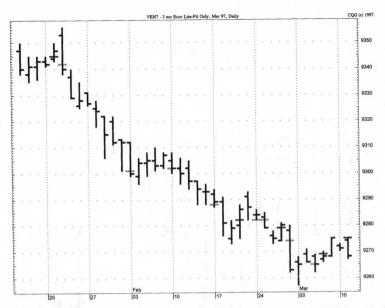

**Figure 6.19** TD Trap requires an open that is less than or equal to the previous trading day's high and greater than or equal to the previous trading day's low. Whichever direction price breaks out is the direction in which the trade should be taken. Qualifiers, such as the close one trading day ago less than either the close two trading days ago or the open one trading day ago for an upside move or the close one trading day ago greater than the close two trading days ago or the close one trading day ago greater than the open one trading day ago for a downside move. TD Trap is designed to supplement those TD Open trading opportunities which do not occur because of the position of the current trading day's opening price.

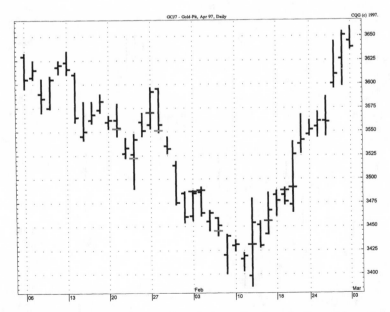

**Figure 6.20** TD Trap indications are identified on the chart both upside and downside. The current trading day's opening price must be contained or 'trapped' by the previous trading day's price range. The same qualifiers as described in Figure 6.19 are applied.

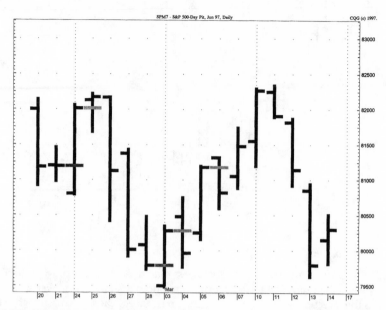

**Figure 6.21** TD Open requires that the current trading day's open be less than the low *x* trading days earlier or that the open be greater than the high *x* trading days earlier. This chart identifies those occasions when the open was less than the previous trading day's low or high and then proceeded to exceed that same trading day's closing price. TD Open can be adapted to relate the opening price to highs and lows other than one trading day ago. TD Open is designed to present opportunities that do not appear with TD Trap, TD CLOP, or TD CLOPWIN.

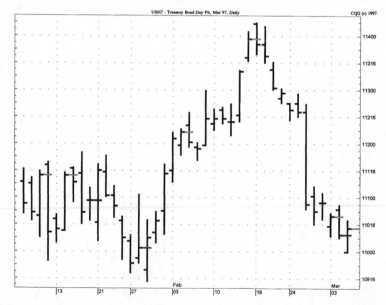

**Figure 6.22** TD Open often works best when trades are exited on the close the day of entry or when used in conjunction with other indicators. The same qualifiers applied to Figure 6.21 are applied to this example.

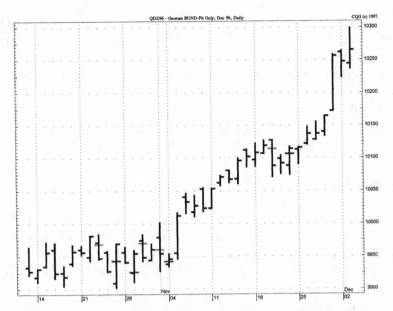

**Figure 6.23** TD Open was changed from relating the current trading day's open to the low or high one trading day ago to the low and high three trading days ago. This relationship can be extended to other trading days' lows or highs or even combinations of them for purposes of confirmation or for additional trading opportunities.

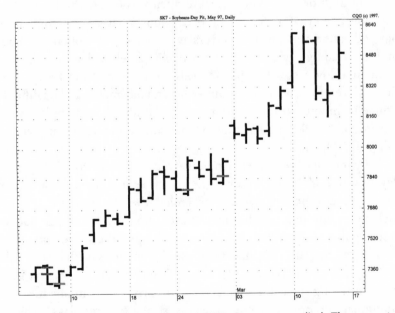

**Figure 6.24** In this example, two versions of TD Open are applied. The current trading day's open is related to the low and high either one or two trading day's earlier. Other comparisons can be made and qualifiers can be simply introduced, such as the close versus close one trading day ago or close versus open one ago.

to TD Open and, consequently, it is recommended that they be used in conjunction with one another. Whereas TD Open provides low-risk entry levels at prior price bottoms and tops, TD Trap low-risk entries occur later at prior price tops and bottoms and consequently, are accompanied by a higher level of risk. Additionally, TD CLOP, TD CLOPWIN, and TD Pivot should be included within this assortment of short-term pattern techniques in order to fulfill the entire suite of trading opportunities (see following).

# TD Open™

Almost 24 years ago, I spent a considerable amount of time researching and comparing the relationships between various price levels and their perceived impact upon the ensuing trading day's price movement. At approximately the same time, Larry Williams, a well-respected market timer, was conducting similar research of his own. A series of phone calls and meetings shortly thereafter developed into a business and personal relationship that exists to this day. We have exchanged research ideas since that time, and I credit Larry with the inspiration to develop and share my ideas with fellow analysts and traders in the industry. One price pattern we both observed in the silver futures market in 1972 (and which I referred to at that time as a "reentry pattern") related the opening price to the previous trading day's intraday high or low. Whenever the open was below the previous trading day's low and price traded the same day above that low, a potential low-risk buy indication was given. Conversely, whenever the open was above the previous trading day's high and price declined below that high the same day, a potential low-risk sell indication was given. Aside from Larry's contribution, I developed and applied numerous enhancements and qualifiers to this simple technique to filter potentially bad trades. The template created to accommodate all the variations of this simple market timing approach is called TD Open.

First of all, the reference points were increased from just the previous day's low or high to the low or high two, three, four, five, six, seven, or more days earlier. Immediately, this expanded the range of this indicator to include trading day possibilities far exceeding the limited frequency provided by the basic comparison of open and high or low one trading day ago. In other words, the open may be above the previous day's low or below the previous day's high, but this would not disqualify a low-risk entry indication from occurring since TD Open could still produce from one to six or more additional options over the previous seven trading days, which could develop into a low-risk entry indication as well. Furthermore, with the TD Open indicator, numerous other possibilities or options arise by revising the reference requirement from low and high to open, close, midpoint, average, and so forth. In other words, the indicator becomes more liberal in its requirements when the number of days for possible entry increases from one to seven, as they do likewise when the specified low-risk entry levels change from a price low to a higher price level for an upside move or, conversely, from a price high to a lower price level for a downside move, thereby enabling the open to take place above the previous trading day's low for an upside move or below the previous trading day's high for a downside move and still providing low-risk entry indications. Also, the introduction of a second criterion other than the reference price perfects the low-risk entry selection. For example, not only must the open be less than the low or greater than the high $x$ trading days earlier, but the high must also be greater than or the low less than a prescribed level such as the previous trading day's price midpoint, average, close, open, and so forth, depending upon whether an upside or downside move is qualified. Additionally, a specified percentage penetration of a previous trading day or a percentage of a group of days' trading ranges can be added or subtracted to the current day's open or previous day's close to also perfect the low-risk entry level. TD Sequential or TD Combo on a 1-, 5-, or 10-minute basis can also be low-risk entries introduced to ensure that the penetration of the threshold level, whether it be a low or a high or any other price selection, does not occur coincident with a Setup or Countdown completion, suggesting a contradictory short-term market move and thereby forcing postponement of entry until a subsequent penetration when the market is not short-term overbought or oversold. Furthermore, the specific day of the week can be identified and researched to determine its TD Open performance results for that particular trading day.

One research nugget uncovered when developing TD Open and subsequently applied as a qualifier to other indicators as well is something I call the market's TD Dead Zone™. Specifically, this is the area between the closing price and the intraday low at a price bottom and the closing price and the intraday high at a price top. With the exception of TD CLOP (see following), most short-term indicators generate a high propensity of failure should price open in this zone on a trade day. In other words, if price at a suspected low opens less than the previous day's low, then the market is opening weak, and if price opens above the previous day's close, then the market is opening strong, but any opening between this zone—yesterday's low and close—produces ambiguous market indications. Conversely, at a presumed top, any open within the previous day's high and close is uncertain as well, and you should be skeptical of any market activity that originates with such an opening. This relationship can be applied to versions of TD Open that relate to trading days other than one trading day ago and to other indicators with equal success.

## TD CLOP™ and TD CLOPWIN™

Both TD Trap and TD Open define the two possible breakouts that can occur after the opening of trading by producing a low-risk buy entry at the previous trading day's low or a low-risk sell entry at the previous trading day's high. Whereas TD Open is generally accompanied by a news development and a potential trend exhaustion and price reversal since the opening price must either exceed downside the previous trading day's low or upside the previous trading day's high, TD Trap is characterized by a more subdued opening price, which is contained within the previous trading day's price range. TD CLOP and TD CLOPWIN are counterparts to TD Open and TD Trap. It seemed that the basic TD Open was equipped to deal with price openings that occurred outside the previous trading day's range or any specified day or series of days' highs or lows. In those instances in which the opening price occurred, or was trapped, within that same price range, TD Trap seemed quite capable of identifying low-risk trading opportunities. Subsequently, the goal was to develop hybrids of these two primary trading models in order to perfect and confirm TD Open and TD Trap, as well as to take advantage of other trading situations that would not avail themselves to a trader limiting his or her scope to just these two techniques. Consequently, TD CLOP and TD CLOPWIN were developed.

TD CLOP requires the current day's open to be less than the previous trading day's close and open for a low-risk buy entry and the current day's open to be greater than both the previous day's close and open for a low-risk sell entry. TD CLOPWIN requires the current day's open and close to be contained within ("win") the confines of the previous day's open and close price parameters for both a low-risk buy and a low-risk sell. The condition "or equal to" can be added to each indicator's qualifiers. In the case of TD CLOP, if the current trading day's open is less than the two previous reference points—the previous trading day's open and the previous trading day's close—and the high is greater than both price levels, then a low-risk buy entry is indicated. Conversely, if the current trading day's open is greater than the two reference points—the previous trading day's open and the previous trading day's close—and the low is less than both these price levels, then the low-risk sell entry is defined. Other refinements can be simply introduced. In the case of TD CLOPWIN, the relative position of the reference day's close versus the reference day's open dictates whether a TD CLOPWIN low-risk buy or low-risk sell entry is operative. If the close is greater than the open, then expect a low-risk buy. If the close is less than the open, then expect a low-risk sell. However this expectation is not always the case and it is often prudent to await the ensuing trading day's price movement to initiate the low-risk entry. In addition, the next trading day's price action will help confirm any trade that may have been executed, since a higher high the ensuing day suggests upside follow-through, and a lower low the same day indicates downside follow-through. Furthermore, the TD Critical Qualifier is always available to make certain that the suspected breakout was not a result of a short-term price disequilibrium, which is quickly corrected the ensuing trading day.

TD CLOP and TD CLOPWIN examples appear in Figures 6.25 through 6.29.

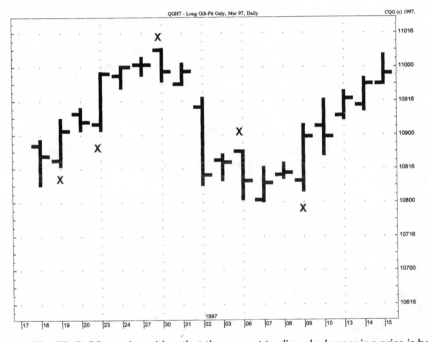

**Figure 6.25**    TD CLOP requires either that the current trading day's opening price is below both the previous trading day's open and close and the current day's high is greater than both price levels *or* the current trading day's opening price is greater than both the previous trading day's open and close and the current day's low is less than both price levels. The TD CLOP upside indications are marked with an *X* below the price bar and the TD CLOP downside indications are marked with an *X* above the price bar.

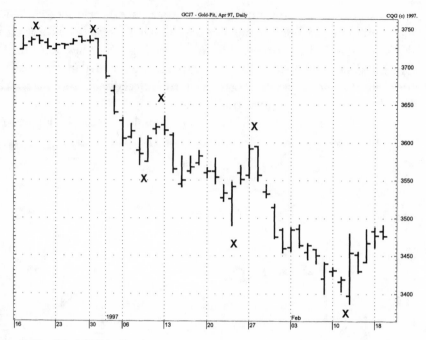

**Figure 6.26**  TD CLOP indications are marked with an *X*. Other family members of TD CLOP include TD CLOPWIN, TD Open, and TD Trap. Any one of these could possibly offset a TD CLOP open position.

**Figure 6.27**  The TD CLOP indications are marked on the chart with *X*s.

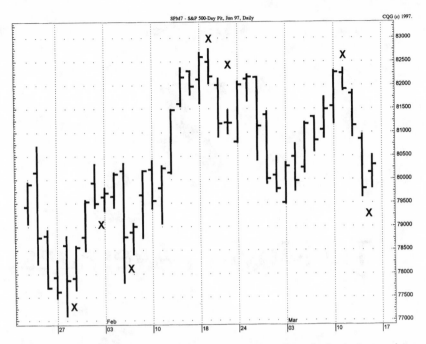

**Figure 6.28** TD CLOPWIN requires that the current trading day's closing and opening prices are contained within the opening and closing price one trading day ago. If the close is greater than the open, the move should be upside and if the close is less than the open, the move should be downside.

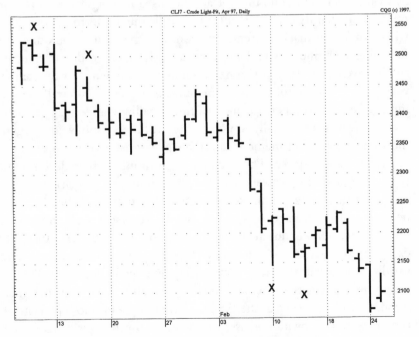

**Figure 6.29** TD CLOPWIN indications are identified with an *X*.

# Chapter

# 7

# TD Moving Averages

## TD Moving Average I™

Most traders have at one time or another used moving averages to initiate trades or to identify a trend. While historically the results may appear worthwhile whenever markets trend up or down, the results for other trend-following techniques would more than likely have produced comparable results given a similarly positioned trading environment over the same time period. By the same token, most any moving average works well in a trending market, but the performance within a trading range market for most moving averages is usually abysmal. My attitude is ambivalent regarding most trend-following methods and their performance when market trends are defined and in force. The dilemma confronting most traders lies in correctly differentiating between trending and trading range markets.

In a trading range market, just about the time price breaks above or below a moving average, it is usually time to reverse a position rather than initiate one. This is due to the fact that most markets, with the possible exception of cartel world markets such as copper, sugar, cocoa, tin, and oil usually operate within a trading range. My research indicates that 80 percent of the time this is the case, and of the other 20 percent in which markets trend, 12 to 14 percent of the time they trend up and 6 to 8 percent of the time they trend down. This is a result of the psychological reinforcement associated with the initial correct decision to buy and subsequent decisions to add to positions with the increase in margin availability and the trading conviction that prices will continue higher and, on the other hand, the single decision typically associated with selling. During the 1970s and early 1980s when an inflationary environment existed, trends were more pronounced, persistent, and prevalent. Frustrated by the frequency of many false starts, by the time an actual trend is about to begin the financial punishment inflicted by so many failures would have most traders too gun-shy to pull any trigger when an opportunity arises. This trading predicament is the same whether the moving-average approach applied or calculated is simple, exponential, centered, or displaced. Initially, because of the innate skepticism I developed throughout the years toward any type of moving average, I elected to use moving averages only as a stop-loss discipline as a result of these obvious shortcomings. Occasionally, I would revisit this methodology, and then in the early 1980s when markets were beginning to display more tendencies to operate in trading ranges, the realization hit me that using some of my trading techniques to identify price breakouts in combination with the application of a moving average might offer a viable alternative to the conventional moving average approaches and that applying this methodology might generate trading success. The combination of the two dissimilar approaches proved effective. Monitoring its performance and observing others who applied it profitably to identify low-risk entries proved that the results warranted acceptance and usage for both applications. The by-product of this research produced TD Moving Average I.

The concept behind TD Moving Average I is simply that if markets have a tendency to operate within trading ranges, then applying a moving average to markets within this environment would be an invitation to get whipsawed by trading. Consequently, the only prudent time to employ a moving average is when the market's context has been transformed from sideways to trending. The real feature of this indicator is its ability to speak only once potential price breakouts arise and to maintain trading silence or dormancy during nontrending markets. In order to capitalize on only those markets that are potentially trending, I installed a unique moving-average approach that is activated only once the prospects for a breakout and the establishment of a trend arise and then is extinguished after a short period of time if market behavior fails to confirm the continuation of the trend and the reversion to a trading range. One technique used to differentiate between the two types of markets is to determine whether either a low has been formed that is greater than all previous 12 trading days' lows, and if it has, then a five-day moving average of the lows is calculated for a period of four trading days. If succeeding lows greater than the previous 12 trading days' lows are formed as well, this process of calculating a five-day moving average is continued for a period of four trading days (including the current trading day). Once the series of 4 trading days has expired without a continuation of new 13-day high low (low greater than all previous 12 days' lows), then TD Moving Average I of the lows is extinguished. Conversely, TD Moving Average I of the highs is constructed similarly but in reverse. A high must be formed that is less than all previous 12 trading days' highs, and then a five-day moving average of the highs is calculated for a period of 4 days. If a subsequent high lower than all 12 previous days' highs is recorded, this process is continued, and the calculation of the moving average is suspended three days after the last occurrence of a high less than all previous 12 highs is recorded until the pattern is repeated again. In other words, I place a meter on price activity, and as long as a price trend is perpetuated the calculation is continued. Once the sequence of higher lows or lower highs is interrupted, the possibility of a trading range exists and TD Moving Average I vanishes, thereby reducing the likelihood of being whipsawed by in-and-out trading. TD Moving Average I will remain connected as long as the series of higher lows or lower highs persists. Once this pattern fails to appear after three trading days, it is suspended.

TD Moving Average I should be applied to markets as a stop-loss discipline, as well as a low-risk entry qualifier in conjunction with other indicators presented throughout this book. If a trade is entered based upon this indicator, entry should be taken on a closing basis and the following trading day's opening price should be monitored closely in case the TD Critical Qualifier is activated. In other words, the trade is suspect if a closing price exceeds the TD Moving Average I and then the following day's opening price fails to confirm the breakout by exceeding the level of the previous day's breakout as well. Figures 7.1 through 7.3 display TD Moving Average I.

## TD Moving Average II™

By definition, conventional moving averages will identify market bottoms and tops after they are formed. By displacing or projecting moving averages into the future a specified number of trading days, this process can be improved somewhat if the market's trend is decelerating or the market is in a trading range. Also, by calculating a series of moving averages of price highs, lows, and closes, and even multiplying the high and low values by a percentage that is added to the highs and subtracted from the lows (much like constructing a channel and possibly projecting these values into the future), the process of identifying high and low turning points becomes more precise, but at the same time, unless filters are introduced, the indicator is fraught with many false starts. The following admonition is not given lightly; it comes from a great deal of research and study regarding moving averages:

**Figure 7.1** Originally, TD Moving Average I was used as a stop loss for outstanding positions. However, the results using this approach for low-risk entries, especially for short-term charts, such as 1-, 5-, or 60-minute intervals, as well as daily has been very good. In order to make it effective, a closing price penetration must be confirmed by an opening in the following price bar as well. The breakout indications are marked with an *X*.

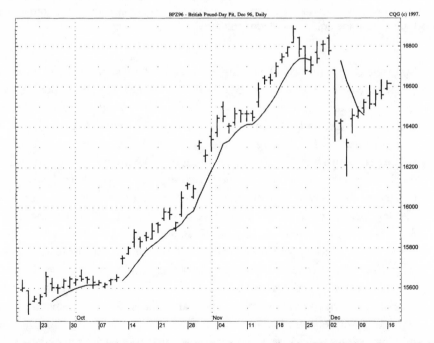

**Figure 7.2** It's uncanny how price activity is often repelled by TD Moving Average I. Usually, closes above or below the moving average that are confirmed by the following price bar's opening price indicate a valid breakout.

247

**Figure 7.3**   Price has demonstrated a tendency to hug TD Moving Average I until the time it penetrates the moving average on a closing basis, confirms the next trading day, and then breaks in the other direction. The moving average is not displayed every day because there must be an obvious attempt for the market to record a breakout. Intraday price penetrations above or below the moving average are not legitimate breakouts and are often merely opportunities to trade against or "fade" the break.

With the exception of TD Moving Average I, which surveys the market environment to ensure that the potential for a market trend exists before entering the market, there is only one other reliable method of calculating a moving average, and this approach is called TD Moving Average II.

Whereas TD Moving Average I awaited the breakout of a trading range before introducing a moving average, TD Moving Average II is always displayed on the price chart. In fact, two moving averages of closes are calculated and displayed on a chart, one short term (3 days) and one long term (34 days). In order to assume a positive or bullish outlook on the market, the 3-day moving average must be positioned above the 34-day moving average, and conversely, to view the market in a negative or bearish context, the short-term moving average must be less than the long-term average. Once the overall perspective of the market has been defined as potentially bullish or bearish, the two moving average values are related to their respective counterparts a defined number of trading days earlier. In the case of the 3-day moving average, the current day's value is compared with the value two trading days earlier, and in the case of the 34-day moving average, the current day's value is compared with the calculation one trading day earlier. Therefore a rate of change of moving-average values is calculated for both the long- and short-term periods. On the chart, each moving average is colored blue when their rates of change are advancing and red when they are declining. It is simple to determine visually when the short-term average is above the long-term average and vice versa. That is all that is required for a trader to evaluate the market's trend and to arrive at his or her market outlook. Obviously, as with other moving averages, your entry into or out of the market is delayed until price has already turned. However, by introducing two moving averages, making certain that the shorter-term is above the longer-term average in an advancing market or below the longer-term one in a declining market, and also requiring that the rate of change of each is increasing in an up market or declining in a down market before entertaining entry, the trading precautions will have been properly installed. Furthermore, depending upon your preferences, the time series of the moving averages, as well as the lookback for the rate of change calculations, can be adjusted. Figure 7.4 displays TD Moving Average II.

**Figure 7.4**  TD Moving Average II requires the construction and comparison of two distinct moving-average time periods. In this example, a 3-day and a 34-day moving average are displayed. Both moving averages turned up together in September and the short-term average was above the long-term. Until the short-term average declines below the long-term and both averages' rate of change decline, the market is expected to move higher.

# Chapter

# 8

# Market Timing Systems and Systems Development

*Observation:* At the time we met, both Paul Tudor Jones and Peter Borish from Tudor Investment were young, aggressive, open-minded, consumed by the markets, and determined to research and experiment with all sorts of market timing techniques. It was my assignment to test and develop trading systems for Tudor, and I created four primary trading systems. Their names neither describe their methodologies nor the concepts upon which they are based, because they are named after my four eldest children: TD TJ, TD Carrie, TD Meghan, and TD Rocke.

Peter and I were in charge of systems trading development. The company had only recently begun a concerted effort to develop mechanical systems to trade the markets. Paul and Peter had previously established themselves as successful discretionary traders and it was their intention to do likewise within the realm of systems trading. Prior to accepting a position with the company, I had researched, created, and applied a set of mechanical trading systems that Peter had traded successfully real time for a period of approximately 12 to 18 months. They were impressed with the results and confident that this successful performance record justified not only the continuation of trading these systems with increased funds, but also the concerted effort to develop a library of additional mechanical trading systems. Once that decision had been made, the nucleus for Tudor Systems was formed. It was the company's goal to dedicate a significant budget and staff to this project. It was my job as executive vice president to deploy my years of market timing research and experience to test and create additional turn-key trading systems.

The common denominator of all the trading methods created for Tudor was the simplicity of their construction and use. At all expense, customizing and tailoring systems to specific markets was avoided. This process is called *optimization*, and I have never subscribed to its implementation. Although each market traded is different in composition (equity, fixed income, wheat, gold, oil, etc.), collectively, the traders operating in each market possess the same emotions, expectations, and goals, as well as similar trading habits and methodologies. Consequently, my techniques are designed to apply pervasively to all markets without any adjustments or adaptations. Although there's no need to share with you all aspects and every nuance of these systems, their basic components will be discussed and presented for your consideration and review in the context of indicators, as well as the possibility of any part of these techniques being introduced into your own trading toolkit. Just as with all the other market timing techniques presented in this book, it is incumbent upon you to apply the critical trigger mechanisms required to activate signals. In a sense, you'll be provided with a cameo appearance of each technique, detailing the basics in general terms without an extended discussion of specific details.

Each of the systems was composed of a series of rules for entry, exit, profit taking, stop loss, and money management. Initially, the performance results were immensely successful, and prior to the suspension of trading, some systems continued to produce a respectable positive return. However, the significant returns generated in the first few years diminished somewhat over the ensuing four to five years. Both Paul and Peter were generous in allowing me to participate in those returns.

Two key ingredients to the success of these systems, as well as any system for that matter, are the introduction of a reasonable money management methodology and a disciplined, unemotional approach to the execution of mechanically generated trades. In Chapter 13, a simple and logical approach to money management will be presented. As far as discipline is concerned, systems could no doubt best be implemented by an unemotionally, detached third party such as a computer or a robot, since both are immune to the series of roller-coaster emotions generally responsible for the financial disasters suffered by traders. By having traders execute the trades, an element of risk exists as a result of their attachment to trades or of their propensity to introduce their own outlook, biases, or experiences into the trading process. In order to counteract this potential negative influence of override, Peter initially hired a young professional and some recent college graduates to execute the trades. This arrangement worked well since it reduced the risk of a trader's emotions unduly influencing the execution of the orders generated by the systems.

The goal here is not to describe each and every aspect of the trading systems developed and traded at Tudor, but to illustrate the general construction and structure of these systems in order to give you an appreciation for their simplicity and trading utility. In no way whatsoever are they intended to be ready-to-install timing devices for your immediate trading. They are to serve merely as models for you in your effort to design and craft your own trading methods and you should accept these ideas within that intended context only.

# TD TJ™

This trading model is designed to capture short-term opportunities in the market by identifying potential price exhaustion levels that arise when traders concede a losing position in a market by capitulating at the opening price. Specifically, given an initially incorrect or ill-timed trading decision coupled with adverse market psychology and unfavorable news as a backdrop, which only serve to refute the prudence of a trader continuing to hold a losing position, as well as the potential for additional losses accumulating, it is not uncommon for traders in the market to emotionally and financially throw in the towel, thereby creating a price opening that exceeds downside the previous day's low or upside the previous day's high. When such situations arise they imply emotional liquidation and, consequently, often present exceptional trading opportunities for an alert trader. Similar to TD Open (discussed in Chapter 6) but more specific, TD TJ is designed to identify and capitalize on these emotionally driven market turning points.

TD TJ requires an opening price that is outside the previous trading day's price range parameters (i.e., the previous trading day's high or low). In other words, the opening price is required to be either below the previous trading day's low for an upside move or above the previous trading day's high for a downside move. Furthermore, to qualify for a price advance, the high one trading day ago must be greater than or equal to the low two or three trading days ago. To qualify for a price decline, the low one trading day ago must be less than or equal to the high two or three trading days ago. Finally, to identify a low-risk buy entry zone, the current trading day's opening price must be at least 38.2 percent times the previous trading day's price range less than the previous trading day's low price and, at the same time, greater than 100 percent times the previous trading day's true price range less than the previous trading day's low price, and the current trading day's high must exceed upside the previous day's low by at least one price tick. Conversely, to identify a low-risk sell entry zone, the current trading day's opening price must be at least 38.2 percent times the previous trading day's price range greater than the previous trading day's high price and, at the same time, less than 100 percent times the previous trading day's true price range greater than the previous trading day's high price, and the current trading day's low must exceed downside the previous day's high by at least one price tick. In those instances in which the current price open is less than the previous trading day's low price but not less 38.2 percent times the previous trading day's price range minus the previous trading day's low, then the low-risk buy entry zone is elevated to the previous trading day's closing price plus one price tick. Conversely, in those instances in which the current price open is greater than the previous trading day's high price but not greater than 38.2 percent times the previous trading day's price range added to the previous trading day's high, then the low-risk sell entry zone is lowered to the previous day's closing price minus one price tick.

Another variation of TD TJ enters the market partially at the 38.2 percent level upside if the opening is below the level described above and enters the market partially at the 38.2 percent level downside if the opening is above that level. These entries are in addition to the conventional entries that are at the previous trading day's low and previous trading day's high as previously described.

Additional qualifiers and filters can be introduced to perfect this methodology, and we experimented and improved upon this basic structure by including other variables. But only the general approach and design of the technique is described and presented for your review. In order to improve upon this base you may prefer to experiment with TD Open (see Chapter 6), which is a dynamic indicator template utilizing the general TD TJ methodology but which places it within a much broader and dynamic trading shell, thereby enabling a user to apply and exploit unlimited additional qualifiers and filters to arrive at an improved market timing indicator.

## TD Carrie™

This trading model is designed to participate in breakouts by identifying critical price levels that previously served as important levels of price resistance and support. Although it is more likely to identify short-term market direction, occasionally it will highlight the inception of significant long-term price moves. TD Carrie complements TD TJ in the sense that instead of identifying emotionally driven price exhaustion turning points, it focuses upon breakout points and is more of a trend-following approach to trading. Just as TD TJ is a derivative of TD Open, so, too, TD Carrie is more akin to TD Trap. The requirements for a low-risk TD Carrie entry zone indication are as follows: an open less than or equal to the high four trading days earlier for an upside breakout and an open greater than or equal to the low four trading days earlier for a downside breakout. Additional trading rules are as follows:

1. For an upside breakout, the close one trading day ago must be less than the close two trading days ago, and for a downside breakout, the close one trading day ago must be greater than the close two trading days ago.

2. For an upside breakout, the true high four trading days ago (the high four trading days ago or the close five trading days ago, whichever is greater) must be greater than the high two, three, or five trading days ago, and for a downside breakout, the true low four trading days ago (the low four trading days ago or the close five trading days ago, whichever is less) must be less than the low two, three, or five trading days ago.

3. For an upside breakout, the current high must exceed the true high four trading days ago by at least one price tick, and for a downside breakout, the current low must exceed the true low four trading days ago by at least one price tick.

Obviously, other refinements and enhancements can be included and applied to improve the success of this approach significantly, just as they will when applied to the other techniques.

## TD Meghan™

This trading model is of a short-term variety and is designed to capitalize on price patterns and price relationships that appear frequently in most markets. Once again, the major components of this market timing technique are simple and straightforward. First of all, the price range from true high to true low one trading day ago must be less than the true range three trading days ago in order to qualify both upside and downside low-risk trading opportunities. (The *true range* is defined as the high or the prior trading day's close, whichever is greater, and the low or the prior trading day's close, whichever is less.) Next, for an upside move, the close one trading day ago must be less than or equal to the low three trading days ago, or the current opening price must be less than the low three or four trading days ago, *and* the current opening price must be greater than or equal to the close one trading day ago, or the current opening price must be less than or equal to the low one trading day ago. The reason for this requirement relates to an observation made many years ago, called the TD Dead Zone. (See page 239.) For an upside move, this refers to those occasions in which the opening price occurs within the price area between the previous trading day's close and the previous trading day's low. Such occurrences are generally associated with unreliable and unpredictable market price follow-through for an upside move. For a down-side move, the close one day ago must be greater than or equal to the high three trading days ago, or the opening price must be greater than the high three or four trading days ago, *and* the current opening price must be less than or equal to the close one trading day ago, or the current opening price must be greater than or equal to the high one trading day ago. Once again, the TD Dead Zone refers to the price area between the previous trading day's high and the previous trading day's close. In the case of an upside move, the high must be above the previous trading day's high. In the case of a downside move, the low must be below the previous trading day's low. The low-risk buy entry levels are calculated by adding the current day's open plus the range one trading day ago for an upside move and the current day's open minus the range one trading day ago for a downside move. As with the other trading techniques and described in this book, other reference prices can replace the ones cited. For example, the high and low two trading days ago can replace "one trading day ago." Additionally, various price relationships can serve to qualify and filter these basic components and will assist in the construction of a workable market timing approach. Other considerations such as stop loss, profit taking, and money management considerations should also improve this technique, as well as the introduction of any combination of the many other indicators presented throughout this book.

## TD Rocke™

This trading model is a short-term timing technique, and its construction and design are basic. The composition of this approach is simple and straightforward, similar to the other techniques presented. For an upside breakout above the high two trading days ago, either the high two trading days ago must be less than the high four trading days ago or both the high three trading days ago must be less than the high four trading days ago and the high two trading days ago must be less than the high three trading days ago. Furthermore, for an upside breakout, the close one trading day ago must be less than the open one trading day ago and the current open must be less than the high two trading days ago. Conversely, for a downside breakout below the low two trading days ago, either the low two trading days ago must be greater than the low four trading days ago or both the low three trading days ago must be greater than the low four trading days ago and the low two trading days ago must be greater than the low three trading days ago. Furthermore, for a downside breakout, the close one trading day ago must be greater than the open one trading day ago and the current open must be greater than the low two trading days ago. As you can see, the low-risk entry levels, depending on whether upside or downside, are the high and the low two trading days ago. Once again, other refinements to this trading base can be introduced, and adding such additional filters will serve to enhance the performance of the model as well as the accuracy of identifying low- and high-risk entry zones.

You now have the core of a series of market timing techniques that were implemented and traded successfully for an extended period of time at Tudor. If you use them, you may not enjoy comparable success, since markets change and occasionally a trader must review price behavior to determine the prudence of adapting an indicator by introducing qualifiers, filters, and refinements. There are no guarantees in this business, and there is no assurance that these adaptations and adjustments will produce profitable trading results. Keep in mind that many extraneous considerations foreign to the creation and implementation of a market timing system contribute to trading success: money management skills, market discipline, portfolio selection, and a key, though often overlooked, element called *luck*. Nevertheless, with the numerous indicators presented in this book, you should be able to combine these market timing indicators to improve your chances of trading success and profitability.

# Chapter

# 9

# TD Triangulation™ and TD Propulsion™

*Observation:* My professional career began on the institutional "buy side" of the investment business. While working for a large investment advisory firm, I realized that most "sell side" (brokerage house) market timers or technicians spoke the same language and used the same boring market timing tools. Oftentimes they were so preoccupied traveling and visiting clients that they failed to develop any original market timing techniques and were content to utilize the methods they had learned and had been accustomed to for years. Consequently, it didn't take long to discover that most of the original, creative market timing work was being done in the futures or commodity side of the business. Leverage, low margins, and volatility were the hallmarks of these markets, and they attracted individuals who were willing to accept the challenge of trading with an open mind and with the analytical ammunition essential for trading success. A 25-year friendship with Larry Williams evolved into a business arrangement as well. Larry possessed a keen insight into the markets that other market technicians lacked. We were compatible and worked closely on research projects for an extended period of time, and even to this day we share ideas and research projects. Among them are two market timing models: TD Triangulation and TD Propulsion. At the time they were developed, they were described as being elements of Thrust Dynamics.

Both TD Triangulation and TD Propulsion were developed with unique market timing principles in mind. For example, TD Triangulation operates on the premise that subsequent to a market advance or decline, prices generally experience retracements, which serve to relieve overbought and oversold conditions. While in its retracement mode, market prices tend to surpass critical price thresholds, and the momentum created and required to break these price barriers usually propels prices to the next level of resistance or support, which can be mathematically calculated. Just as many years ago TD REBO was the first attempt to provide formulas and structure to volatility and breakout market timing approaches, so, too, TD Triangulation has served as the genesis or catalyst for many other analysts' pattern recognition analysis techniques, since it was the first attempt to catalog price and pattern relationships. TD Propulsion, on the other hand, uses a similar price momentum model, only in reverse, and attaches a less significant role to price patterns and more to market thrust. Specifically, TD Propulsion operates on the premise that repetitive price movements in the same direction have a tendency to replicate one another. In other words, given a rally, then a price correction, the next attempt to rally will meet resistance at a prescribed percentage of the previous rally's movement, and once these levels are exceeded, often the price advance will continue to the next resistance level, which is also a percentage of the previous up move. Conversely, in a declining market, a successive price decline has a tendency to repeat a previous decline in percentage increments, and whenever key support levels are violated, prices generally gravitate to the next support level.

## TD Triangulation

There are basically eight types of market timing approaches that can be applied to markets. These methods include trend following, cyclical and seasonal, pattern recognition (chart formations), anti- or contratrend, oscillator- or indicator-driven, measurement, volatility, and momentum. TD Triangulation is an element of market thrust or momentum coupled with a heavy emphasis upon pattern recognition. A simple analogy should describe the thrust component of this market timing concept. Assume you are driving a car at 70 miles per hour and you turn off your ignition and, at the same time, apply the brakes. The car will continue to move forward despite your attempts to stop it. The same idea applies to the markets. If price is accelerating and surpasses a specified threshold level, momentum should propel the market's price movement farther to its next objective or target zone. By introducing specific ratios, a trader can arrive mechanically and mathematically at predetermined, calculated price objective zones. However, TD Triangulation as a system unto itself isn't recommended just because a trader is able to arrive at precise entry and price objective levels. Rather, TD Triangulation is useful as an indicator because it can be applied in conjunction with other indicators in this book to confirm your suspicions regarding future price activity.

TD Triangulation is a distinctive market timing technique in the sense that, at the time of its release close to two decades ago, it was the first technical method to employ not only pattern recognition techniques but also Fibonacci-derived ratios as its core. Despite the fact that TD Triangulation is trend following by design, it provides a higher degree of precision than traditional trend-following approaches since it establishes both definitive entry and exit price levels. Because of its trend-following nature, it is recommended as a tool to confirm existing trades in which positions currently exist or are about to be taken. At the same time, you may act in contradiction to those price entries that may not be qualified at price objective levels.

There are four stages to the TD Triangulation process: (1) identification of reference highs and lows; (2) selection of operative price patterns; (3) implementation of appropriate mathematical formulas, and (4) application of rules to determine trade suitability.

TD Triangulation is designed to identify both low-risk entry levels after a reaction bottom has been formed in an uptrend and low-risk entry levels after a reaction top has been made in a downtrend. The selection process of these critical price levels is conducted in a systematic, objective manner. In fact, the identification of these price levels is accomplished similarly to the procedure employed to identify price points for TD Relative Retracements— that is, at a price low, refer to the left of the chart to the last time a price high was recorded that was less than that low, and conversely, at a price high, refer to the left of the chart to the last time a price low was recorded that was greater than that high. The next step is to locate the highest price recorded between the day in which the high is lower than the recent reference low for an upside move and the lowest price recorded between the day in which the low is higher than the recent reference high for a downside move. This price-level selection process is complete once these two points have been identified. The next phase is to "triangulate" the third critical price in between these two price levels, which is the high for an upside move and the low for a downside move. Once this stage is completed, the starting point is initialized. Research suggests that the effectiveness of Triangulation diminishes if your reference price to the left of the chart occurs more than 144 trading bars ago.

The next task is to evaluate the specific price pattern associated with the current market. Seven different buy and sell price patterns exist in a market. These patterns are described next.

### Buy Patterns

You should examine and study the specific relationships between intraday highs, lows, and closes in order to appreciate the distinctions between these sets of price patterns. For upside moves, the following price patterns are operative:

For pattern 1 the low range day has ascending lows and ascending closes, both the day preceding and succeeding it.

For pattern 2 the low range day has ascending closes on both the day preceding and the day succeeding it, as well as descending lows.

For pattern 3 the low range is surrounded the day before and the day after with descending lows and descending closes.

For pattern 4 the low range day is surrounded by lower closes. Pattern 4a has ascending closes and descending lows. Pattern 4b has ascending closes and ascending lows.

For pattern 5 the low range day is surrounded by lower closes. Pattern 5a has descending closes and lows. Pattern 5b has descending closes and ascending lows.

For pattern 6, which is a four-day pattern, the lowest close occurs subsequent to the lowest low and day 4 is an up close versus the previous day's close.

For pattern 7 the lowest close occurs before the lowest intraday price low.

The following price levels are critical to each pattern:

Pattern 1—the close of day 2
Pattern 2—the close of day 3
Pattern 3—the low on both days 2 and 3
Pattern 4—the closes
Pattern 5—the lows
Pattern 6—the low of the fourth day
Pattern 7—the low of day 2 (the lowest day)

For downside moves, the patterns and price levels are reversed (see following).

## Sell Patterns

Once again, it is recommended that you review the specific relationships between intraday highs, low, and closes in order to fully understand the differences between the following price patterns, which are reciprocal patterns to the ones presented for the buy patterns. For downside moves:

For pattern 1 the high range day has descending highs and descending closes both the day preceding and the day succeeding it.

For pattern 2 the high range day has descending closes both the day preceding and succeeding, as well as ascending highs.

For pattern 3 the high range is surrounded the day before and the day after with ascending highs and ascending closes.

For pattern 4 the high range day is surrounded by higher closes. Pattern 4a has descending closes and ascending highs. Pattern 4b has descending closes and descending highs.

For pattern 5 the high range day is surrounded by higher closes. Pattern 5a has ascending closes and highs. Pattern 5b has ascending closes and descending highs.

For pattern 6, which is a four-day pattern, the highest close occurs subsequent to the highest high and day 4 is a down close versus the previous day's close.

For pattern 7 the highest close occurs before the highest intraday price high.

The following price levels are critical to each pattern:

Pattern 1—the close of day 2
Pattern 2—the close of day 3
Pattern 3—the high on both days 2 and 3
Pattern 4—the closes
Pattern 5—the highs
Pattern 6—the high of the fourth day
Pattern 7—the high of day 2 (the highest day).

For upside moves, the patterns and price levels are reversed (see previous).

To calculate price objectives for TD Triangulation, adhere to the following procedure. This example will serve to illustrate the selection process in an advancing market. Assume price has declined from a high of 100 to a low of 50. On the same day that the 50 low is recorded, the closing price is 51. Assume pattern 1 applies. The three components of Triangulation have been defined—a high of 100, a low of 50, and a close of 51. Had pattern 2 occurred and the close been 53, the three prices would have been 100, 50, and 53. All patterns except pattern 3 use only one figure. In the case of pattern 3, a price from day 3 is used for entry and a price from day 2 for the target level. Conversely, in a declining market, the process is reversed. Assume price has advanced from a low of 50 to a high of 100. On the same day that the 100 high is recorded, the closing price is 99. Assume that pattern 1 applies. The three components of Triangulation have been defined—a low of 50, a high of 100, and a close of 99. Had pattern 2 occurred and the close been 97, the three prices would have been 50, 100, and 97. All patterns except pattern 3 use only one figure. In the case of pattern 3, a price from day 3 is used for entry and a price from day 2 for the target level.

The formula for TD Triangulation Buy Entry is as follows:

$$1.00 - \frac{\text{recent price low}}{\text{recent price high}} \times 0.236 + 1.00 \times \text{pattern price} = \text{low-risk entry price (buy)}$$

For example, assuming that the price high is 100, price low is 50, price close is 51, and a pattern 1 exists, the formula for Entry would read as follows:

$$1.00 - \frac{50}{100} \times 0.236 + 1.00 \times 51 = 57.018 \text{ (buy entry price)}$$

Further, the formula for the TD Triangulation Buy Target or Price objective is essentially the same formula as Entry *except* that 0.4472 replaces 0.236.

*Note:* The Entry price should be rounded off and a tick added to ensure price penetration, and the target price should be rounded off and the objective shaved by at least one tick. A price tick is the minimum price fluctuation of a market.

The formula for TD Triangulation Sell Entry is as follows:

$$1.00 - \frac{\text{recent price high}}{\text{recent price low}} \times 0.236 + 1.00 \times \text{pattern price} = \text{low-risk entry price}$$

Further the formula for the TD Triangulation Sell Target or Price objective is essentially the same formula as Entry, *except* that 0.4472 replaces 0.236.

*Note:* The Entry price should be rounded off and a tick added to ensure price penetration, and the Target price should be rounded off and the objective shaved by at least one tick. A price tick is the minimum price fluctuation of a market.

Additional criteria critical to the TD Triangulation process include the following:

1. If either both the closes one day before and after the intraday low or intraday high are equal or if two consecutive closes within the TD Triangulation pattern set are equal, then an invalid TD Triangulation pattern exists.
2. If two or more consecutive days within the TD Triangulation pattern set have equal intraday lows or highs, this group of days is treated as if one day and the last day's close is operative if needed in the formula.
3. If a buy or sell indication is generated by price exceeding the intraday Entry levels but price fails to hold above/below the Entry level on a closing price, the factor used to calculate the Target is readjusted from 0.4472 to 0.3354.

4. If subsequent to entry, in the case of a buy, price declines into the zone between the lowest low and the close that day, the Target must be recalculated and the ratio 0.3354 must replace the 0.4472 factor. In the case of a sell, if price rallies up to the zone between the highest high and the close that day, the same factor adjustment must be made.

5. If price equals the Entry level but fails to exceed the Entry level by at least one price tick, the trade is not effected regardless of whether price exceeds that level the next day (if the opening price on the following trading day exceeds the Entry level, the trade is possible, but price exceeds the opening price by one or two ticks).

6. If the close on the third day of the set of pattern 2 fails to close within the range three days earlier, the trade is no longer operative.

7. If the close on the buy Entry day is higher than the highest of the three closes prior to Entry (or if the close of the sell Entry day is lower than the lowest of the three closes prior to Entry), then the trade is invalidated—the explanation is that the market has become too strong (too weak) and unsupported short covering (panic selling) has occurred.

8. If Entry occurs on the second day of the three-day set, then the range—high or low—must intersect the range two days earlier, and if not the trade is invalidated. If Entry occurs on the third day of the set, the range that day must intersect the range three days earlier.

9. If the close of the Entry fails to close above at least one of the previous three lows for a buy (below at least one of the previous three highs for a sell), then liquidate on the close that day.

Furthermore, apply Triangulation only to the futures contracts with the largest open interest. Finally, if Entry occurs on day 2 of pattern 7—the most common of all TD Triangulation patterns—the price Target must be hit the same day or the stop loss must be adjusted to one tick below the low of the entry day for an upside move and one tick above the high of the entry day for a downside move for that trading day as well as the next trading day. The standard Stop Loss should be reinstated thereafter.

These, then, are my TD Triangulation rules. If you are an inactive trader, you may not wish to take those trades that occur while the pattern is developing. By concentrating upon major price moves of more than just a few points, investors can take advantage of TD Triangulation just as traders are able to do likewise when they focus upon potential trades of a shorter duration.

## Stop Losses

Obviously, if a contradictory signal occurs at any time, the previously active signal should be exited and the position reversed.

There are three original stop losses I developed over 20 years ago. Not only are they applicable to TD Triangulation, but also to systems you may currently be using. The key reference levels for the stops for the first two are based upon the extreme low and extreme high depending upon whether the TD Triangulation projection is up or down. For TD Stop Loss 1: (a) when projecting upside and long the market, calculate the difference between the lowest intraday low price from the first price level selected for TD Triangulation calculation and the close that same trading day and subtract that difference value from the first price level selected for TD Triangulation calculation and (b) when projecting downside and short the market, calculate the difference between the highest intraday high price and the close that same day and add the difference to the highest intraday high. In order to trigger the stop loss for a low-risk buy indication, the closes for two consecutive trading days must exceed the calculated Stop Loss price level downside. In order to trigger the stop loss for a low-risk sell indication, the closes for two consecutive trading days must exceed the calculated Stop Loss price level upside. TD Stop Loss 2 uses the same intraday high and low, but instead of the close that same day, it uses the true low and true high. This difference is then subtracted from the intraday low or added to the intraday high, depending on whether the position taken is long or short the market. Once again, if the close exceeds this calculated level, the stop loss is activated. In this case, I await only one close to exceed the stop loss level. TD Stop Loss 3 is my TD Two Day Stop™, which can be applied to TD Propulsion (see following) and other methods as well. In fact, it is almost a technique unto itself. The stop requires two consecutive down closes versus the respective previous trading day's close if you are long the market and two consecutive up closes versus the respective previous trading day's close if you are short the market. The only other requirement is that the close of each day of this two-day set be contained by the price range two days earlier. Specifically, if long the market and the close one trading day ago is less than the close two trading days ago and today's close is less than the close yesterday and both closes are contained by the true price range (the true high and the true low) two trading days prior to each, then exit on the close. Conversely, if short the market and the close one trading day ago is greater than the close two trading days ago and today's close is greater than the close yesterday and both closes are contained by the true price range (the true high and the true low) two trading days prior to each, then exit on the close.

### Refinement to TD Two Day Stop

Pyramiding, or adding to a market position is not something I recommend. However, if you are so inclined, you might try a variation of the TD Two Day Stop to time your addition to an outstanding market position. A key component of this stop loss is the requirement that the closing prices be contained by the price range two trading days earlier. If, however, a trader is long the market and two consecutive down closes occur and both are less than the low two trading days prior to each, then a trader could consider adding to his or her position. On the other hand, if you are short the market and two consecutive up closes occur and both are greater than the high two trading days prior to each, then you could consider adding to your position as well. This pyramiding technique, however, is not operative if a contradictory signal is generated the same day.

## TD Propulsion

Whereas TD Triangulation identifies entries and price targets for reactionary price moves—rallies after a downtrend or declines after an uptrend—TD Propulsion is designed to operate in the direction of the overall price trend. In other words, if the market rallies for a period of time, experiences a price decline that does not violate the low marking the inception of the previous advance, and then subsequently resumes its rally, ideally TD Propulsion will identify the inflection price level, at which time sufficient momentum or thrust has been generated to indicate that price will likely continue to advance to at least the price target zone. In other words, the law of physics is applied to the markets—an object set in motion tends to remain in motion. The only question is at what point in time the market is "set in motion." Two ratios that are derivatives of Fibonacci numbers are key to determining the threshold zone required to gather sufficient momentum. One is responsible for establishing the low-risk entry zone. The other is important in determining the likely area of trend exhaustion or, in other words, the target area. They are 0.236 and 0.4472. The first number was derived by multiplying and calculating the differences between two household Fibonacci ratios: 0.618 and 0.382. In other words, $0.618 - 0.382 = 0.236$ and $0.618 \times 0.382 = 0.236$. There exists a relationship between the mathematical ratio pi (0.1416) and 0.236. By dividing pi (0.1416) by 6, the calculated value is 0.236. Also, the square root of 5 is 2.236, and by dividing the Fibonacci ratio 0.618 by 5, the calculated value is 1.236. As you can readily see, there are numerous derivations that will produce this same ratio 0.236 or variations of it.

There are three components to TD Propulsion: (1) the identification of the major market movement, swing, or thrust, (2) the application of the TD Propulsion formula and calculations, and (3) the establishment of the stop loss.

To calculate the entry level for a price move upside, subtract the difference between the most recent price high and a previous low that was preceded by a price decline from a prior high day's close of at least 0.236 of that difference. Conversely, to calculate the entry level for a price move downside, subtract the difference between the most recent price low and a previous price high that was preceded by a price advance from a prior low day's close of at least 0.236 of that difference. This process qualifies an entry-level calculation. In summary, to qualify and initialize a price low and establish a buy entry level, a decline from a recent high day's close of at least 0.236 of the distance from a recent high to a prior low that was preceded by a decline from a prior high day's close of at least 0.236 must have occurred. To qualify and initialize a price high and establish a sell entry level, an advance from a recent low day's close of at least 0.236 of the distance from a recent low and a prior high that was preceded by an advance from a prior low day's close of at least 0.236 must have occurred.

Contrary to the many price patterns used to calculate the entry and price objective levels for TD Triangulation, TD Propulsion requires the identification of only two price patterns. An *Inverted Pattern* occurs at a low of a three-day set when the middle (second) trading day of the set is the lowest low of the three trading days and the close that day is above the previous trading day's close (first) and less than the close of the last trading day (third). In addition, the high of the low day must not be above the previous day's high—in other words, an "outside day" must not occur. Any other pattern at the low is a *Standard Pattern*. On the other hand, an inverted pattern occurs at a high of a three-day set when the middle (second) trading day of the set is the highest high of the three trading days and the close that day is below the previous trading day's close (first) and greater than the close of the last trading day (third). In addition, the low of the high day must not be below the previous day's low—in other words, an "outside day" must not occur. Any other pattern at the high is a Standard Pattern. At the low or the high, if any two consecutive days have equal closes, then the pattern is invalid and Propulsion cannot be applied. In addition, if price, subsequent to the completion of the three-day set, declines below any of the three-trading-day-set closes at a low or advances above any of the three-trading-day-set closes at a high, then the pattern is invalidated and Propulsion cannot be reapplied until a lower intraday low is recorded for an upside move or a higher intraday high is recorded for a downside move.

The TD Propulsion formula for a Buy Entry is as follows:

1. Inverted Pattern: Current close of the price low ÷ (1.00 − the previous price low ÷ the prior price high × 0.236 + 1.00)
2. Standard Pattern: Current close of the price low × (1.00 − the prior price high ÷ the previous price low × 0.236 + 1.00)

The TD Propulsion formula for a Buy Target is as follows:

1. Inverted Pattern: Current price low ÷ (1.00 – the previous price low ÷ the prior price high × 0.4472 + 1.00)
2. Standard Pattern: Current price low × (1.00 – the prior price high ÷ the previous price low × 0.4472 + 1.00)

The TD Propulsion formula for a Sell Entry is as follows:

1. Inverted Pattern: Current close of the price low × (1.00 – the prior price high ÷ the previous price low × 0.236 + 1.00)
2. Standard Pattern: Current close of the price low ÷ (1.00 – the previous price low ÷ the prior price high × 0.236 + 1.00)

The TD Propulsion formula for a Sell Target is as follows:

1. Inverted Pattern: Current price low × (1.00 – the prior price high ÷ the previous price low × 0.4472 + 1.00)
2. Standard Pattern: Current price low ÷ (1.00 – the previous price low ÷ the prior price high × .4472 + 1.00)

Furthermore both Entries should be rounded off and an additional price tick added to ensure price penetration of key levels and Targets should be rounded off to the lower number for an upside target and to the higher number for a downside target, as well as shaven by a tick. A price tick is the minimum price fluctuation of a market.

An additional entry rule is called the TD Final Filter™, which is a variation of Qualifier 3, which I use to qualify intraday entries for TD Lines, Relative Retracements, and so forth. The TD Final Filter is calculated each day to determine whether too much anticipation of a price breakout already exists and, consequently, diminishes the likelihood of a breakout. In other words, if traders are already positioned for an imminent breakout, then who is left to precipitate the breakout, figuratively speaking. Therefore each day prior to a buy entry, calculate the difference between the previous trading day's close and that same day's true low (the low or the close the prior trading day, whichever is less) and then add this value to the previous trading day's high. If Entry is within that filter, a buy exists only if the close exceeds the TD Final Filter value. Conversely, prior to a sell entry, calculate the difference between the previous trading day's close and that same day's true high (the high or the close the prior trading day, whichever is greater) and then subtract this value from the previous day's low. If Entry is within that filter, a sell exists only if the close exceeds the TD Final Filter value. You can apply the TD Final Filter or variations of it to trading ideas of your own, qualifying trades and removing expectations that arise due to a frenzied market and price conditions.

## Stop Losses

At the risk of being redundant, please refer to the Stop Loss options described in the preceding discussion of TD Triangulation.

## Refinement to TD Two Day Stop

Once again, refer to the description of the TD Two Day Stop presented in the earlier discussion of TD Triangulation.

# Chapter

# 10

# Additional Indicators and Ideas for System Development

## TD Trend (TDT)™

Although not a market timing trend follower, I have researched and developed a number of market momentum models. One technique created with the expectation that it would enable me to identify important price breakout levels produced results, in fact, that contradicted my expectations. The output of this research experience will similarly surprise any reader who is inclined to buy strength or sell weakness and be classified as a trend follower. Originally, TD Trend (TDT) was developed as a trend-following method, but it quickly became apparent that it is more suitably classified and applied as an exhaustion or contratrend indicator. Research and application of TDT indicated that by the time the market reaches key threshold levels, oftentimes the move is exhausted and about to reverse its trend. Consequently, what was perceived to be a level at which price should accelerate its trend often turned out to be the termination of a move instead. Further studies confirmed that TDT is best utilized as a trend-anticipation technique. Although the variables used to construct TDT are dynamic and can be changed depending upon a trader's preference, basic or default settings are described here.

To apply TDT upside and thereby identify a price trend exhaustion level and what should be a prelude to a short-term price decline, a trader must locate the last three successively lower (with respect to one another) intraday true highs with closing prices the same day that are also less than the previous trading day's close. Conversely, to implement TDT downside and identify a downside price trend exhaustion level and what should be a prelude to a short-term advance, a trader can perform the same process, only in reverse. A trader must locate the last three successively higher (with respect to one another) intraday true lows with closing prices the same day that are greater than the previous trading day's close. Once the inception level of the series for the upside (the highest close) and the inception level of the series for the downside (the lowest close) are established and a subsequent closing price exceeds these key levels, a short-term price reversal often ensues.

Examples of TDT appear in Figures 10.1 and 10.2.

There is no requirement that the preceding selection of time periods defined and comparisons described are the proper ones. Other relationships can no doubt be introduced that are equally effective, and you are encour-

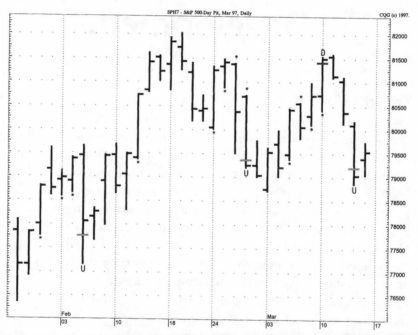

**Figure 10.1**    TDT is designed to identify potential areas of price exhaustion and short-term trend reversal. The comparison is made between the current trading day's high and the third most recent down close versus the previous trading day's close whose intraday high that same day is less than the previous count day's high. Conversely, at a potential exhaustion low, the comparison is made between the current trading day's low and the third most recent up close versus the previous trading day's close whose intraday low that same day is greater than the previous count day's low. In order to perfect the identification of the high or low, TD Diff, TD Open, TD Trap, etc., can be applied as well. Other qualifiers can be introduced. The asterisks identify those trading days used in comparisons.

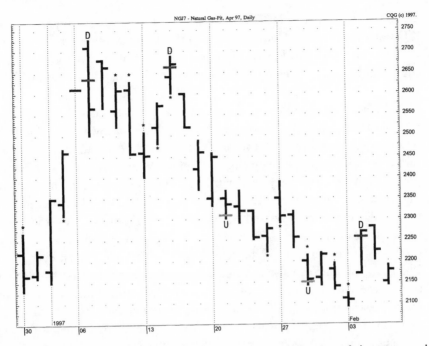

NGJ7 - Natural Gas-Pit, Apr 97, Daily                                                CQG (c) 1997.

**Figure 10.2**  In some instances, TDT is precise in the identification of short-term exhaustion levels. At other times, it is premature. Therefore it is best to experiment with different time periods and price relationships. Also, it is prudent to use TDT in conjunction with other indicators.

aged to experiment and apply these adaptations. However, keep in mind that my intention in developing this indicator was to identify trend breakouts, and it subsequently migrated to an identification of completely the opposite market condition—the termination of a trend or a price exhaustion zone. By experimenting with this process, you will certainly find variations to accommodate your own trading style. Since the advent of computers and sophisticated software, this process has become considerably more simplified than the condition that existed when it was developed many years ago—namely, visual inspection and trial and error.

## TD Pivot™

TD Open is somewhat rigid in the sense that the critical reference day(s) are established arbitrarily (e.g., one trading day ago, two trading days ago, three trading days ago). In order to counteract this inflexibility and arbitrariness, TD Pivot was created. TD Pivot adapts to the dynamics of the marketplace itself by using recently formed TD Points as reference levels. For example, whereas TD Open may use the low or high one, two, or three trading days earlier as a reference point, TD Pivot uses that low or high only if it is also a TD Point low or high. Consequently, TD Pivot requires that the selection of an important previous low or high be a result of price activity itself rather than an arbitrarily selected reference price level, which is the case with TD Open.

In fact, with TD Pivot there are various critical prices depending upon whether the option selected is an orthodox TD Point low or TD Point high or an unorthodox TD Point low or TD Point high. An example of a low-risk buy entry will help to explain the principles involved. In order to identify a possible low-risk buy entry level within a defined period of $x$ number of trading days ago, the nearest TD Point low is identified by a low preceded the trading day before and the trading day after by higher lows. Now the current day's open can be either "below" the most current TD Point low or "above" it or possibly equal to it. If the selection made is "below most current TD Point low" or what can also be referred to as "below most current last valley," then if the current open is not less than (or possibly equal to, depending upon the selection) that TD Point low, no potential low-risk buy entry exists on that particular day. However, if the choice is merely open "below the most current higher TD Point low" or "below the last higher valley," then a potential low-risk buy entry could occur that day regardless of whether the current day's open is below the most recent TD Point low or not. Assuming the current open is less than the TD Point low—either "last valley" or "last higher valley"—then the low-risk buy entry can be at that TD Point low or some other price level above the TD Point low on that same trading day if selected. In addition, the selected TD Point low can be level 1, 2, 3, and so on. Furthermore, the low-risk buy entry point can be adjusted to any of a number of days before or after the TD Point low provided that the current day's open is less than (or equal to) that trading day's low and the current day's high is greater than the low-risk entry point, whether it be the TD Point low or $x$ number of days before or after the TD Point low. Finally, instead of requiring the open to be less than the TD Point low, an unorthodox option can be selected, such as the open "below the most recent TD Point high" or $x$ day(s) before or after the TD Point high and the high greater than the most recent TD Point high or $x$ days before or after TD Point high. In other words, in this example the most recent TD Point high can be referred to as either the "last peak" or the "higher peak" and the current open must be less than (or possibly equal to, depending upon the selection) that reference price or $x$ day(s) before or after, whichever may be selected. As you can readily see, all sorts of options exist as to what reference point to select.

Conversely, to identify a low-risk TD Pivot sell entry within a prescribed period of $x$ number of previous trading days, reverse the conditions described above. First locate the closest TD Point high, or in other words, for a TD Point level 1, a high preceded the day before and the day after by lower highs. The current day's open can be either "above" the most current TD Point high or "below" it, or possibly equal to it. If the selection made is "above most current TD Point" or "above most current last peak," then if the current open is not greater than (or possibly equal to, depending upon the selection) that TD Point high, no potential low-risk sell entry exists on that particular day. On the other hand, if the choice is merely open "above the most current lower TD Point High" or "above the last lower peak," then a potential low-risk sell entry could occur that day regardless of whether the most recent TD Point high is above the current day's open. If, for example, the current open is greater than the TD Point high—either "last peak" or last higher peak"—then the low-risk sell entry can be at that TD Point high or some other price level on that same day if selected below the TD Point high. Furthermore, the selected TD Point high can be level 1, 2, 3, and so on. The low-risk sell entry point can be revised to any number of days before or after the TD Point provided that the current day's open is greater than (or equal to) the TD Point high and the current day's low is less than the entry point, whether it be the TD Point high or $x$ number of days before or after the TD Point high. Finally, instead of requiring the open to be greater than the TD Point high, an unorthodox approach can be chosen, such as the open "above the most recent TD Point low" or $x$ day(s) before or after the TD Point low and the low less than the most recent TD Point low or $x$ days before or after the TD Point low. In other words, in this example the most recent TD Point low can be referred to as either the "last valley" or "lower valley" and the current open must be greater than (or possibly equal to, depending upon the selection) that reference price $x$ day(s) before or after whichever may be selected.

Figures 10.3 and 10.4 display TD Pivot.

As you can readily see, the various setting selections for TD Pivot are numerous. The feature of this variability is the fact that a trader can test and choose combinations which suit his or her trading style. Whereas you might be uncomfortable entering the market on an upside reentry indication once price exceeds a previous TD Point low, you can introduce an additional filter, such as the high exceeding the TD Pivot day's close to confirm strength. Furthermore, higher-level TD Points can be used, and the key reference days can be adjusted to either $x$ number of days before or after the TD Point low. The combinations and filters that can be introduced are endless. Once again, however, by becoming too restrictive with many filters and rules, the risk of optimization or "historical price fitting" exists, and consequently the predictability and effectiveness of an indicator's performance can diminish in the process.

**Figure 10.3**    TD Pivot refers the current trading day's opening price to the most recent TD Point High or Low. If the opening is above the intraday high or below the intraday low and price penetrates these levels, the most basic form of TD Pivot has been defined. TD Pivot is an alternative indicator to TD Open, which is totally static since it relates to a specific trading day regardless of whether a turning point (TD Point) existed at that time or not. The TD Point references have been marked with an *X*.

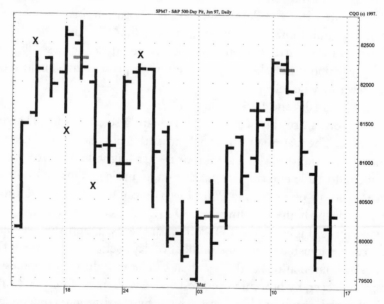

**Figure 10.4**    TD Pivot in this example compares the current trading day's opening price with the most recent lower TD Point high and most recent higher TD Point low. The low-risk entry indication is shifted to the right by one trading day. The reference TD Point highs and lows are marked with an *X*, but the entry level is one bar to the right.

# TD Diff™

One manifestation of my obsessive market research efforts into price patterns is an indicator called TD Differential or TD Diff. Not only is it important what this indicator says, but it is equally important what TD Diff does not say. By definition the lowest closing price at a market's low must be a down close, since subsequent closes must fail to exceed that low close or it would no longer be the lowest close, and if any close did perchance record a lower close, then it would become the new low close until it is violated. Conversely, the highest closing price at a market's high must be an up close, since subsequent closes have to fail to exceed that high close or it would no longer be the highest close, and if any close did happen to record a higher close, then it would become the new high close until it is likewise violated. To identify a potential short-term price bottom, TD Diff evaluates the price relationship between the low and the close recorded on a particular trading day and compares it with the price relationship between the low and the close recorded the prior trading day. In order to identify a potential short-term top, TD Diff evaluates the price relationship between the high and the close recorded on a particular day and compares it with the price relationship between the high and the close recorded the prior trading day. TD Diff applies to those closing price relationships that can be expressed as follows: (1) At a potential low, the current trading day's close is less than the previous trading day's close (i.e., close today is less than the close yesterday) and the previous trading day's close is less than the prior trading day's close as well (i.e., yesterday's close is less than the close two days ago). (2) At a potential high, the current trading day's close is greater than the previous trading day's close (i.e., close today is greater than the close yesterday) and the previous trading day's close is greater than the prior trading day's close as well (i.e., yesterday's close is greater than the close two days ago). In other words, TD Diff surveys the market looking for those instances in which two consecutive trading days record down closes (closes less than each respective previous trading day's closes) or up closes (closes greater than each respective previous trading day's closes). Once identified, the value of the price difference between the close and the low for each day (if consecutive down closes) is recorded and the value of the price difference between the high and the close for each day (if consecutive up closes) is recorded. The two-day set of differences is compared, and if the current trading day's value is greater than the previous trading day's value and two consecutive down closes are recorded, then there exists a good chance that the current day's low will not be exceeded on the following trading day. If the current trading day's value is greater than the previous trading day's value and two consecutive up closes are recorded, then there exists a good chance that the current day's high will not be exceeded the following trading day. Exhaustive research suggests that in those instances in which two consecutive down closes or two consecutive up closes occur, TD Diff plays an important role. To reiterate, if the current one-day differential is greater than the previous day's difference, then there is a greater likelihood that a possible bottom or top has been formed with the current trading bar, depending on whether price is at a low or a high. Conversely, had the current differential been less than the previous day's difference, then there is a stronger chance that the trend will continue over the near term. In summary, if the trading day before a down close versus the previous trading day's close is an up close, there is a chance that a short-term bottom has been made. Conversely, if the trading day before an up close versus the previous trading day's close is a down close, there is a chance that a short-term top has been formed. However, if both consecutive closes are down or up, then TD Diff can be applied to determine the possibility of a continuation or an interruption of the ongoing trend. Should TD Diff imply a resumption of the trend, research suggests that this should occur within the ensuing three trading days, and more likely than not, the next trading day.

Although TD Diff is not an infallible indicator that will accurately forecast the ensuing trading day's market direction, it is nevertheless an effective predictor of what price behavior to expect in the market on the next trading day. Many years ago I observed the market's tendency to broadcast its price disposition when this pattern occurred. At that time, I referred to TD Diff as my "sleep indicator." This expression seemed appropriate because when I was trading a particular market and was uncomfortable holding this position overnight for fear the price action the following trading day might destroy me financially, TD Diff would provide me with the confidence necessary to be able to sleep that night. In fact, when I shared this technique with my good friend Charlie DiFrancesca, the largest trader on the Chicago Board of Trade in the late 1980s, he was impressed enough with the results to hold positions overnight that he may have liquidated in the past because of short-term market uncertainty. His brother John has introduced TD Diff into his trading discipline and uses this technique in his own floor trading to this day, often liquidating or holding overnight positions in various markets solely because of TD Diff.

Extensive research has helped to distinguish between those price patterns and relationships generally associated with trend reversals and those price patterns and relationships that typically occur during trending markets and are thereby merely price reactions within ongoing trends. One such pattern which rarely appears at a market bottom or top is the occurrence of two or more consecutive equal closing prices marking the completion of a trending market decline or advance. By discounting the possibility that a price bottom or price top will be formed coincident with this price pattern—equal closing prices—a trader generally can look for a subsequent lower close to form a price bottom or a subsequent higher close to occur at a price top. Having discounted the appearance of an "equal" closing price pattern proposition at a market bottom or top, besides TD Diff, one other price pattern and price relationship exists that possesses a degree of predictability accompanying its appearance. By definition, the lowest close and the highest close occur when a market reverses trend from down to up and up to down. If the day before the lowest close in a downtrending market is an up close versus the previous day's close and if the day before the highest close in an uptrending market is a down close versus the previous day's close, there is a possibility that the price trend has been exhausted and a suspected price reversal in the market is imminent. You should be vigilant to such a development whenever this price pattern appears. Namely, compare the previous trading day's close with the prior trading day's close and the current trading day's close with the previous trading day's close. If the current trading day's close is less than the previous trading day's close and yesterday's close is greater than the close the trading day prior to it, then the potential of a short-term low exists. Conversely, if the current trading day's close is greater than the previous trading day's close and yesterday's close is less than the close the trading day prior to it, then the potential of a short-term high exists. At the time TD Triangulation (see Chapter 9) was developed, Larry Williams researched a price pattern he called "valise." Simply described, valise is a series of four closing price comparisons—at a price bottom, the most recent closing price is less than the previous trading day's close, and the trading day prior to the lowest close is an up close compared to the close two days before the lowest close, and both the trading days immediately prior to the up close are down closes versus each respective previous trading days' close. Conversely, at a price top, the pattern is reversed, since the most recent closing price is greater than the previous trading day's close, and the trading day prior to the highest close is a down close compared to the close two days prior to the highest close, and both the trading days immediately prior to the down close are up closes versus each respective previous trading days' closes. I have developed a number of refinements for both patterns. Since either TD Diff, the valise (the last two trading days), or "equal" closes are the only three possible price patterns that can occur at a market bottom or top, I have addressed and exhausted all conceivable price pattern possibilities. The general distinction between these patterns is obvious, but it is critical to differentiate between various versions of these two price patterns similar to computing a value difference for TD Diff. Since equal closes occur infrequently in markets at significant price tops and bottoms, there remain only the other two price pattern options for additional research study and analysis.

For examples of TD Diff see Figures 10.5 and 10.6.

**Figure 10.5**  TD Diff calculates the difference between a trading day's closing price to that same trading day's low price and relates that value to the previous day's value, provided both are down closes versus the previous trading day's close. Conversely, TD Diff calculates the difference between a trading day's high and that same trading day's close and then compares that value with the prior trading day's value, provided both days are up closes versus the previous trading day's close. If the current trading day's value is less than the previous trading day's value, price should go lower intraday the following trading day at a low and should go higher at a high. The value for the prior trading day appears with a hash mark on the chart and if the close is above the mark and two consecutive up closes appear, price should go higher intraday the next day and if the close is below the hash mark at a low, then price should decline intraday the following trading day.

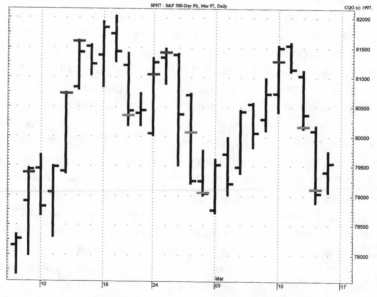

**Figure 10.6**  Without exception, TD Diff described the likelihood of price following through either upside or downside the trading day after the indication.

# TD Pressure™

It is fascinating to study the relationships within and between various markets, whether they be specific prices, price levels, price patterns, time periods, or any other conceivable price- and time-related combination. It has been emphasized repeatedly throughout this book that a key or "critical" component of many of my indicators and formulas, as well as price filters, is the opening price. Granted, the other price levels such as high, low, and close that are published by most of the media and followed by most traders are important as well. However, the opening and the closing prices are the two most important price levels. Consequently, I often use the opening price as a reference point and use the close that same day for confirmation purposes, or I use the closing price and the opening price the following trading day for confirmation purposes. In fact, for a number of years, I have been critical of the way in which daily price changes are reported both on the various data networks, as well as in the daily newspapers. For example, should you call your broker to receive a price quote, the current price is always related to the previous day's close and if a significant news event or corporate announcement occurs after the previous day's close and prior to the current day's opening price, the current day's close could misrepresent what has actually taken place in the market. If the news is released late yesterday after the previous trading day's closing price and it is favorable, and the current day's closing price subsequently closes above the previous trading day's closing price, then the impression is that accumulation or buying has been dominant today. However, if the current day's close is, at the same time, below the current day's opening price, then since the open, the trading activity in that marketplace can be characterized as having been under distribution and not accumulation as you might presume to be the case. In other words, often in volatile, as well as inactive markets, the open can be exaggerated or controlled by news events or aggressive buying or selling campaigns, and despite the fact that the close that same day may be above or below the previous trading day's close, if its comparison versus the current day's opening price does not confirm by recording a closing price above the open that same trading day as well, then there is an obvious conflict. For example, I have inserted this comparison of close versus the previous trading day's close and close versus the current open into the TD Plurality indicator shell to evaluate this comparison (see Chapter 1 under TD Plurality). However, if the opening price is significantly above or below the previous day's close, then by introducing an adjustment factor, you are able to account for this anomaly and adjust for this explosion in demand or supply and account for it in an accumulation/distribution model index should it be necessary. Nevertheless, the key message here is that the opening price is an important market variable, and when analyzing the current trading day's price movement, it is more valuable as a reference price than the previous day's closing price level.

Once again, most traders seem to be unduly influenced by market convention, since they accept commonly used reporting practices such as those used by the media and quote services. Industry convention or standards require that all price movement be referenced to the previous trading day's price close, and that is the accepted reporting practice. A more accurate method would be to relate the current day's price with the current day's opening price. Often a news item will influence or distort the level of the opening price and the market will quickly adjust by filling the price vacuum from the previous day's close. Although price may close up versus the previous day's close but less than the current day's opening price or may close down compared with the previous day's close but at the same time greater than the current day's opening, the true picture of accumulation or distribution operating within the market will be misperceived and misrepresented. My work is comprehensive and both simple and complex at the same time, depending upon the level of analysis a trader may desire. A sophisticated model called TD Pressure has numerous components that address these various approaches. Not only is TD Pressure valuable when relating price change and relationships between opening and closing prices but it is also helpful for incorporating volume and rate of change (of volume, price change, and a combination of volume and price change) into the equation. Consequently, I have developed a series of approaches to assist in evaluating accumulation and distribution in markets: (1) price change, (2) volume, (3) volume and price change combined, (4) comparisons of price change and a combination of volume and price change, (5) relationships between these variables, and (6) the rate of change of accumulation and distribution of this statistical information.

The accumulation/distribution models I developed in the early 1970s used the opening price as the focal point for all the formulas. Initially, I applied these formulas to stocks, perfected the techniques, and then used the same approaches in the futures markets. The chronology of the methodology is as follows:

1. *On-balance-volume analysis:* A cumulative index is constructed as a result of adding all the daily volume if the trading day's closing price is greater than the previous trading day's closing price level and subtracting all the volume if the trading day's closing price is less than the previous trading day's closing price level.

2. The current trading day's opening price is substituted for the previous trading day's closing price level in the on-balance-volume formula.

3. A ratio is introduced whereby a percentage of the price movement is allocated to either buying or selling pressure (i.e., the "current trading day's

close *minus* current trading day's open" *divided by* the difference between the "current trading day's high and current trading day's low").

4. The ratio calculated in item 3 is multiplied by that same day's volume.

5. The cumulative index is derived by summing the daily values calculated in item 4.

6. All the positive values calculated in item 4 are added together. Over a specified number of trading days, such as 55 or 89 trading days, and this value becomes the numerator, and this value is in turn divided by the absolute value of all the positive values calculated for the numerator *plus* all the negative values (absolute value) to arrive at a percentage of buying pressure over the total amount of buying and selling pressure combined in order to be able to relate one market to another.

7. The rate of change (ROC) of the ratio presented in item 6 is calculated to measure the intensity of the buying pressure—13-day rate of change for 55 trading days and 21-day rate of change for 89 trading days.

8. A trading band defining overbought/oversold threshold levels for the ROC is installed to define low-risk trading opportunities.

Whenever an opening price gap greater than or less than the previous trading day's close of 8 percent is recorded, it is recommended that an alternative or adjustment formula be used to compensate for the heavy inflow of demand or supply. Instead of using the open formula, I introduce the *difference between* the following two values, which serve as proxies for buying and selling pressure, respectively:

1. The difference between the current trading day's high *minus* the previous trading day's close *plus* the difference between the current trading day's close and the current trading day's low.

2. The difference between the current trading day's high *minus* the current trading day's close *plus* the difference between the previous trading day's close and the current trading day's low. At the same time, I ignore all negative values. This comparison is similar to TD DeMarker II (see Chapter 1).

Variations of TD Pressure have been comprehensively described for your consideration and review. Any one of these variations can stand on its own research and trading merits. You should experiment and apply each version to the markets and then incorporate one or all, as your comfort level may dictate, into your trading toolkit. In regard to its application to futures markets, three adaptations are recommended. Since actual volume is typically reported a day late, estimated volume can be substituted. Whenever price trades to its daily limit and trading is suspended since the market is "bid or offered" limit up or limit down, the limited trading volume fails to reflect true demand. In these instances, either substitute the highest volume over the previous month's trading as a proxy or combine that trading day's price range with the following trading day's range and volume and use this activity as a trading range and volume proxy. Finally, since futures have an open interest component which stocks do not, by dividing volume by open interest and then calculating a ratio which in turn is multiplied by volume a clearer picture of buying and selling pressure is presented. Examples of TD Pressure appear in Figures 10.7 through 10.9.

**Figure 10.7**  TD Pressure calculation of 55 days with a rate of change of 13 days when applied with price only and not volume yields this indicator presentation. Price indicator divergence is presented, but another approach is to install an overbought/oversold indicator band.

**Figure 10.8**   This chart is identical to Figure 10.7 with the exception that the indicator includes price and volume.

**Figure 10.9**   This chart is identical to Figures 10.7 and 10.8 with the exception that no rate of change is calculated and the indicator is a cumulative index of price change and volume.

# Chapter

# 11

# Methods to Calculate
# Price Objectives

## TD Trend Factors™

*Observation:* Subsequent to the release of my first book, *The New Science of Technical Analysis*, I was contacted on separate occasions by two individuals who had doctorate degrees and who had questions regarding TD Trend Factors. Coincidentally, both individuals lived in England. In the first instance, the caller asked if I had a degree in structural engineering. He indicated that TD Trend Factors used ratios similar to those applied in the construction of bridges. I had no background whatsoever in engineering and was surprised to hear of such a connection. The second person posed a question regarding my education as well, but in this case he quizzed me regarding my training in molecular biology. Amused by his question, I likewise indicated to him that I possessed no background in this area. Both episodes implied a basis for my market timing research that extended further than the trial-and-error process conducted to uncover these ratios and their application to market activity and price behavior. It came as a complete surprise to learn of the connection and the application of these ratios to areas of science and mathematics. That was not the genesis of my research. Although the precision witnessed throughout the years by applying this tool to price projections has often been eerily and uncannily accurate, the derivation of the TD Trend Factor process has been more mundane and innocent than the sophisticated and complex attributes assigned by some highly educated people. While their compliments are gratifying, they are entirely undeserved.

Using my calculator to make price comparisons between price highs and lows, I discovered that a series of ratios defined levels of price resistance and support. Regardless of which market was analyzed, these ratios appeared to work well. In the late 1970s I described these ratios as "Magic Numbers," and shortly thereafter as Trend Factors. I arrived at these specific numbers through a combination of Fibonacci ratios and trial and error. Here's how. The two popular Fibonacci ratios are 61.8 and 38.2 percent. By subtracting these two values, you arrive at 23.6 percent. In turn, divide that value by 4, since market moves generally occur in price legs and the indication of the inception of a price leg is a market move of approximately 25 percent of the prior price leg (see TD Propulsion, Chapter 9). By dividing 23.6 percent by 4, you get 5.9 percent. By applying this percentage to various markets and conducting a lengthy period of testing, it became apparent that 5.56% was a more effective ratio to use. Further variations of this ratio are presented in the discussion of Propulsion. As a result of more research, I found that additional resistance and support levels are identified by using multiples of 5.56 percent (0.9444 is the difference between 100.00 and 0.0556). More tests indicated which specific price levels to use as a base to arrive at price objectives. Just as with both TD ROC I and II, when applying Trend Factors to less volatile markets or price levels that are in decimals, an additional decimal place is added to 1.056 (multiply fraction by 0.1) to arrive at 1.0056 and concurrently increase 0.9444 to 0.99444. Whereas the base price of 0.0556 (or for smaller price levels 0.00556) is used in each calculation of Trend Factor price objectives upside, when performing the exercise for the downside Trend Factor objectives it is not quite the same process, since each TD Trend Factor price objective is in turn used as the next base to calculate the next downside level (each respective increment is in turn multiplied by 0.9444, or for smaller price levels, 0.99444). Consequently, 5.556 percent is multiplied for upside moves and 94.44 percent is multiplied for downside moves (for smaller price levels 0.5556 and 0.9944 percent are used).

In order to "initialize" or determine whether a price low qualifies as a Trend Factor base, you should make certain that from a recent intraday high to subsequent intraday low, price has declined by at least 5.556 percent. In order to determine what price high qualifies as a Trend Factor base, you should make certain that from a recent intraday low to subsequent intraday high, price has advanced by 5.556 percent (adjust to alternative percentages for smaller price levels). The most recent price move of at least 5.556 percent either upside or downside determines whether the TD Trend Factor objective is calculated up or down. The important element is the proper selection of the specific price levels to use when making price projections. Originally, at a reversal low (low less than the previous trading day's low and the close above the previous trading day's close), the first TD Trend Factor upside projection was derived by multiplying 1.0556 by the close and all subsequent projections to the intraday low. The same process only in reverse was applied at a high—the close of the reversal high trading day (high greater than the previous trading day's high and the close less than the previous trading day's close) was used to make the first TD Trend Factor downside projection and the intraday high of that same day was used for all subsequent projections. In those cases where a price reversal is not recorded at a low or a high, the low was used for all upside price projections and the high for all downside price projections. However, there are now more occurrences of variations of these patterns, and consequently I am experimenting with combinations of other selections, as well as multiplying both the high and close for downside projections and both the low and close for upside projections. In addition, the distance between TD Trend Factor levels can be subdivided by 2 to arrive at additional, interim potential levels of support and resistance.

Figures 11.1 through 11.10 display various TD Trend Factor examples.

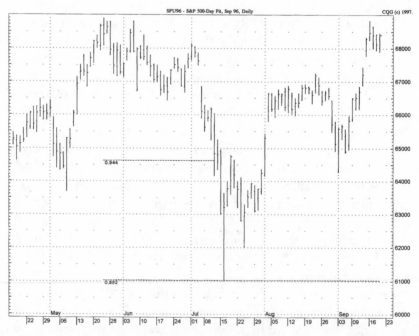

**Figure 11.1** By applying TD Trend Factors to the highest day's closing price the two downside price objectives were displayed. The lower objective was 610.25, which was the precise market low to the tick. When price hit that objective, the futures were locked down limit at 610.25. The breakout to lower price levels was not qualified, thereby indicating a low-risk entry indication and likely price reversal at the price objective level.

**Figure 11.2** Coincident with TD Sequential or TD Combo low-risk buy or sell indications, TD Trend Factors can be applied to arrive at price objective areas. The two generated off of the intraday low on November 13 were hit precisely—one at $100^{23}\!/_{32}$ and the other at 106. Similar situations are not uncommon. The five examples displayed in Figures 11.3 through 11.7 for various Treasury bond futures demonstrate TD Trend Factors' uncanny ability to pinpoint these price objectives with precision.

**Figure 11.3** To update the TD Trend Factor price objectives through June 1995, you must refer to the November 1994 low and apply it to the September 1995 contract and the price objectives presented on this chart. The December 1994 objective is more correctly derived by applying it to closer expiration contracts. In March the TD Trend Factor was exact, as it was in May. In June it identified the upside exhaustion level. The subsequent decline into August is shown in Figure 11.4.

**Figure 11.4**   This chart enlarges the decline from July through August. The TD Trend Factor objective was hit on the reaction low day. The TD Trend Factor was calculated off of the high day's close. In order to determine whether a price level is qualified for a TD Trend Factor calculation either upside or downside, the market's most recent move either upside or downside must encompass a price distance of at least 5.56% from intraday low to intraday high or from intraday high to intraday low.

**Figure 11.5**   Once again, notice how exact the second TD Trend Factor level was in December 1995. The low day's close was used to calculate this objective.

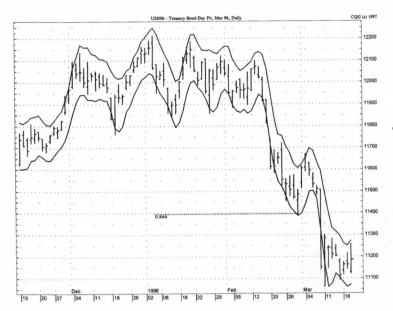

**Figure 11.6**  The January highest trading day's close was used to calculate the TD Trend Factor downside price objective, which was hit exactly. The possible breakout downside was not qualified and price rallied. TD Channel II identified a short-term low at the same price level.

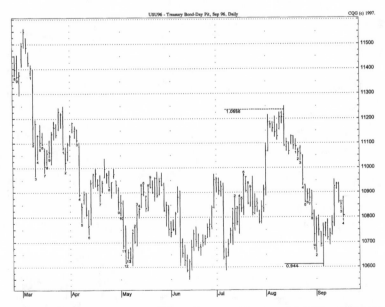

**Figure 11.7**  To continue from the previous figures, this chart identifies the TD Sequential low-risk buy indication in May and the subsequent TD Trend Factor objectives in August and September. The June low day's close was used to calculate the upside objective, and the August high was used to make the downside objective in September.

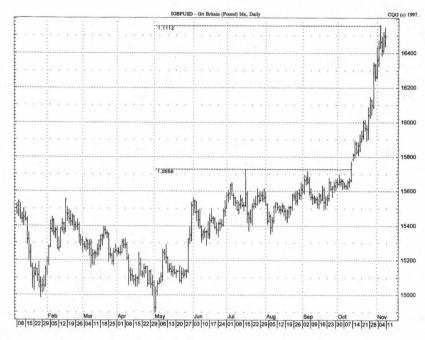

**Figure 11.8**  The two TD Trend Factor objectives displayed on this chart are consistent with the TD Trend Factor objectives calculated for the British pound futures contracts.

**Figure 11.9**  All the TD Trend Factor price objectives provided good price support and translated into price levels from which the market rallied.

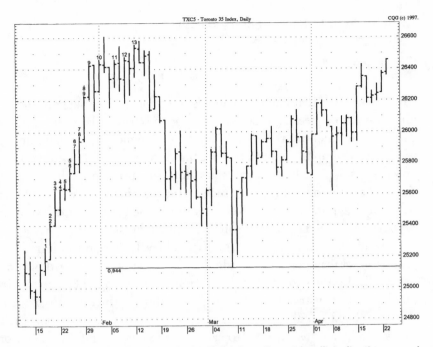

**Figure 11.10(a)**  The TD Combo 9-13 high-risk buy (low-risk sell) indication was given in February. From the intraday February high, the downside TD Trend Factor objective was realized.

**Figure 11.10(b)**  TD Sequential generated low-risk sells in October and in April and a low-risk buy in December. "Ignore smaller true high/true low" Recycle option was selected. The TD Trend Factor objective was satisfied in December, and the TD Trend Factor objectives were met upside with the peak objective of 2½ TD Trend Factor satisfied in April. One-half TD Trend Factor levels are positioned one-half the distance between objectives.

## TD Channel I™

Most techniques that employ channels to establish price support and resistance are suspect because they depend upon the current day's price activity to calculate and identify these price levels. Consequently, by definition, if a market timer employs a series of price highs to arrive at an upside projection and a series of price lows to arrive at a downside projection, then the objectives are continuously being revised as price continues to record intraday a new daily high or a new daily low. As a result, the research conclusions misrepresent what is taking place in the market by suggesting that a trader would have executed a trade at the channel level when in fact intraday that channel level may possibly be redefined by being upgraded or downgraded repeatedly. In order to combat this serious shortcoming, TD Channel I was developed. Its construction may appear unorthodox, since a ratio to calculate the upper band is multiplied by a series of price lows, and a series of highs is multiplied by a different ratio to calculate the lower band. In other words, the larger ratio is multiplied by an average of the lows and a smaller ratio is multiplied by an average of the highs. In actuality, this process understates the performance results of this indicator, since as price records new daily highs or new daily lows the channel adjusts up and down. In any case, remarkable precision and price synchronization has occurred when applying TD Channel I. For TD Channel I, the ratios applied are 103 percent multiplied by a three-day moving average of the three most recent trading days' lows and 97 percent multiplied by a three-day moving average of the three most recent trading days' highs. There is a high degree of accuracy when this indicator is applied to higher-priced, actively traded markets such as S&Ps and Treasury bonds. Due to the fact that most individual stocks are low-priced and much less volatile than futures, it is beneficial to increase the lower channel parameter from 103 to 111 percent and decrease the upper complement from 97 to 89 percent while continuing to multiply the former revised ratio by the average of the lows and the latter revised ratio by the average of the highs. Figure 11.11 displays TD Channel I.

## TD Channel II™

Superficially, TD Channel II may possess the serious flaw associated with most channel techniques and described in the discussion of TD Channel I. Experience, however, indicates that the ratios and time periods I have selected have a higher incidence of accuracy and precision than most conventional approaches. This is due to the fact that price often seems to synchronize with the TD Channel II projected price levels, especially when applied to higher-priced, actively traded markets such as S&Ps and Treasury

**Figure 11.11**  Price infrequently exceeds the TD Channel I either upside or downside. Whenever it occurs, it is usually an opportunity to enter or exit the market. Instances in which the channel was exceeded are marked with an *X*.

bonds. The ratios preferred are 100.5 percent multiplied by a three-day moving average of the highs (current day's high and the previous two trading day's highs) and 99.5 percent multiplied by a three-day moving average of the lows (current day's low and the previous two trading days' lows). For stocks you should revise the channel settings. In this case, applying 105 and 95 percent is recommended. Figures 11.12 through 11.14 illustrate TD Channel II.

## TD Channel III™

By selecting the central tendency of price range activity over a defined number of trading days and then multiplying the high and the low of the trading day selected by factors or ratios, a trading channel can be constructed. Rather than apply some sophisticated mathematical formula to calculate the average or typical values over the time period, this task is performed simply by identifying the median or middle trading day's high and the median or middle trading day's low over the period selected, multiplying an average of the median day's highs by 101.5 and an average of median day's lows by 98.5 to construct TD Channel III. Usually, you might want to select an odd num-

**Figure 11.12**  TD Channel II indications are marked with an *X*. The penetrations occur infrequently, but when they appear, they are usually coincident with a major turning point.

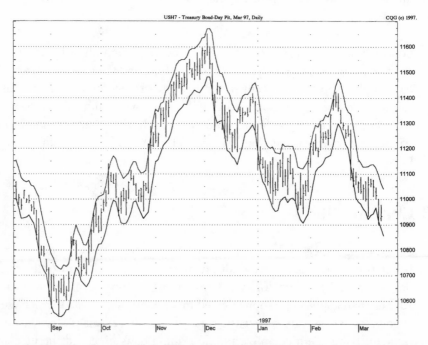

**Figure 11.13**  TD Channel II usually defines the parameters for a daily price move. Although it is a three-day average of highs and lows, highs and lows are usually synchronized to the channel. Should price close outside the channel, it usually returns within the channel the following trading day.

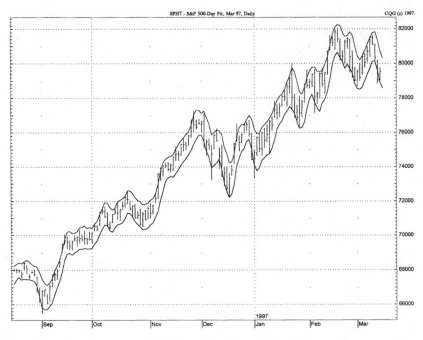

**Figure 11.14**   The sensitivity and ability of TD Channel II to define price tops and bottoms intraday is obvious on this chart.

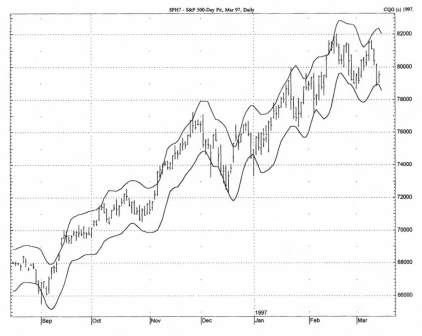

**Figure 11.15**   TD Channel III creates a wider band than TD Channel II and the price moves outside the band identify potential trading opportunities.

ber of days for your lookback period, such as five days (thus the median or middle day's high would be three, and consequently the third-highest (or third lowest) high and low over that period of time would be selected). For the purpose of calculating the moving average of median highs and median lows, three trading days is suggested. Figure 11.15 shows TD Channel III.

# Chapter

# 12

# Market Myths
# and Misconceptions

## Point and Figure

Every few years a fad within the trading community becomes fashionable and its use becomes widespread. One recent practice is to apply point and figure charts to long-term trading in the futures markets. Having been introduced to point and figure charting almost 30 years ago by an individual named Abe Cohen, I subsequently subscribed to his Chart Craft publication, as well as both Morgan, Rogers, and Roberts charting service and Jim Dines' Paflibe publication. While there is merit to applying point and figure to stocks, its application to futures is questionable for a number of reasons. First of all, these markets are highly leveraged and the supply is virtually unlimited. It is not uncommon to see the entire open interest turned over in a matter of two to three trading days, given the daily trading volume. Consequently, a prudent trader more than likely has liquidated his or her position by using tight trailing stop losses. The high volatility due to the leverage in these markets suggests that most traders do not withstand a large loss, and it is common for big losses to be inflicted whenever a price range is large. Furthermore, it may be likely with stocks where margin requirements are higher, short interest is limited, and volatility is less pronounced that support and resistance levels are legitimate, but my research suggests otherwise with futures.

## Confusion Regarding Graphic Presentation of Overbought and Oversold Oscillators

Although it is possible when a runner in a race anticipates the start and jumps the gun to restart and try again, in the markets such activity is not possible. When first introduced to real-time market graphics in the late 1970s with a Comtrend machine, I wanted to go back in time and restart my trades. As an experiment I bought and sold a market based solely upon the crossover of an indicator from oversold and overbought thresholds. Historically, on a chart this process appeared potentially profitable but, in actuality, an important lesson emerged: that anticipating moves of an oscillator before its time interval completion is a dangerous trading practice. Upon first exposure, you may disagree and argue that an intraday move out of overbought or oversold territory is not anticipation, but an explanation and a real-time experience should clarify this point for you. Reviewing the historical results of trading in this fashion, I was confident of a trading opportunity once the oscillators (it was probably Ralph Dystant's Stochastics Indicators) moved from oversold to neutral and from overbought to neutral. Upon the penetration of the threshold into the neutral zone from the oversold zone, I contacted my broker and placed an order. Lo and behold, before my very eyes the indicator once again appeared beneath the band in the oversold zone. Consequently, I called my broker and exited the trade. Within minutes, the oscillator traveled into the neutral zone again. Struggling to reconcile this fact, I even called the vendor of the real-time charting package. Quickly, it became apparent that the analysis conducted was done in retrospect on daily charts—I was operating at the time on an intraday basis. The two processes and time periods are not compatible. It is not uncommon to record a successive series of "false starts" throughout a trading day, and that is why the bottom line does not appear on a chart until the last entry of the day or the closing price, since it is a daily calculation and all the machinations and anticipation exerted by operating on an intraday basis are not only time-consuming, but oftentimes expensive. If a daily-basis calculation is made, it is incorrect to introduce intraday oscillator readings and then to extrapolate what the end of day will produce or look like. By attempting to do so, you are contaminating your data and processes. It is strongly suggested that if you use an oscillator in this manner to determine entry levels, you should review the historical results in the context of relating the oscillator value with the closing price on the same day, ignoring the intraday highs and lows since they do not play a role in most oscillators' construction. The only determinant factor in entry is the closing price. Anticipating where the oscillator will align itself on the close is an effort in futility and fraught with restarts. For this very reason, qualifiers are introduced to perfect low-risk entry zones (review, for example, TDPOQ, which is discussed in Chapter 1).

## Short-, Intermediate-, and Long-Term Definitions

Market prices change from day to day, and trends can be classified as seasonal, cyclical, or secular. Seasonal trends are defined as a result of historical tendencies in various markets to rally or decline during the same time period each year. Most attention in this regard has been focused upon the various commodities markets, but there are similar tendencies in the financial futures markets and in the individual equities' markets. Those analysts who argue that no application of seasonal analysis can be applied to these markets are operating under a misconception.

By referring to short-, intermediate-, and long-term opportunities in the market and by describing these terms in a temporal sense rather than in terms of a percentage return context, traders are overlooking opportunities in the marketplace. For example, historically, stock markets have not demonstrated the volatility they have demonstrated in recent years. Whereas moves of 20 percent or more in the past would require at least six to twelve months to accomplish, 10 to 20 percent moves three to six months, and moves of 5 to 10 percent up to three months, these moves are being realized in a matter of trading *days* in the current market. By applying only the time consideration for trading purposes, traders are required to hold a position longer than they might if they defined the terms short-, intermediate-, and long-term in relation to percentage price movement.

## New Highs, New Lows

Upon first entering the investment business, I concentrated on buying those stocks that were trading at new lows and selling those stocks that were trading at new highs. Looking back, I am chagrined by my foolishness. This practice is akin to betting on the "long shots" at horse races. Stocks that trade at yearly lows have many unhappy owners who would be tickled to break even, and would likely do so when prices advance (if they do). Stocks that trade at yearly highs, conversely, have many happy owners and there is limited overhead supply. When this situation became apparent, I concentrated my attention upon purchasing the new highs and liquidating the new lows. In particular, if a stock is recording a new high at the time the overall market is at a new low, the stock will likely be a leader on the upside when the overall market reverses trend upside. On the other hand, if a stock is making new lows at the same time the market is at a new high, once the market reverses downside the stock should be a leader in the decline. In regard to the latter proposition, I conducted research to determine the prospects for those stocks recording new lows simultaneous with a market high and then subsequent to the market decline. Initially, it was surprising to see that many of these stocks disappeared from the data sheets, and I could not reconcile this development. Then it became clear that these stocks were delisted. Many had filed for bankruptcy and consequently could not be found in data files. My conclusion from this exercise is that the likely leadership for stocks off a market low are those stocks recording new highs simultaneous with the market lows, and the likely candidates for the downside and potential bankruptcies are those issues making new lows coincident with the market recording new highs.

## Price Reversals

It's amazing how many traders expound upon the benefits of price reversals or "key" price reversals and associate them with significant market turning points. In *The New Science of Technical Analysis*, a chapter is devoted to a series of price patterns that have predictive value, referred to as *Waldo Patterns*, since they blend in with the chart background much like the cartoon character Waldo blends into his environment. The discussion of price reversals indicated that most of these reversals were characteristic of short-term or floor trader activity that was being conducted to take advantage of short-term overbought or oversold opportunities. Typically, it is assumed that at a low, if price records a reversal (a lower low than the previous day's low and an up close) or what some describe as a "key" reversal (a lower low than the previous day's low and a close greater than the previous trading day's high), that price will continue higher. My research suggests otherwise. Usually, lows are recorded when not only the low is less than the previous day's low, but also the close is less than the previous day's close. The only exception I could uncover occurred when the close of the reversal day is above all four previous trading days' closes and the following trading day's high exceeds the reversal day's high. At a price high, these patterns are reversed (i.e., the close of the reversal day is below all four previous trading days' closes and the following trading day's low exceeds the reversal day's low).

In a similar situation you can often compare the current market close with the close four trading bars prior to the most recent TD Point low or TD Point high. Some readers may confuse this relationship by comparing the current closing price with the close four trading bars prior to a recent TD Point low or high. Generally, these levels are the same, but it is possible to record a TD Point low and then a subsequent higher TD Point low or a TD Point high and a subsequent lower TD Point high similar to TD Double TD Point. In this situation, the recent TD Point low or TD Point high is used as the reference level, and the close four trading bars prior to that current low or high becomes critical since it is the revised reference price level.

In fact, it is possible that the current bar's low or high may qualify as a new TD Point low or TD Point high, but this conclusion cannot be made until the succeeding bar's low or high is formed, at which time the TD Point low or high will be revised and a new reference low will be defined. (See Chapter 6, TD Double TD Point.)

## Price Gaps and Price Laps

*Price gaps* are those trading days in which a particular trading day's low price is above the previous trading day's high price or those trading days in which a particular trading day's high price is below the previous trading day's low price. *Price laps* are those trading days in which the low is less than the previous trading day's high but greater than the previous trading day's close or those trading days in which the high is greater than the previous trading day's low but less than the previous trading day's close. My research indicates that the only distinction between a price *gap* and *lap* is the first letter of each word. I treat them as if they were the same.

It is common to hear many market timers say that all price gaps are filled. I disagree. Tell this to the short seller of Chrysler in 1932 or to the DJIA short seller just after the low in January 1975. This was not the case. The TD Gap™ indicator identifies those price gaps that occur on Mondays, which are critical trading days much different from other trading days of the week since a weekend gives traders an opportunity to premeditate and make their trading decisions less emotionally. Furthermore, if a price gap is not filled within 11 trading days and trading days 8, 9, 10, or 11 either record a higher high than all trading days 1 through 7 for an upside move or record a lower low for a downside move, then the gap is usually not filled until the trend is reversed, if at all.

## TD One Tick One Time Rule™

Many traders view the fact that a market may trade a certain price level more than one time as an opportunity to buy at, or prior to, that level since it has proven to be supported in the past or as an opportunity to sell at, or prior to, that level since it has proven to be resistant in the past. This is an obvious misperception of price behavior, which can be abrogated by using the TD One Tick One Time Rule.

Using time and sales data retrieved from the exchanges, I identified a phenomenon that served to confirm potential short-term price tops and bottoms. A remarkable price pattern became apparent by reviewing all instances in which price recorded equal lows or highs at significant price turning points. In the research for repetitive prices, there were few instances in which this pattern coincided with the inception of significant market moves, leading to the conclusion that if it occurs infrequently, the likelihood is that when it does occur it is likely soon superseded, thereby providing an alert trader with an opportunity not available to others. Specifically, at the lowest price level at which there is a price tick, most highs and lows are recorded when price trades at that level only one time. From reviewing endless time and sales reports, it became apparent that meaningful price lows and highs were recorded as price moved in one direction, and an extreme price tick was made and price reversed quickly. This observation was shared with two large floor traders in the Treasury bond pit. They agreed that it appeared to be valuable information but offered that it was impractical to apply to floor trading since they were unable to determine when it occurred while they traded on the floor of the exchange. In fact they described it as a price blur where bids and asks are all that appear to them. Sure, they could have looked at the exchange's wall boards, but that would have distracted them from their trading. But you can be assured that whenever they were off the floor and their trading focus was upon this trading phenomenon, they were aware of this trading pattern. It struck me as a great opportunity for "upstairs" traders to have a distinct edge over floor traders, since they were able to apply this technique whereas floor traders were not. More research indicated that if a specific price level is hit only one time, and subsequently price advances (declines) from that level without trading at that level again, then a potential low (high) has been made. Conversely, if a price is hit and the market upticks (downticks) from that level and then declines (advances) to that level once again, the chance is great that the price will be exceeded downside (upside). The TD One Tick One Time Rule is difficult to apply if you are a floor trader, but it is relatively simple if you have a price chart (or at least time and sales data) at your disposal. Typically, trading at a price level one time occurs at the culmination of a price decline or price advance. Although short-term charts such as a one-minute chart demonstrate this event often, even daily charts are instructive in showing that it is unlikely to witness equal lows or highs at price extremes. The reason for this fact is that eventually price will exceed a level equaled at least one time. In other words, turning points in price are typically associated with price trading at that level only one time since they occur coincident with price exhaustions. Consequently, prior to or coincident to entering a trade, you should make certain that the TD One Tick One Time Rule is operative and that price is able to bounce off the price level and that it fails to trade that level again to ensure the chance of a significant exhaustion price point having been hit. This same approach can apply to daily price charts with equal success of confirming price highs or lows.

## Strong versus Weak Markets

The market is strong or weak if the current trading day's high or low is double the previous day's price range either added to or subtracted from the previous trading day's close. This statement is true only in reverse. Research indicates that after a price advance, if a high is recorded and it is more than double the previous trading day's true price range added to that same trading day's close, then a short-term high is likely being formed. Conversely, after a price decline, if a low exceeds two times the previous trading day's true price range subtracted from that same trading day's closing price, then a short-term low is likely being formed. This pattern can be helpful for trading when it is applied to TD Diff (see Chapter 10). I refer to this measure as the TD Double Price Range™.

## A Broker or a Market Commentator Predicts a Buyout

Despite the fact that the government is actively prosecuting those traders who use inside information regarding stock buyouts, the willingness of the public to attempt to trade based upon these rumors never ceases. To take advantage of an opportunity illicitly gained is personally disconcerting, so I have always avoided trading on any such rumors. First of all, no one should be trading on inside information. Psychologically, it removes the challenge associated with investing. (In my days of playing basketball, I would forego an easy layup and elect to reposition myself a distance from the basket in order to make the shot more difficult.) You could almost wager that no more than 1 percent of all the rumors of buyouts ever materialized. It just doesn't happen that way. Using the TD Pressure (Chapter 10) indicator enabled me to predict many buyouts in the late 1970s and early 1980s. Contacting management and informing them that my work indicated such activity seemed an amusing game at the time, earning me the moniker of the "grim reaper" within investment circles. Rumors should be ignored, or you should sell positions whenever rumors arise. To dissuade traders and friends from buying based upon this speculation, there is a simple technique you can use to differentiate between bogus and real information regarding a buyout. The reasoning is as follows: Assume you are the first to hear of suspected takeover news. Then research to determine how many shares of the company's stock have been issued. Next calculate 25 percent of this total, and each day add the daily volume until that amount has been exceeded in cumulative volume. Since SEC rules require an announcement of the buyer's intentions if any purchase totaling more than 5 percent of the company's stock occurs, if no announcement has been made, it is unlikely that it will. Any corporate banker who is advising a prospective buyer would not be performing well if he or she had not accumulated 5 percent by that time. Consequently, assume the buyout rumors are merely that—unsubstantiated rumors, opportunities to sell not buy.

## Elliott Wave Analysis Is Definitive When Identifying Market Tops and Bottoms

If this phrase is applied to the wave interpretation of the market retrospectively and is unqualified, it may be a valid statement, but it is unquestionably without merit if related to market movement and price activity concurrently as the waves unfold. This is an effort in futility, somewhat akin to trying to catch smoke—you are able to see it, but unable to grasp it. Since conventional wave analysis and Fibonacci numbers are connected, my research resulted in an approach to wave analysis called TD D-Wave™. Simply described, you identify a 21-day low (a low that is less than all previous 20 trading days' lows) and once "initialized," you await the first high greater than the previous seven trading days' highs (eight-day high) to identify D-Wave 1. Once a low below the previous four trading days' lows (five-day low) is recorded, D-Wave 1 is identified by the highest high of that price move. Then you await a 13-day high (a high greater than all previous 12 trading days' highs), and D-Wave 2 has been defined as the lowest low. Once an 8-day low is recorded (a low less than all previous 7 trading days' lows), D-Wave 3 has been identified; D-Wave 4 is completed as soon as a 21-day high is recorded (a high greater than all previous 20 trading days' highs); D-Wave 5 is completed once a 13-day low is recorded. It is also required that each up wave (D-Waves 1, 3, and 5) is successively higher and that the low of reaction D-Wave 4 is greater than the high of D-Wave 2. The reaction D-Waves (a, b, and c) are formed after the D-Wave 5 price high occurs with a 13-day low (a), an 8-day high (b), and a 21-day low (c). The beauty of this type of approach is the value derived in calculating price projections based upon the length of the various price waves. (See Figures 12.1 and 12.2.)

## It Is Impossible to Make Daily Price Projections for Markets

The formula for TD Daily Range Projection™ provides a trader with a consistent and mechanical methodology to calculate the following trading day's projected price range (high and low). The formula to project tomorrow's high and low is as follows: The current trading day's high *plus* the current trading day's low *plus* the current trading day's close. Depending upon

**Figure 12.1** TD Wave measures from the low in August to the completion of Wave 1 in September and multiplies by 1.618 and when this value is added to the low of Wave 2 to arrive at the price objective at the completion of Wave 5.

**Figure 12.2(a)** The same measurement and calculations as in Figure 12.1 are applied in this example. There are two price objectives—one in July and the other in October—that fulfilled the objectives of Wave 3 and that were close to the completion of Wave 5. By introducing TD Sequential or TD Combo Setup or Countdown, TD Wave indications can often be improved.

**Figure 12.2(b)**    Subsequent to the downside correction completed in August, price rallied and completed a TD Wave 1 through 5 count coincident with the fulfillment of the upside price objective.

whether the current trading day's close is less than, greater than, or equal to the current trading day's opening price, the high, low, or close is doubled. If the close is greater than the open, the high is doubled. If the close is less than the open, the low is doubled. If the close is equal to the open, the close is doubled. In order to project the high, divide the four-value sum by 2 and subtract the current day's low. To project the low, subtract the current day's high. If price should open the following trading day above the projected high or open the following trading day below the projected low, then price is likely to break out that trading day in the direction of the opening price gap. Often, if the breakout is upside, the original projected high becomes the revised projected low, and if the breakout is downside, the original projected low becomes the revised projected high. On the other hand, if the open is contained by the high- and low-projected range, usually the projected high serves as price resistance and the projected low serves as price support for that trading day, and the closing price usually gravitates to the area in between the projected high and low. Occasionally, you may want to use the daily range projections and apply them to TD REBO to arrive at low-risk entry opportunities (Chapter 6). In the early to mid 1980s, I appeared daily on Financial News Network (FNN) and forecast the daily range projection for T-bonds and S&P futures. This is the technique I used and I refer to it as TD Daily Range Projection. (See Figure 12.3.)

## Price Patterns Do Not Repeat Themselves

If this were in actuality the case, my research work would have been in vain. After a respite of 10 years, TD Analog™ has been resurrected as an object of research. Rather than spend a lengthy discourse on TD Analog, I prefer to describe in general terms its construction and purpose. It has been said that history has a tendency to repeat itself. Although the characters and the settings may not be the same, the events and the outcomes do appear to repeat themselves throughout history. Likewise in the marketplace, various price patterns seem to repeat, and often their implications are similar as well. At the time these observations were made over 20 years ago, the technology was not sufficiently advanced to produce and catalog these repetitive price patterns. New technology has enabled me to research and develop a series of relationships to facilitate comparisons between various markets and price patterns in order to extrapolate price behavior. The product of this effort is TD Analog.

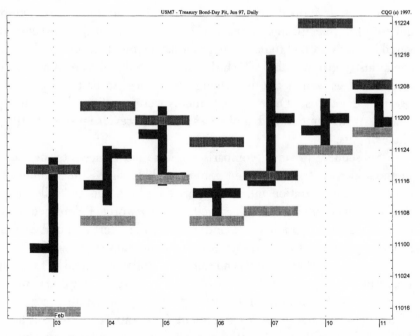

**Figure 12.3**  The TD Range Projection defines the daily price parameters for markets. It's a simple formula, but the results often are precise. Statistically, it is rare to project a daily high or low, but this chart indicates its ability to accomplish this feat.

TD Analog is designed to take a snapshot of current price activity and then superimpose that price movement upon previous, similar price pattern activity to locate a match. For example, you can compare the current market's open, high low, and close with the previous trading day's comparable price levels, as well as the trading days 2, 3, 5, 8, 13, 21, 34, and 55 trading days earlier. Additionally, you can relate the closing price versus the opening price for each day and compare the relative prices of each of these trading days with each as well as with the other trading days. Next, determine whether a buy or a sell Setup (à la TD Sequential or TD Combo) has most recently occurred to define whether the trend is up or down. Then apply TD Moving Average I to evaluate and confirm whether price is in a short-term up or down trend. Finally, decide what percentage of these various price relationships you prefer to have exist and then compare the price activity to draw conclusions regarding future price movement.

## Only the Option Writers Make Money Trading Options

There is a heavy price to be paid for developing techniques to trade options successfully. My tuition payments were first made when the Chicago Board of Options Exchange opened for trading in the early 1970s. Initially, stock calls were listed. Subsequently, puts were added. In order to control my emotions, I developed a trading checklist and attempted to religiously adhere to it. Specifically, in order to buy a call option the market as measured by an index had to be trading that day below the previous day's close, the industry group within which the stock traded had to be down, and the stock itself, as well as the underlying option, had to be trading below the previous day's close. Once these elements were satisfied, the call was purchased. At the same time, I applied a similar but reverse process to the purchase of puts.

Subsequently, some comparisons were introduced to perfect this methodology when put trading commenced. I related the volume of the nearby option expiration and striking price for both puts and calls and compared the open interest of each as well. In other words, I identified the closest striking price option series and selected the nearby option expiration month—generally, this set is identical to the most active put and call options for that market. Then the puts and calls were dollar-weighted by multiplying their value by the volume. Each was divided by its respective dollar-weighted open interest. Finally, these ratios were divided by one another to get a sense of the market expectations or sentiment. This ratio or value is called TD Dollar-Weighted Put/Call Ratio, and it has proven to be an effective compass for near-term market direction.

## Wait for the Closing Price to Enter a Suspected Price Breakout

To trade otherwise would result in many false breakouts and trading losses. Although the TD Qualifiers have been discussed throughout this book in regard to various indicators, they are sufficiently significant to deserve more attention at this time. TD Qualifiers came about as a result of my own experiences in trading and observing market behavior. If you are actively involved in the markets, you have no doubt been confronted with similar experiences. Having been burned often by first anticipating and then entering at suspected price breakout levels intraday only to see price fail on the close that same day, initially I (and no doubt many other traders) elected to await a closing price that exceeded my breakout levels. The outcome was invariably predictable. On those occasions in which I awaited the closing price to ensure a breakout, I forfeited the price move from the breakout level to the closing price. In those instances in which I entered intraday, I wished that I had awaited the close for confirmation. The dilemma was obvious. Invariably, when I expected price to break out through a critical price level intraday, it was because the previous day's price activity made me predisposed to expect such a follow-through. On those occasions when I expected a failure, it was because I extrapolated the previous day's price activity and erroneously concluded that the market's price behavior would continue. In other words, if the general expectation of investors is for the market to behave in a specific manner, then it is a logical conclusion to expect that they have already established their positions, and their market activity is consistent with their expectations. In other words, their money is where their market sentiment is. It is possible to qualify intraday entries into the market dependent upon the degree (level) of anticipation associated with the price activity expressed the trading day prior to the suspected price breakout or at the opening that trading day. Specifically, the degree of price movement occurring the day before and the closing price that same trading day in relation to the previous trading day's closing price, as well as the current day's opening price relative to the breakout level and the previous day's close, are critical in evaluating a price breakout and the potential of price follow-through. For further information, refer to the qualifier descriptions provided in Chapters 4 and 5 (TD Lines and TD Retracements).

## It's Impossible to Anticipate Trend Changes

This statement contradicts the design and expectation of most of the indicators presented in this book. A brief recapitulation of some of these indicators will put this matter in proper perspective. TD Sequential and TD Combo have been developed to identify opportunity zones associated with price exhaustion and are associated with the element of time. TD Trend Factors, TD D-Wave, and TD Retracements provide a price objective element to the equation. TD Disqualified Lines, TDST, TD LV, TDT, TD Diff, and reverse TD REBO can be used as contratrend indicators. TDPOQ used in conjunction with the various oscillators will identify short-term exhaustion areas, as will TD Critical Qualifier. The various TD Channels and TD Range Projections provide an additional dimension to identify price peaks and troughs. In addition TD Open, TD CLOP, TD CLOPWIN, and TD Trap also enable a trader to take advantage of price exhaustion opportunities as they arise.

## Trading Price Breakouts Is a Simple Way to Participate in Market Trends

Keep in mind that the "trend is your friend unless the trend is about to end." An effective technique to locate short-term price exhaustion zones is to identify TD Point lows or highs that are level 10 or greater. If the first two consecutive trading days in which price exceeds upside a level 10 or greater TD Point high record consecutively higher closes and if both trading day's closing prices are consecutively higher than the close of the TD Point high trading day, then the first subsequent trading day in which a low is recorded that is less than the previous trading day's low is often an indication of a downside price reversal or a consolidation phase. On the other hand, if the first two consecutive trading days in which price exceeds downside a level 10 or greater TD Point low record consecutively lower closes and if both trading day's closing prices are consecutively lower than the close of the TD Point low trading day, then the first subsequent trading day in which a high is recorded that is greater than the previous trading day's high is often an indication of an upside trend reversal or a consolidation phase. Conversely, if these patterns suggest trend reversals, then most other breakout highs and lows that exceed TD Point highs and lows of less than level 10 or that exceed TD Point highs and lows of greater than level 10 and that are not consecutively higher highs and closes or consecutively lower closes and lows would imply the possibility of the opposite condition; namely, the likely continuation of the price trend. My conclusions regarding this price behavior have to do with the fact that initially stop losses are triggered at the previous TD Point high or low on the first day's breakout, and then long-term investors enter after that first day's breakout once the closing price is able to close in the direction of the breakout. Once they have entered the market the succeeding trading day, and if they are sufficiently aggressive, there is usually a price exhaustion shortly thereafter accompanied by a trend reversal or a period of price consolidation. Other considerations such as TD Diff and TD Sequential Setup are important factors as well. In any case, the key and operative phrase is to be price-pattern vigilant for such price conditions to arise and to take advantage of them.

## Once an Entry Technique Is Tested and Perfected, Trading Success Will Follow

Not true! Exits and stop losses are critical. Research indicates that it's relatively simple to develop a mechanical entry for a trading system. The difficult elements of successful trading are stop losses, profit-taking levels, and exit techniques. There are a number of effective stop-loss techniques. Among them are (1) a standard dollar stop loss, (2) a percentage of the previous day's or series of days' ranges, (3) a measure of price volatility subtracted from a recent price low or added to a recent price high or from the current trading day's open, and (4) the series of stop losses presented in Chapters 2, 3, and 9.

In addition to the various exits described in previous chapters, recommended exits include (1) three consecutive up or down closes including the entry bar, (2) the first profitable open price subsequent to the entry price, (3) a "stop gain" of a specific dollar amount, and (4) any high (upside) or low (downside) which is at least double (200 percent times the previous trading bar's price range added to or subtracted from the previous bar's close). Furthermore, stop losses and exits can each be generated by TD REBO, TD Overlap, TD Open, and TD Moving Average I, as well as the many other indicators presented in this book.

A price decline has a tendency to exhaust itself short term once three consecutive down closes versus the previous trading day's close are recorded and the following trading day's open is greater than the previous trading day's close and that same day's low is less than the previous trading day's close. Similarly, this can occur once three consecutive up closes versus the previous trading day's close are recorded and the following trading day's open is less than the previous trading day's close and that same day's high is greater than the previous trading day's close. At times this pattern identifies exceptional opportunities to exit an outstanding position. This pattern is called TD Exit 1.

# Chapter

# 13

# Money Management

An essential element to success in trading is ignored in almost all trading or market timing books or articles. It's surprising given its importance that very few writers devote any time to the discussion of money management practices and principles. This chapter will present one approach to money management that is general and could be easily supplemented by other methods if you desire. The goal here is to provide recommendations for a simple, viable approach to allocating funds and managing your portfolio.

This book is not intended to include a course on money management. However, if there is one subject within the realm of trading that is vital to a trader's financial survival and at the same time totally overlooked as critical, it is the discipline of money management as it applies to trading success. If market indicators and systems were always precise in identifying tops and bottoms, the necessity for prudent money management skills would not exist. Unfortunately, such is not the case. Even if a system were 99 percent accurate, the 1 percent failure rate could conceivably wipe out a trader who did not apply money management methodology. The following techniques for your consideration in designing a prudent and viable money management program may appear simplistic upon first glance. However, making procedures complex serves only to obfuscate the obvious, easy, and straightforward approach to sound money management. These recommendations regarding the design of a money management methodology are a compilation of various techniques I have developed and employed successfully throughout the years.

Before you enter any trade, you should be convinced that the trading event will prove to be profitable. Otherwise, why even attempt the trade? Obviously, no decision in life is always correct and this applies invariably to the markets. In the case of the markets, however, you are not able to undo a bad decision and recover your losses from a trade. This lesson came early in my career. Discretionary decisions or trading hunches or guesses may prove profitable on occasion, but how do you quantify and duplicate this decision-making process in the future? Consequently, the following suggestions are directed not only toward developing a series of mechanical, objective approaches to trading decisions and money management but also to enable you to replicate your decision-making process regardless of the time period and the number of markets followed. The primary considerations are consistency, objectivity, and portability. Additionally, you need to be sensitive to diversification of market timing techniques, as well as markets monitored. By implementing a number of unrelated methods, you will be able to sufficiently diversify your portfolio and thereby reduce your level of risk. In other words, by applying a combination of market timing approaches, each of which uses a different trading philosophy, you will be able to operate as if you had a number of trading advisors managing your funds. Obviously, these techniques should be applied on paper before introducing them real time into your trading regimen. Once the techniques have been sufficiently tested to ensure performance results and nuances, the money management disciplines must be introduced. The other chapters of the book pertain to the methodologies, so this discussion is devoted to a basic approach of managing trades and your investment.

First, you should allocate percentages of capital equally to various mechanical market timing models. Therefore, if you have developed and decided to use three noncorrelated mechanical approaches, then you should designate the same percentage participation to each. You may choose to vary this approach. For example, if one system is two times more effective than another, then you would double by position size or if the frequency of trading for one method is twice as active as another technique, you may wish to reduce portfolio commitment by 50 percent. However, for sake of discussion, assume that all systems are equally effective. Assuming a total of 100 percent, you may not wish to allocate in total more than 30 percent to these systems collectively at any one time. Also assume for purposes of simplicity that you have elected to follow 10 individual markets for each system. Consequently, your maximum exposure would be no greater than 30 percent of your beginning equity, and that is only if each model has its maximum investment exposure of 10 markets at any one time and each market is being traded simultaneously at the same time (10 markets times 3 trading methods times 1 percent apiece equals 30 percent exposure).

How are you to measure your investment commitment in terms of number of futures contracts, for example? Rather than subscribe to an esoteric portfolio management methodology with numerous complicated variables connected by advanced statistical formulas, you should rely on the market itself to dictate your level of exposure at any point of time. Specifically, the various futures exchanges determine the margin requirements to trade markets. Typically, as trading activity becomes volatile, the margin requirements increase. At that time, you should reduce your exposure because you would have specifically allocated only a 1 percent commitment to that market for this particular market timing method. Conversely, when price activity becomes inactive and less volatile, you would increase your investment exposure, hopefully, awaiting a breakout and increased volatility. Consequently, margin requirements serve as a barometer for fund allocation. To clarify this process, the market itself is the best source for dictating market exposure. This measure can easily be determined through simple calculations. The various futures exchanges evaluate the volatility and volume of markets continuously. If for any reason, they believe that the potential exists for wide daily swings in the market and, concurrently, the risk of erosion of a trader's margin, then, typically, they will be inclined to raise margin requirements. Therefore, whenever margin requirements are raised, market exposure as measured by the number of contracts traded should be adjusted accordingly. In other words, say you assume a portfolio size of $1 million, the use of three trading systems, and the limitation of trading only 10 markets in each. The maximum exposure can be no greater than $300,000 dollars, since that amount accounts for 30 percent of $1 million, the maximum account size defined above. It is unrealistic to assume that positions will exist in each and every market at any one period of time, however. In any case, this allocates $100,000 to each of three markets. In turn, this would imply that for each method, each market would represent $10,000 dollars. Now suppose the margin requirement in one market is $1,000. Then 10 contracts could be traded at any one time. If volatility increases, the exchange may decide to raise margin requirements by an additional $1,000 to $2,000, thereby forcing you to reduce your position size to five contracts ($5 \times 2,000 = \$10,000$ and $10 \times \$1,000 = \$10,000$). What has effectively occurred is a portfolio contract-size adjustment of 50 percent due to a 100 percent increase in margin requirements. If the volatility has increased sufficiently that the exchange is compelled to raise margin requirements, and you are still positioned in the market and have not been stopped out of the trade, then it is likely that the market has moved in your favor. In that case, the money management discipline and methodology described here requires closing out profitable positions, and prudent trading would also dictate profit taking. The initial exposure was a function of margin requirements, and the change was made as a result of market volatility and potential risk as defined by the increase in margin requirements.

Once in a trade, stop losses must be introduced. Generally, you should apply a standard stop loss and not risk any more than 1 percent of your portfolio on any one trade. Should you desire to increase this stop loss, you should reduce accordingly the size of the position or exposure you have in that market and at that method at that particular time. For example, you should always maintain a 1 percent risk level, but if you wanted to increase the dollar stop loss to double that amount, you should reduce your market exposure by 50 percent. All other increases in stops would be adjusted accordingly as well.

As the portfolio size in one method and in one market increase, you should adjust your stop loss and profit-taking levels and make certain that your exposure does not constitute an undue weighting in the portfolio. In fact, as the profit in a position increases, you should reduce the position size to maintain a maximum portfolio exposure and, ideally, in effect you will be investing only the profits generated in the trade.

The approach described here is simplistic but effective. High-tech mathematical modeling and sophisticated statistical techniques can be introduced, but experience indicates that minimal improvements will be produced. Although this approach to money management is devoted to high-margin futures, a similar approach can be easily applied to stock portfolios.

In conclusion, it is critical that a trader design and implement a methodology that is capable of being measured for performance statistics historically. Once confident of the results and comfortable with the implementation, a trader should paper-trade the method and then apply it real time to the markets with funds in small lots or shares. As you gain experience and confidence with the method, the position size can increase. Discipline is a prerequisite. If you conform to the general money management guidelines discussed in this chapter and then add improvements to the schedule to fill in any blanks in procedure, a difficult and critical component of trading success will have been addressed and satisfied.

# Chapter

# 14

# Conclusion

No system or indicator is or will ever be perfect. Markets respond and behave subject to the inputs driving traders to buy or sell. Just about the time you might believe that you have solved the market puzzle and have elevated yourself to "master of the universe" status, prepared to take on the trading community with your great set of indicators or market timing systems, it is probably the time the market will come down upon you with its humbling blow. The market operates impartially and takes no prisoners. Despite your confidence and intentions to trade successfully, unless you are prepared to accept the verdict of the marketplace, which at times will prove you wrong, you will not be successful. We live in an imperfect world, and the various markets are merely a microcosm of this dynamic, imperfect activity as well. No certainty exists, and the only gauge we have regarding future price behavior is past market activity. Although it is possible to measure the impulses expressed in the marketplace by traders by evaluating the intensity of both selling and buying pressure, contingencies must be introduced to protect against unknown factors. The detailed presentation of indicators in this book proves the extent to which one person will go to decode the dynamics of the markets and to establish an objective and rigid approach to applying market timing indicators: This process has consumed my life! Hopefully, the fruits of my labor will benefit you in your research and trading.

You have participated in a medley of my favorite market timing tools. By no means has this discussion been complete. In many instances, an entire book could be devoted to additional descriptions and explanations of these indicators. Instead, may this sampling lead you to conduct further research and analysis of your own. This book's presentation of my indicators is like a sports car. Although the horsepower may be more than required to operate the vehicle, and the speedometer gauge may accommodate higher speeds, it is unlikely that these levels will ever be tested. So, too, the likelihood of your becoming conversant in all the indicators presented is unlikely; nevertheless, perhaps I've shared enough ideas to pique your interest in selective areas sufficiently to encourage you to experiment with techniques of your own.

Unfortunately, neophyte traders often believe all that is necessary to be successful is to adopt an indicator or a system with a proven track record. Nothing could be further from the truth. It is imperative that traders recognize the additional significance of sound management principles and discipline, as well as the necessity to continually test and refine their own indicators and systems. Consequently, an appreciation of the statistical probabilities of various events repeating themselves, as well as an attitude of detachment, must be introduced into the trader's psyche and portfolio toolkit. It is a rare individual who is able to combine these three important elements and then translate them into trading success. I have known a number of bright portfolio managers who were able to design investment strategies with specific objectives in mind for their clients. However, they relied upon their research departments to select the specific investment vehicles to accomplish these goals and, at the same time, were dependent upon their trading departments to execute the trades. Other individuals may be great analysts but are ineffective traders and poor portfolio managers. Some believe, since they were creators of the systems or indicators, that they possess the license to interfere with their methodology and to introduce variations without proper testing and support. Some choose to override or interfere with the execution of the trades. It is not essential that a trader be an expert in any one of the areas presented in this book. However, an individual who possesses average aptitude in each should likely enjoy trading success.

Traders can be classified as either discretionary or systematic. In reality, most are probably a combination of the two approaches. I have attempted to provide you with one aspect of the trading process by presenting a series of market timing indicators for your review and consideration. By no means are these techniques intended to be turnkey systems. Rather they are indicators. Preparation, consideration, and attention to other factors such as indicator composition and weightings are necessary to accomplish the elevation of these indicators to the status of systems. This outstanding "assignment" is yours to ponder. It should be a relatively simple undertaking to customize these techniques and develop systems by introducing variables of your own. Consequently, the selection and application of the indicators presented throughout this book are discretionary. By introducing parameter settings and selection criteria of your own, including entry and stop-loss levels, the process can become mechanical. And finally, by integrating both money management and mechanistic trading disciplines, the trading process should be complete.

The scope of indicator coverage presented in the book is extensive. I have attempted to address every aspect of market timing analysis in a logical and an objective manner. The goal has been to mechanize and thereby simplify the indicator process. In retrospect, it is virtually impossible to construct an indicator checklist and require that each element presented be considered before a trade be entered. The time and the effort required neither permit nor justify such an ambitious and unrealistic process. Consequently, you should concentrate upon, and become proficient in, selective areas of analysis. Ideally, you will then be able to deal with specific indicators and the nuances associated with their appearances and application to the markets. Just as a physician is likely to become a specialist in a particular field of medicine, so, too, should you specialize in your business of trading. At the same time, your familiarity with and understanding of the other indicators presented will enable you to apply, or at least locate, other techniques outside your areas of expertise whenever necessary. Even in my own analysis of the markets, I tend to rely upon various indicators to establish an overall perspective before honing in on specific indicators to fine-tune my entries and exits. You will become partial to various indicators and approaches once you develop proficiency and comfort in their usage, just as I have my own favorites.

Trading is like any other endeavor. In order to be successful, it requires that an individual thoroughly understand and appreciate all aspects of the subject matter and possess a passion for the profession. I possess a voracious appetite to accumulate knowledge and conduct research regarding price patterns and market behavior. As a vocation and avocation, I am absorbed with researching the markets. A trader must possess more skills than an analyst, but his or her degree of market timing sophistication need not be as extensive as described in this book. By properly addressing the role of money management and discipline, the importance of developing a perfect trading system diminishes accordingly. Athletes who specialize solely in three-point shooting in basketball or who are designated hitters in baseball are limited in their contributions to a team. So, too, is an expert analyst limited. Provided a basketball player is also a good ball handler, rebounder, and blocker and a baseball player is both a good fielder and a runner, their play can be described as well-rounded and their value increases commensurately. Likewise, being an above-average analyst, trader, and money manager, rather than excelling in any one aspect of the investment business, is definitely an important criterion for trading success.

In conclusion, a trader must cease to look for explanations as to why a market behaved a certain way at any particular time. That's the job of a reporter. Excuses or reasons other than those attributable to the dynamics of the market itself are, in the final analysis, meaningless. A market will respond to the same news differently dependent upon its predisposition at the time. Many tools required to decode market price activity have been provided in this book. You should study and apply these trading techniques. Other parameter selections and indicator variations exist that will likely produce better results than the ones presented. In any case, in order to be a successful trader, the proper attitude and resilience are required and you should expect trading losses to occur. No methodology is without its shortcomings. By spending time addressing the various pitfalls that may arise, you will mature as both a researcher and a trader. In the meantime, I will continue my pursuit of the ideal trading indicators . . . since my job as a researcher is never finished.

# Appendix

# TD Indicator™ Settings

The following presentation provides a generic description, as well as the various default settings, for the first generation of TD Indicators for the approved versions of Windows and MS-DOS software. Other selections may be more suitable, and you are encouraged to experiment and to establish your preferences.

## TD REI

| | |
|---|---|
| Period to be used in calculating the REI | 5 |
| Number of bars to be used for duration analysis | 6 |
| Upper oscillator band | 45.00 |
| Lower oscillator band | 45.00 |

### Advanced TD REI

| | | | |
|---|---|---|---|
| Price to be used when comparing to previous highs | High | Open<br>Close<br>(High + Low + Close) / 3 | Low<br>Midpoint |
| Price to be used when comparing to previous lows | Low | Open<br>Close<br>(High + Low + Close) / 3 | High<br>Midpoint |
| Number of bars back to be used when comparing to previous highs | 2 | | |

| | | |
|---|---|---|
| Number of bars back to be used when comparing to previous lows | 2 | |
| Should "equal" be used when comparing prices? | Yes, use equal when comparing | No, use only greater than or less than |
| Type of moving average to be used on prices *before* the comparisons are made | None | Simple Exponential Centered |
| Period to be used in calculating the moving average | 0 | |
| Number of bars to be used for moving average smoothing | 0 | |
| Should an adjustment be made if the period for the calculations is less than 8 bars? | No, don't adjust | Yes, make the adjustment |

# TD ROC I

| | |
|---|---|
| Period to be used in calculating the Rate of Change | 12 |
| Number of bars to be used for duration analysis | 16 |
| Upper oscillator band | 102.50 |
| Lower oscillator band | 97.50 |

## *Advanced TD ROC I*

| | | | |
|---|---|---|---|
| Price to be used when comparing to previous bars | Close | Open<br>Low<br>(High + Low + Close) / 3 | High<br>Midpoint |
| Type of moving average to be used on prices *before* the comparisons are made | None | Simple Exponential Centered | |
| Period to be used in calculating the moving average | 0 | | |
| Number of bars to be used for moving-average smoothing | 0 | | |

# TD ROC II

| | |
|---|---|
| Period to be used in calculating the Rate of Change | 12 |
| Number of bars to be used for duration analysis | 16 |
| Upper oscillator band | 102.50 |
| Lower oscillator band | 97.50 |

### *Advanced TD ROC II*

| | | | |
|---|---|---|---|
| Price to be used when comparing to previous bars | Close | Open Low (High + Low + Close) / 3 | High Midpoint |
| Type of moving average to be used on prices *before* the comparisons are made | None | Simple Exponential Centered | |
| Period to be used in calculating the moving average | 0 | | |
| Number of bars to be used for moving-average smoothing | 0 | | |
| Value of TD ROC I to be used when substituting alternate prices | | | |
| Upper threshold | 100 | | |
| Lower threshold | 100 | | |
| "Alternate price" to be used when the upper threshold is exceeded | High | Open Low (High + Low + Close) / 3 | High Midpoint |
| "Alternate price" to be used when the lower threshold is exceeded | Low | Open Low (High + Low + Close) / 3 | High Midpoint |

## TD DeMarker

| | |
|---|---|
| Period to be used in calculating the DeMarker | 8 |
| Number of bars to be used for duration analysis | 16 |
| Upper oscillator band | 60.00 |
| Lower oscillator band | 40.00 |

### *Advanced TD DeMarker*

| | | | |
|---|---|---|---|
| Price to be used when comparing to previous highs | High | Open Close (High + Low + Close) / 3 | Low Midpoint |
| Price to be used when comparing to previous lows | Low | Open Close (High + Low + Close) / 3 | High Midpoint |
| Number of bars back to be used when comparing to previous highs | 1 | | |
| Number of bars back to be used when comparing to previous lows | 1 | | |
| Type of moving average to be used on prices *before* the comparisons are made | None | Simple Exponential Centered | |
| Period to be used in calculating the moving average | 0 | | |
| Number of bars to be used for moving-average smoothing | 0 | | |

## TD Plurality

| | |
|---|---|
| Period to be used when making price comparisons | 5 |
| Upper oscillator band | 2.50 |
| Lower oscillator band | −2.50 |

| First price to be used | | Condition | Second price to be used | | Value to be used when condition is true |
|---|---|---|---|---|---|
| Price | Bars back | | Price | Bars back | |
| Close | 0 | < | Close | 1 | −1 |
| Close | 0 | < | Open | 0 | −1 |
| Close | 0 | < | Close | 3 | −1 |
| Low | 0 | < | Low | 2 | −1 |
| Close | 0 | > | Close | 1 | +1 |
| Close | 0 | > | Open | 0 | +1 |
| Close | 0 | > | Close | 3 | +1 |
| High | 0 | > | High | 2 | +1 |

| | | | |
|---|---|---|---|
| First price to be used when comparing to previous prices | Close | Open | High |
| | | Low | Midpoint |
| | | (High + Low + Close) / 3 | |
| Relationship to be used when comparing the "First" price to previous prices | Greater than | Equal to or greater than | |
| | | Less than | |
| | | Equal to or less than | |
| Number of bars back to apply when selecting the "First" price | 0 | | |
| Value of the previous price to be used when comparing the "First" price | Close | Open | High |
| | | Low | Midpoint |
| | | (High + Low + Close) / 3 | |
| Number of bars back to be used when comparing the "First" price to previous prices | 1 | | |
| Value to be used when this condition is true | +1 | | |

## TD Absolute Retracement

| | | | |
|---|---|---|---|
| Price to be used when making projections | Close | Open | High |
| | | Low | Midpoint |
| | | (High + Low + Close) / 3 | |
| Display the 1.382 level when making projections | Yes, display the 1.382 level | No, don't display the 1.382 level | |
| Display the 1.618 level when making projections | Yes, display the 1.618 level | No, don't display the 1.618 level | |
| Display the 0.618 level when making projections | Yes, display the 0.618 level | No, don't display the 0.618 level | |

| Display the 0.382 level when making projections | Yes, display the 0.382 level | No, don't display the 0.382 level |

## TD Relative Retracement

| Price to be used when making projections | Close | Open                         High<br>Low                          Midpoint<br>(High + Low + Close) / 3 |
|---|---|---|
| Number of ticks required for a line penetration | 1 | |
| Display the 0.382 level when making projections | Yes, display the 0.382 level | No, don't display the 0.382 level |
| Display the 0.618 level when making projections | Yes, display the 0.618 level | No, don't display the 0.618 level |
| Display the 'magnet' level when making projections | Yes, display the 'magnet' level | No, don't display the 'magnet' level |
| Display the 1.382 level when making projections | Yes, display the 1.382 level | No, don't display the 1.382 level |
| Display the 1.618 level when making projections | Yes, display the 1.618 level | No, don't display the 1.618 level |
| Display the 2.236 level when making projections | Yes, display the 2.236 level | No, don't display the 2.236 level |

(See following for qualifiers and cancellations for this indicator.)

### TD Relative Retracement Qualifiers and Cancellations

| (The following conditions apply to upward projections; reverse this logic for downward projections) | | |
|---|---|---|
| A down close the bar before an upside breakout will qualify the breakout | Yes, use this qualifier | No, don't use this qualifier |
| An open above the breakout line will qualify the breakout | Yes, use this qualifier | No, don't use this qualifier |
| If the distance between the previous bar's close and its low, when added to the close, is still below the line, it will qualify the breakout | Yes, use this qualifier | No, don't use this qualifier |
| If the next open after the breakout is below the breakout line, the breakout is canceled | Yes, use this condition | No, don't use this condition |
| If the next high after the breakout is below the breakout bar close, and then closes below the breakout line, the breakout is canceled | Yes, use this condition | No, don't use this condition |
| If the next high after the breakout is below the breakout bar high, the breakout is canceled | Yes, use this condition | No, don't use this condition |

# TD Trend Factor

| | | | |
|---|---|---|---|
| Price to be used when making projections | Close | Open<br>Low<br>(High + Low + Close) / 3 | High<br>Midpoint |
| Display the 1.0556 level when making projections | Yes, display the 1.0556 level | No, don't display the 1.0556 level | |
| Display the 1.1112 level when making projections | Yes, display the 1.1112 level | No, don't display the 1.1112 level | |
| Display the 1.1390 level when making projections | Yes, display the 1.1390 level | No, don't display the 1.1390 level | |
| Display the 1.1668 level when making projections | Yes, display the 1.1668 level | No, don't display the 1.1668 level | |
| Display the 1.2224 level when making projections | Yes, display the 1.2224 level | No, don't display the 1.2224 level | |
| Display the 1.2780 level when making projections | Yes, display the 1.2780 level | No, don't display the 1.2780 level | |

# TD Sequential

## *Setup*

| | | | |
|---|---|---|---|
| Number of consecutive bars to be used for Setup | 9 | | |
| Number of bars back to be used for comparing prices | 4 | | |
| Price to be used for comparing to previous closes | Close | Open<br>Buy high<br>Buy low<br>(High + Low + Close) / 3 | Midpoint<br>Sell low<br>Sell high |
| Should "equal" be used when comparing | No, don't use equal | Yes, use equal when comparing | |
| Rules for Intersection | Intersection not required | Required *only* during Setup<br>Required during *or* after Setup | |
| Starting bar for Intersection | 8 | | |
| Rules for Recycling | *Before, on* or *after* the completion of Setup | *Before* or *On* the completion of Setup<br><br>Only *After* the completion of Setup<br>Only *Before* the completion of Setup<br>Smaller or larger high to low<br>Smaller or larger true high to true low<br>Ignored—Recycling is *not* considered | |

| | |
|---|---|
| Factor to be used in determining "larger" Setups | 2.00 |
| Rules for canceling a Setup | Any close above the true high of the current Setup |

(Expressed for a "Buy" Setup
   Reverse this logic for "Sell" Setups)

Any high above the
   highest close of the
   current Setup
Any high above the
   highest high of the
   current Setup
Any close above the
   highest close of the
   current Setup
Any close above the
   highest high of the
   current Setup

## Countdown

| | | | |
|---|---|---|---|
| Number of consecutive bars to be used for Countdown | 13 | | |
| Number of bars back to be used for comparing prices | 2 | | |
| Price to be used for comparing to previous highs and lows | Close | Open<br>High<br>(High + Low + Close) / 3 | Midpoint<br>Low |
| Should "equal" be used when comparing | Yes, use equal when comparing | No, don't use equal | |

## Advanced TD Sequential

Additional TD Sequential Qualifiers and Cancellations
(Expressed for "Buy" Setups, reverse this logic for "Sell" Setups)

| On or Off | First price to be used | | | Condition | First price to be used | | | And/Or |
|---|---|---|---|---|---|---|---|---|
| | Price | Bar number | Phase | | Price | Bar number | Phase | |
| On | Close | 13 | Countdown | > or = | Close | 8 | Countdown | And |
| | Open | 13 | Countdown | > | Close | 8 | Countdown | |
| On | Close | 8 | Countdown | > | Close | 5 | Countdown | |

# TD Moving Average I

| | | |
|---|---|---|
| Period to be used in calculating the moving average | 5 | |
| Type of moving average to be used | Simple | Exponential<br>Centered |

| | | | |
|---|---|---|---|
| Number of bars to be used for moving-average smoothing | 0 | | |
| Price to be used for the higher average | Low | Open / Close / (High + Low + Close) / 3 | Low / Midpoint |
| Price to be used for the lower average | High | Open / Close / (High + Low + Close) / 3 | High / Midpoint |
| Factor to be applied to the higher average | 100.00 | | |
| Factor to be applied to the lower average | 100.00 | | |
| Number of bars to look back for new highs or new lows | 12 | | |
| Number of bars back to be plotted | 4 | | |

## TD Moving Average II

| | | | |
|---|---|---|---|
| Period to be used in calculating the first average | 13 | | |
| Period to be used in calculating the second average | 55 | | |
| Type of moving average to be used | Simple | Exponential / Centered | |
| Number of bars to be used for moving-average smoothing | 0 | | |
| Price to be used for the moving averages | Close | Open / Close / (High + Low + Close) / 3 | Low / Midpoint |
| Factor to be applied to the first average | 100.00 | | |
| Factor to be applied to the second average | 100.00 | | |
| Number of bars to be used in the first average for comparison | 3 | | |
| Number of bars to be used in the second average for comparison | 1 | | |

## TD Channel I

| | | | |
|---|---|---|---|
| Period to be used in calculating the moving averages | 3 | | |
| Type of moving average to be used | Simple | Exponential / Centered | |
| Number of bars to be used for moving-average smoothing | 0 | | |
| Price to be used for the higher average | Low | Open / Close / (High + Low + Close) / 3 | Low / Midpoint |

| Price to be used for the lower average | High | Open<br>Close<br>(High + Low + Close) / 3 | High<br>Midpoint |
|---|---|---|---|
| Factor to be applied to the higher average | 103.00 | | |
| Factor to be applied to the lower average | 97.00 | | |

## TD Channel II

| Period to be used in calculating the moving averages | 3 | | |
|---|---|---|---|
| Type of moving average to be used | Simple | Exponential<br>Centered | |
| Number of bars to be used for moving-average smoothing | 0 | | |
| Price to be used for the higher average | High | Open<br>Close<br>(High + Low + Close) / 3 | Low<br>Midpoint |
| Price to be used for the lower average | Low | Open<br>Close<br>(High + Low + Close) / 3 | High<br>Midpoint |
| Factor to be applied to the higher average | 100.50 | | |
| Factor to be applied to the lower average | 99.50 | | |

## TD Channel III

| Period to be used in calculating the moving averages | 3 | | |
|---|---|---|---|
| Type of moving average to be used | Simple | Exponential<br>Centered | |
| Number of bars to be used for moving-average smoothing | 0 | | |
| Price to be used for the higher average | High | Open<br>Close<br>(High + Low + Close) / 3 | Low<br>Midpoint |
| Price to be used for the lower average | Low | Open<br>Close<br>(High + Low + Close) / 3 | High<br>Midpoint |
| Factor to be applied to the higher average | 101.50 | | |
| Factor to be applied to the lower average | 98.50 | | |

## TD Open

| | | | |
|---|---|---|---|
| Number of Bars Back for Reference Price for "Up Moves" | 1 | | |
| Value to be used for Reference Price for "Up Moves" | Close | Open | High |
| | | Low | Midpoint |
| | | (High + Low + Close) / 3 | |
| Number of Bars Back for Reference Price for "Down Moves" | 1 | | |
| Value to be used for Reference Price for "Down Moves" | Close | Open | High |
| | | Low | Midpoint |
| | | (High + Low + Close) / 3 | |
| Should "equal" be used for comparisons? | No, don't use equal when comparing | Yes, use equal when comparing | |

## TD Trap

| | | | |
|---|---|---|---|
| Number of Bars Back for Reference Price for "Up Moves" | 1 | | |
| Value to be used for Reference Price for "Up Moves" | Close | Open | High |
| | | Low | Midpoint |
| | | (High + Low + Close) / 3 | |
| Number of Bars Back for Reference Price for "Down Moves" | 1 | | |
| Value to be used for Reference Price for "Down Moves" | Close | Open | High |
| | | Low | Midpoint |
| | | (High + Low + Close) / 3 | |
| Should "equal" be used for comparisons? | No, don't use equal when comparing | Yes, use equal when comparing | |

## TD Gap

| | | | |
|---|---|---|---|
| First bar after the gap to begin the confirmation | 8 | | |
| Last bar after the gap to end the confirmation | 11 | | |
| Price to be used when looking for a price lap | Close | Open | High |
| | | Low | Midpoint |
| | | (High + Low + Close) / 3 | |
| Day of the week to be highlighted with a "+" mark | Monday | Tuesday | Wednesday |
| | | Thursday | Friday |

# TD Pressure

| | |
|---|---|
| Period to be used in calculating TD Pressure | 55 |
| Period to be used for TD Pressure Rate of Change | 13 |
| Formula to be used for the calculations | (Close – Open) / (High – Low) |
| | Close – Previous close |
| | Close – Open |
| | (Close – Prev close) / (High – Low) |
| | (Close – Prev close) / True Range |
| | (Close – Open) / True Range |
| Data to be used for the calculations | Price only          Price times volume |
| | Volume only |
| Percent to be used for adjusting extreme gap openings | 8.00 |
| Display the TD Pressure Index | Yes, display the TD     No, don't display the |
| | Pressure Index         TD Pressure Index |
| Display the TD Pressure ROC Ratio | Yes, display the TD     No, don't display the |
| | Pressure ROC Ratio     TD Pressure ROC Ratio |
| Display the TD Pressure ROC | Yes, display the TD     No, don't display the |
| | Pressure ROC           TD Pressure ROC |

# Index

*DeMark indicators introduced by "TD" are registered trademarks, although the standard trademark symbol will be omitted here*

*Page numbers for exhibits are in italic type*

# Special Demo Disk Offer!

Free TD Indicator* demo diskette to readers of this book.

You can receive a free copy of this informative software for Windows "end-of-day" or TradeStation/SuperCharts by calling Futures Learning Center at 1-800-601-8907 ext. 2509 or 319-277-6341 ext. 2509 or by sending your name and address to:

> Demo Diskette—TD Indicators
> Futures Learning Center
> 219 Parkade
> Cedar Falls, Iowa 50613

Or you can receive a free copy of this informative software for Bloomberg, Dow Jones TradeStation, Windows, or TradeStation/SuperCharts by calling TD Indicators at 714-731-3384 or by sending your name and address to:

> TD Indicators c/o Investment Software
> 1742 Amherst Road
> Tustin, California 92780

* TD Indicators are trademark protected

---

# DeMark Indicator Studies Now Available on the Following Networks:

| | |
|---|---|
| ADP (London): | 011-44-171-971-2500 |
| Aspen Research: | 800-359-1121 or 970-945-2921 |
| Bloomberg: | 800-448-5678 or 212-318-2000 |
| Bridge: | 800-325-3282 |
| CQG: | 800-525-7082 |
| Dow Jones TradeStation: | 800-556-2022 |
| FutureSource: | 800-621-2628 |
| TradeStation/SuperCharts c/o Futures Learning Center | 800-601-8907 or 319-277-6341 |
| Coming Soon: Reuters | |